Other books by Peter Grant:

The Maxwell Saga:
1 – Take The Star Road
2 - Ride The Rising Tide

Coming in December 2013:
3 - Adapt And Overcome

Walls, Wire, Bars and Souls

A Chaplain Looks At Prison Life

Peter Grant

Fynbos Press

ISBN: 0615884393
ISBN–13: 978-0615884394

Although this is a factual memoir, details of all persons
(except the author) and incidents described in this book
have been altered to prevent identification and preserve
individual privacy, for reasons described in the
Introduction (*q.v.*). Therefore, any resemblance to
real people or places is purely coincidental.

Cover image supplied by Dreamstime:
http://www.dreamstime.com

Cover design by Oleg Volk:
http://www.olegvolk.net

Editing assistance by Grace Bridges:
http://hire.gracebridges.co.nz/

This book is dedicated with respect
to all those who work in jails, prisons,
penitentiaries and other correctional institutions,
keeping us safe from those confined inside them.
We owe them all a debt of gratitude.

CONTENTS

FOREWORD

by Ian McMurtrie
Lieutenant, WCSO
Wichita Falls, Texas

I first met Peter Grant by way of the Internet over a decade ago. Since then I have come to know him as a friend, a confidant, and a counselor.

He is a witty and engaging speaker. His tales of Africa often have listeners howling with laughter, and shaking their heads in disbelief. As a child of Africa myself, I've noticed it's the stories that make the average listener shake his (or her) head in disbelief that are the most Africa-esque. If you haven't been in Africa, a lot of the stories he and I tell are, quite frankly, incredible to most.

Much like Africa, to the average citizen of America the Detention/Corrections field is a mysterious world, with its own incomprehensible language; cultural mores that make complete sense to the natives, but are completely illogical to outsiders; a rigid code of behavior; and — like Africa — its own associated myths that, while shocking, are frequently less so than the reality.

For those of us who have Africa in our blood, explaining it to people who have never been there is extremely difficult. The worldview and mindset of the average American makes it hard for them to wrap their minds around the reality of sub-Saharan Africa. The same is true for the Detention/Corrections field. Describing 'gassing' (don't ask); 'trying to find the keister bunny' (you don't want to know); 'chomos'; 'ducks'; 'nuts-'n-butts'; and the other realities of large jail and prison life to someone who has never walked a tier is… difficult, at best.

Finding someone who can draw the mental picture of Detentions/Corrections for Joe Citizen is priceless.

Peter is one such person. As I read this book, I found myself nodding. I have spoken to the people he writes about — well, not those exact people, but I have interviewed a predator just like the one he speaks of. I have seen 'rabbits' identical to the one in these pages, and find his assessment of the average inmate's sense of responsibility for his (or her) actions to be spot-on.

Peter writes this book from the perspective of a combat veteran, a priest and an astute observer of the human condition — an observer who has the uncommon ability to take the results of years of observations and make them comprehensible to the average reader.

What is in this book is not comfortable to think about, but it is reality. If you have a loved one walking a run in a detention center or a prison; if you're interested in Criminal Justice; or if you've been there and you wonder if anyone else saw the things you did; read this book.

Or not. Parts of it may give the average reader nightmares – but that doesn't make it any less true.

Well done, my friend. Well done, indeed.

INTRODUCTION

In these pages, I'll try to give an accurate and unvarnished picture of what it's like to work in a high-security penitentiary, surrounded by some of the most violent and dangerous criminals in the United States. As a chaplain, I've had the advantage of being in a relatively neutral position. Convicts come to chaplains as a matter of routine to deal with personal issues. This gives us a broader insight into their minds, lives and existence than that gained by many Correctional Officers, who also sometimes approach us to discuss problems, and occasionally use us as counselors. We thus see and hear things on and from both sides of the fence — a unique perspective on prison life.

Every event about which you read in these pages, and every detail about convicts and life in prison, is true. I haven't made up a thing — prison life is weird enough to make that unnecessary! Some with long prison experience may frown, and say that a few incidents 'couldn't' or 'shouldn't' have happened, as they're 'against regulations'. To such people I can only say, regulations can't always provide a solution to every problem. Sometimes one has to 'think outside the box' and be creative. I've been blessed to work with Wardens, administrators and executives who weren't afraid to do that. It paid handsome dividends on occasion.

Despite the reality of what I say here — every person exists, every incident happened — I've changed every name in this book except my own. I've also modified details of people and/or their crimes and/or events and/or locations I mention, to prevent their identification. That's necessary for three reasons. First, there are legal protections for the privacy of individuals, even incarcerated convicts. For obvious reasons, I haven't been able to approach every individual for permission to describe them or incidents involving them, so I've had to cloak them in a certain amount of anonymity.

Second, some of the events I describe might attract retaliation, and some of the individuals I discuss might be targeted by other convicts for revenge. I don't want those involved to suffer any negative consequences, so I've made absolutely sure that they can't be recognized. Officially and for the record: any resemblance of anyone named or physically described in this book, to persons living or dead, is purely coincidental.

The third reason to disguise individuals and events is, of course, institutional security. I don't want to give away confidential information about how a prison monitors those it incarcerates, or how its security precautions work. I've been guided by previously published books and Internet resources. If a technique or event has already been described in a public forum, I don't have a problem mentioning it here. However, certain details, procedures, equipment and methods are not well-known, and I've therefore avoided any in-depth discussion of them. I've also omitted certain details from incidents I describe, things that might help to identify their date or location with any precision, to prevent inmates who witnessed them from putting two and two together and learning more than they should.

Such disguising of people, places and events is made easier because I've spent more than fifteen years (abroad and in the USA) in prison ministry and chaplaincy, serving either part-time or full-time in numerous institutions. (In the USA these included a Federal high-security penitentiary and its attached minimum-security camp,

iv

two state medium-security prisons run by private contractors, two state-run prisons [a maximum- and a medium-security unit] and two town and/or county jails.) I've been able to 'mix and match' details, descriptions, people and incidents to give an accurate picture of prison life, whilst simultaneously ensuring that no individual except myself can be identified from these pages. Furthermore, I've waited almost a decade since my enforced medical retirement from full-time prison ministry to publish this memoir, so that the passage of time will also have made identification of individuals, institutions and events more difficult.

I've written this book in sets of three alternating chapters. The first in each set describes part of a duty shift at a Federal high-security penitentiary, illustrating many of the activities that go on there, and offering a personal perspective on a chaplain's job. To do this, I drew on my memories of incidents at more than one prison, taking place over the course of several years. I've combined them into a composite portrait of a typical shift, one that encompasses most of the elements of a chaplain's (and a prison's) daily activities. The people and events I describe are in no way out of the ordinary. Many shifts are less busy than the one I portray, but others may be even busier — not to mention more dangerous. My most hectic day in the penitentiary saw three assaults (one of which threatened to develop into a mass riot), a lock-down of the entire compound, and a whole string of related activities. That was an interesting duty shift, all right — in the sense of the ancient Chinese curse! While the shift I describe here is varied and busy, it's by no means as bad as it can get.

The second chapter in each set of three describes aspects of the people and lifestyle within (and sometimes beyond) prison walls. In the last two, I offer some ideas for evaluating and improving the present state of our corrections system. The third chapter in each set is a short 'Convict to Chaplain' vignette, describing conversations with individual inmates. These are drawn from memory, of course, but they're pretty accurate. One doesn't forget such exchanges, even though in many cases one would prefer to do so!

A word about language. Convicts' speech (and sometimes that of prison staff as well) is usually laden with profanities. I've chosen to disguise this by using asterisks rather than modify the language used, so as to retain an element of realism. Since I'm reporting actual conversations, I felt that leaving the 'raw' language accessible in this way was important to convey the reality of such dialogue. Furthermore, prison slang is an argot all its own; and, to make things even more complicated, there are significant differences in slang from one prison system to another. For example, there are many and varied names given to illegally-produced prison alcohol. What I call 'hooch' is referred to as 'pruno' by a friend of mine, a retired Corrections Lieutenant in another state. Another instance: the term 'punk' may mean a street thug in one prison system, and a homosexual in another. Given such potential for confusion, most of the time I've chosen to use normal language instead of prison slang. I've provided a glossary explaining the relatively few slang terms that I've included, amongst others.

As you read this, spare a thought for the tens of thousands of correctional staff and the millions of prisoners who are behind bars right now. It's a world hidden from most Americans, yet one that has a constant and dramatic impact on our lives through taxation, the legal system, and the enforcement of our laws. Some (including myself) question very seriously whether the way the system is run at this time is producing the desired results. Some even argue about what those results should be! I've tried to address some of those issues in these pages.

I should thank a great many individuals for the help they've given me in learning my way around prison work and ministry. However, if I name individuals, this could lead to the identification of convicts with whom we've worked, which in turn may have less than desirable consequences. For that reason, I won't mention names here: but to those of you in the corrections field who recognize my name, thank you all very much. In particular I thank J.H., T.S. and V.V., fellow chaplains all. Thanks for all you've done for me, my brothers. I hope I've been able to return the favor, both in person and through these pages. Perhaps they'll help your loved ones and others understand what we go through.

Thanks again for joining me in these pages. I appreciate your company. I hope you'll find reading about prison life as interesting as it is to work in such an environment.

Peter Grant

September 2013

FRIDAY — NOON

It's a hot, steamy summer day. The temperature's well into the 90's and the humidity's right up there too. The truck's air-conditioner is keeping me nicely cool inside the cab, but that's about to change. I'm driving through wooded countryside, the last few houses left behind me. It's uncomfortable having to wear my seatbelt over the stiff, unyielding black web belt around my waist. A metal keyholder is digging into my right thigh, and I reach down and adjust it to a slightly more comfortable position.

Ahead a turnoff appears. I slow down, make the turn and drive slowly up the approach road. The speed limit's only 25 on this stretch, and the Warden's been complaining about our driving, so we're all careful — at least for now. In another couple of weeks something else will have gotten his attention, and many will speed up again... until the next crackdown, anyway.

I pass the warehouse. All the food and supplies come in here for processing before being sent up to the complex, and anything shipped out by the prison industry is moved through here as well. Further up the road is the minimum-security camp. It has no walls or fence, as its convicts are not considered dangerous. Over a hundred of them live here. They handle the grounds around the complex, mowing the grass and tending the flowerbeds. Others work in the warehouse. It's a lot cheaper using them for such jobs

1

instead of hiring staff at normal wages. A couple of them have just finished their lunch, and are walking down the grass verge towards the warehouse. One of them recognizes me and waves casually. I wave back as I drive past them.

The entry looms up. I slow down and stop, winding down my window, wincing as the steaming, muggy air of a Southern summer slaps me in the face like a hot wet fish. I look into the security camera that's directed at window height to identify drivers, and wait... and wait... and wait. Either the guard in the tower isn't paying attention, or he's busy with something else. I wait a few more moments, then reach out and press the intercom call button. A brief pause, then the box crackles. "Sorry, Chaplain, I was on the phone." The bar swings up.

I look up at the tower and wave as I turn into the employee parking. The guard up there has a frustrating job. He's got to watch his section of the fence and walls, to make sure none of our unwilling customers are trying to take their patronage elsewhere. He has to control the vehicle entrance, admit those of us who work here, and ask those he doesn't recognize to state their business. It's his decision whether to admit them, or have a roving patrol check them out. He also has other duties, and must fill out his reports and try to stay alert and on top of things. He and the guards in the other towers are our last and most lethal defense against convict escape or rebellion. I remember the dry voice of the instructor at the Training Center: "It's not the walls or the wire or the bars that keep the hard boys inside — it's the guards with the guns in the towers." I've heard our hard-core inmates agree with him, loudly and profanely.

I park, get out of my truck and hoist my black leather bag out of the passenger seat. Already I can feel perspiration breaking out on my forehead and making my black clergy shirt and trousers damp and sticky. They might as well be a solar heating system in this climate. I walk towards the gray breeze-block administration building. Behind it the tall triple perimeter fence, topped with razor wire, filled to above head height between the outer and middle fences with coils of the lethally sharp-edged metal strands, runs to left and right for hundreds of yards before making right-angled turns and vanishing behind the compound walls. About fifty yards inside the inner fence, the outer wall of the penitentiary glowers windowless and somber. I grimace slightly as I draw nearer. Time to ignore the outside world for a few hours and concentrate on my job. If I don't, it's a sure bet that one or more convicts will be watching for precisely such a lack of concentration, and will seize the opportunity to take advantage of it — and me.

I pull open the heavy swinging steel door, straining against the tug of the heavy-duty closer, and greet the guard at the lobby desk as I enter. He smiles and nods at me, but he can't answer. He's holding a telephone to his ear and trying to respond to a caller. I can hear the tired frustration in his voice as he says, "No, Ma'am, inmates are not permitted visitors outside scheduled hours unless it's an emergency situation, and that requires prior verification and approval by the Warden." He's probably lost count of the number of times he's had to politely but firmly lay out the rules on that subject for callers. Many of them can't seem to accept the reality that prisons don't exist for the convenience of visitors, but for the safety of society. Our policies and procedures are set up accordingly.

I walk past him through the metal detector. It beeps at me in irritation, but I don't stop. Visitors would be searched. Staff aren't, under normal circumstances. We've all got key-holders on our belts and other metal equipment that sets it off every time.

I come to the staff board. My name is there, one among many, long serried rows of them, each with a hook below it bearing a token with the staff member's name. At the moment, my token is turned face to the wall, its blank rear surface outwards. I take it from its hook, turn it over, and replace it. It now displays my name. If anything goes down inside the prison, they'll check this board to confirm who's inside, and make sure they can account for all of us.

I move on past the mail slots for each department, scanning them as I pass. Yes, there's a call-out list of names for the afternoon's activities in the Religious Services Department's pigeonhole. I pull it out and slip it into my bag as I come to the Control Center window. It has waist-high breeze-block walls topped with bulletproof glass all round, covered by thick heavy bars as an added security measure. Inside it all radio communications, cameras and sliding doors in the complex are monitored and controlled 24/7/365. You don't fool around with such things in a high-security penitentiary. There's a uniformed officer standing at the window.

"Hi, Tom. Key 236, radio 85 and a spare battery, please."

I drop three round brass chits into the sliding metal drawer beneath the glass. Each has my name stamped on it. Tom nods, slides the drawer open on his side and retrieves them, then turns to the key cupboard beside him. Several door-like partitions on hinges protrude from the cabinet. He moves a couple back to expose the right number sequence, runs his finger down the rows and finds my set of keys. He takes them from the hook, hangs one of my chits on it, then walks to the back of the room where long lines of radios are plugged into their recharging docks. He takes my radio out of its socket, and plucks a spare battery from the rack behind the charging station. He brings the items back to the window, dropping them into the drawer with a clatter, and hangs my second and third chits on the radio and spare battery board respectively.

"There you go, Chaplain."

"Thanks, Tom. Anything happening?"

"No, it's been a quiet day so far."

"Good. Let's hope it stays that way!"

I slide the drawer open and retrieve my keys and radio. I count the keys quickly. There are nine of them. One is a very large security door key, with a flip-up cover shielding its notches from prying eyes. Convicts have been known to manufacture their own keys out of anything that comes to hand, from metal scraps to wood to plastic, so we make sure they can't get a good look at the important ones. There are also eight regular keys, for normal doors and padlocks. I check the two chits on the ring. One displays the keyring number, 236, and the other shows the number of keys that are supposed to be on it. Each keyring is checked and its keys counted multiple times every day, first by those to whom it's issued (if you don't check it as soon as you get it, you're responsible if a key's missing when you return it) and then by the evening shift in the Control Center. If the keyring's been issued, they'll radio or telephone the person concerned and ask for a key count. With the kind of people we've got inside our walls, you daren't take any chances on a key going astray.

I clip the heavy keyring to a long chain fastened to my web belt, then sling it from the key-holder just in front of my right hip. Beneath the key-holder is an oval of heavy cloth, to prevent the oversize prison key from abrading my trousers until they need patching. I take a belt clip from my pocket, and attach it to my radio. You *never* hand in that clip. People are always breaking or losing theirs: so if you leave yours on the radio, as sure as night follows day, sooner or later someone's going to 'borrow' it, and you'll be without one until you can 'borrow' someone else's in your turn. Yes, even chaplains have been known to do that.

I turn on the radio, check the charge light, make sure the channel's properly set and all the switches are in the right positions, then clip it onto my web belt next to the key-holder. The spare battery goes into a deep hip pocket of my trousers. The batteries are supposed to last for a full shift, but many of them are old and have been recharged too many times. I'm usually lucky to get six or seven hours out of a battery — hence the spare. If a serious problem arises inside, I won't have time to run to the Control Center to get one. I've learned that lesson the hard way.

I pick up my bag and walk a few yards to the sliding door next to the Control Center. I have to wait a couple of minutes while three others who came in behind me are issued their keys, radios and equipment. I use the time to scan quickly through the call-out list from the mailbox. It's Friday, so we have Jumah prayer coming up at 12:30 p.m.. Almost two hundred of our convicts list themselves as Muslims of one sort or another, and most of them are on the call-out for today's ceremony. It's going to be a hectic three hours until we get everything wrapped up for the afternoon count. The others join me one by one, scanning their departments' call-out lists to see what's in store for them today.

The four of us wait patiently at the slider. We've all got our equipment and are ready to go, but looking through the windows of the Control Center, we can see the guard at the main console talking into a microphone and pressing various buttons. He monitors dozens of sliders, security cameras and activities throughout the complex from his station. If he's busy with others, we'll have to wait our turn. Eventually the guard from the window moves to the console, mutters something to him and presses a button. The steel-and-glass sliding door in front of us jerks, then slowly rumbles open on its rollers.

We walk through, and move along the side of the Control Center as the slider closes behind us. Another slider blocks our way ahead. Only one can open at a time at this entrance: interlocks prevent them both being open simultaneously, unless an emergency occurs. In that case, a special override command can be issued to allow reinforcements to rush inside. The door behind us clangs closed, and the inner slider slowly opens. We walk out, inside the triple fence, and head for the buildings fifty yards ahead. This open space between the fence and the wall has an official name, but I've heard some guards refer to it as 'the killing ground'. No-one moves here except those passing between the outer and inner entrances, as we are, and occasional work parties. Anyone else sighted in this area without a reason to be here is a potential target for the rifles in the towers. Behind us the slider closes.

As we approach the walls, another slider opens to receive us. Like all those in interior corridors, this one has bars only, no glass or solid panels. That makes it easier to see and/or hear any trouble ahead — and weapons can be fired through the bars if necessary. Two sliders later we're in the main portal, a concrete box with sliders on three sides. I wave farewell to the other three as they move off to their departments on one side. I take the slider on the other side of the portal, heading towards the Chapel area.

I look out onto the compound as I walk down the long concrete-floored corridor, its surface polished bright by convict labor, its walls white and aseptic, the gray bars on the windows intruding on my field of vision. Hundreds of convicts are wandering around the yards digesting their lunch, waiting for the 12:30 move to be allowed to pass from one area of the prison to another, to attend whatever they have scheduled for the next hour or two or three.

I come to the double steel doors leading to the Chapel area. I unhook the keyring from my keyholder, select the big security key, flip open the cover over the lock, insert the key and turn it. With a dull *clank!* the big locking bar rolls back. I tug at the door handle, straining to pull it towards me against the pressure of the closer. Inside, I let it swing closed, re-lock it, and head for my office to put down my bag.

As I pass his office, Ken, my fellow Chaplain, looks up from his desk and waves a greeting. He's been on duty since 7:30 this morning. We'll handle Jumah prayer together. It'll take both of us.

CONVICTS

The men who start out with the notion that the world owes
them a living generally find that the world pays its debt in
the penitentiary or the poor house.
— William Graham Sumner (1840-1910)

It's difficult to portray the convicts one encounters inside prison walls. There are all sorts of official statistics, but they don't give you a true 'feel' for what the individuals behind bars are like. For those who want the numbers, I've included them in the 'Statistics' section. In this chapter I'm going to introduce you to a dozen convicts, to give you an idea of the folks you'll find in our prisons every day.

Those sentenced to terms of imprisonment are usually categorized for security or risk purposes according to the severity of their crime(s), the length of their sentence, and the risk they pose to the general public, to staff, to other convicts, and to themselves. The Federal Bureau of Prisons (BOP) operates five risk classifications of prison. Camps are minimum-security — many don't even have fences or walls. Those sent to them are serving shorter sentences for non-violent crimes (or have only a short time left to serve of longer sentences, and have demonstrated consistently good behavior). They're not considered a danger to the community. There are low- and medium-security correctional institutions for convicts who have committed more serious crimes and/or are more of a risk to others. For the most dangerous there are high-security penitentiaries, and for the worst of the worst there's the Administrative Maximum facility (popularly referred to as 'Supermax') at Florence, Colorado. States have their own classifications, but typically you'll find a mixture of at least three levels: Low, Medium, and High or Maximum Security. Cities, towns and counties will have their local jails.

I've worked in low- and medium-security state prisons as a part-time volunteer whilst serving as a full-time pastor elsewhere, and occasionally been a visiting minister to other state correctional facilities. I've sometimes been asked to work with convicts in local jails. I've worked full-time as a chaplain in a Federal high-security penitentiary and a minimum-security camp environment. I can therefore speak about Federal, state and local corrections environments from first-hand experience, not just based on statistics or academic theories. The convicts described below have been drawn from all of these facilities.

Let me preface my descriptions of individuals by saying that there's a golden rule applied by everyone working in corrections: **_you never, ever trust an inmate_**. That probably sounds harsh: and yes, despite its universality, there are a few (*very* few) exceptions to it. Nevertheless, we've learned from long and bitter experience that most convicts will do anything and everything possible to beguile, deceive, delude, exploit, hoodwink and manipulate those in charge of them. You'll see many examples of such behavior as we go along. There are several books describing it if you'd like to learn more[1]. Thus, in the descriptions that follow, bear in mind that I'm describing how convicts present themselves and how they appear to me — but I can be fooled, too.

Let's begin with a couple of minimum-security convicts. Frank is a man in his late forties, tall, rather fleshy, pleasant-spoken. He ended up in prison through financial crimes at his place of employment, although he protests that he wasn't the real perpetrator — merely the 'fall guy' for the true criminals. The court disagreed. He's a charming man, outwardly very relaxed and friendly. He's far more highly educated than most convicts, with a postgraduate degree, but manages to get along with the others (something a lot of better-educated convicts find very difficult). He helps many of them with their legal studies, appeals and motions.

Frank's told me of his health problems. He claims to have suffered a couple of heart attacks and he's worried about his blood pressure. He's asked me to help him appeal for an early medical release, but that's not my responsibility and I can't assist him. He'll have to go through the medical department and then take his case to the powers that be. They'll probably reject it, because incarceration is imposed as punishment for crimes, irrespective of one's state of health. Only in the most severe and extreme cases — such as imminent death — will they consider an early release on medical or compassionate grounds. Frank's disappointed in me, I can tell, but he's got to learn that a pleasant, engaging demeanor isn't enough to persuade any of us to bend the rules for him.

Mike's another minimum-security convict, but he's 'special' — or so he thinks. You see, Mike was once a prison guard. He got caught up in some of the manipulation I spoke about. One of the convicts claimed to have a young wife with two small children. She was (he said) on the point of divorcing him. He was desperate to prevent this — he 'loved her dearly'. Their wedding anniversary was just a few days away, and he wanted to send her a card: but if he posted it through normal prison channels, it probably wouldn't get to her in time. It might make a difference in saving his marriage. Would Mike please be a human being, and help him out by dropping off the card at his home, which wasn't far away? Very foolishly, and despite all the warnings to prison staff about never putting oneself in a potentially compromising situation, Mike agreed. He took the card with him that evening when he went off shift. He was off duty next day, and drove over to the convict's home to deliver the card. His wife was there, but the kids were 'over at their grandma's place'. She invited him in for a cup of coffee 'to thank him for being such a sweetie'. She was wearing a gown — with nothing on beneath it, as it turned out. She dropped the gown and showed him once they were inside. He fled, highly embarrassed... but too late.

Within a week the convict received a letter from his wife with a coded message telling him of her success. Now he was in control. He told Mike bluntly that he was to bring in drugs and other contraband. If he refused he'd have his wife deliver a video recording to the Warden showing her standing naked next to Mike. He threatened to tell the Warden that Mike had tried to rape his wife. If Mike had been sensible and gone to the authorities at once, he'd certainly have been disciplined — perhaps even fired — but he most likely wouldn't have suffered any further consequences. He hadn't done anything criminal up to that point. Instead, he caved in to the blackmailer and brought in drugs and contraband as instructed. Inevitably, he was caught in due course, and sentenced to a lengthy prison term. The courts don't like law enforcement officers who go bad.

Mike wants me to sympathize with him — after all, he used to be (and still considers himself) 'one of us'. I've tried to make it clear to him that he's a member of the inmate population now, and can't expect to be treated any differently from the rest of them, but he finds this impossible to accept. He sees himself as the victim of criminals, not as a criminal in his own right. He's constantly wheedling me to get him some extra privileges or cut him some slack. He does the same thing to every Correctional Officer with whom he comes into contact. I suspect that before long, the authorities will lose patience with him. He'll probably be transferred to a higher-security institution, with a note on his file that he's manipulative and untrustworthy. He probably doesn't consciously realize it (and would reject any such accusation with contempt, I'm sure) but he's trying to beguile us, just as he was once misled himself. It's not going to work. We learn from the example of people like Mike, and we don't forget.

Then we have Laura. She's serving time for distribution of narcotics. She, too, wants me to sympathize with her. Her husband was the one making crystal meth, not her. He forced her to take the drugs to his customers. If she hadn't done so, he'd have beaten her. She's worried about her kids, who are in foster care. Are they being treated properly? Will they still love her when she gets out in three years? They only come to visit her once a month — can't I organize more frequent visits through Child Protection Services? Can't I arrange to take some of her paintings and drawings out to them? She's their mother, after all — surely I can understand her concerns?

I can indeed. Unfortunately Laura can't accept that she's lost most of the rights she once took for granted. She's behind bars, and can no longer be the mother she doubtless wants to be. It's all very well to put all the blame on her husband (who's also serving a prison term) — it may even be true — but she could have chosen at any time to leave him, and take the kids with her. By electing to stay with him, accept his ongoing abuse (which I'm quite prepared to believe really did happen) and co-operate with him in his criminal activities, she's made herself as much of a felon as he is. It's no use protesting that it was all his fault. She had many opportunities to make her own choices, and she did so. Now she has to live with the consequences of those choices. Sadly, so do her children.

Are you noticing something already? All of the convicts to whom I've introduced you thus far *blame someone else for their crimes*. If there's no-one at whom they can point the finger, they'll accuse 'society' of letting them down somehow, or claim that 'the system' was or is biased against them. They'll allege that racism or some other form of discrimination is behind their incarceration. It's never *their* fault, never *their* responsibility. That's probably the most

12

common factor amongst those with whom we deal. Very, very few of them are willing to look you in the eye and say "Yes, I did it, and I'm responsible for my being here." Those who do — fewer than one in twenty, in my experience — are people we can work with, and we have real hope that they'll be rehabilitated and won't offend again. Those who can't or won't accept this truth… well, we expect to see many of them back behind bars soon after their release. They won't learn, and they'll do it again, and they'll find someone else to blame.

Let's move on to Rodney. In his youth he committed a number of crimes ranging from petty theft through mugging to armed robbery. His actions became more and more violent as he fell deeper and deeper into criminal activity. He was in juvenile court many times, but received no more than the judicial equivalent of a slap on the wrist on most occasions. Once he was sentenced to six months incarceration in a juvenile correction facility, but all that did was put him in the company of others who taught him 'better' criminal skills. In his early twenties he committed a murder during an armed robbery, and was sentenced to death. This was later commuted to life imprisonment.

Rodney's in his fifties now, a wiry man with thinning gray hair and a perpetually quizzical expression on his face. He's become an 'old con', to use a common expression. After almost thirty years behind bars he 'knows the ropes'. He can quote chapter and verse of prison regulations (and frequently does so in order to try to get his way), but also knows the risks involved in irritating or annoying the corrections staff. Regulations notwithstanding, there are ways for them to 'express displeasure' with an inmate who won't stop nagging them, and he's experienced most of them. He knows just how far he can push things, and he'll walk right up to that line… but make very sure that he doesn't cross it. He's also learned to get along with most of the other convicts, many of whom are far more volatile and violent than he ever was. He's a murderer, which gives him significant status in the prisoner hierarchy, and helps to ensure that he's largely left alone by those wanting to push others around. He uses his status to obtain various 'favors' from other convicts, usually in return for helping them in some way.

Rodney and I get along. He knows he's going to be in prison until he dies, and there's nothing he can do about it. He'll attempt to con me in any way he can to get extra favors, but he knows I'm aware of that. He'll try a sob story on me from time to time, and I'll look at him tiredly and say, "Not *again*, Rodney?" Then he'll chuckle, hang his head, shuffle his feet, and admit that he's after a favor. Sometimes he provides me with snippets of information that are very useful to the corrections staff and myself. In return, I'll arrange for him to make an occasional free telephone call to his family, or allow him another minor favor. He knows I'll make sure he doesn't abuse such privileges. It's an armed neutrality, I suppose, but both of us can live with that. We understand one another.

Adam's another murderer, but in an entirely different class. He was an enforcer for the Mob in a major city. He was convicted of several murders, and collected a life sentence for each of them (the judge ruling that they were to run consecutively, apparently to make sure he'll never get out of prison). He contemptuously rejects any notion of feeling guilty over his crimes. Those he killed were 'crooks' who were trying to steal from their criminal bosses. They deserved what they got. He was merely the instrument of 'street justice'. I've spent a lot of time talking with Adam, trying to get him to at least acknowledge an intellectual and moral responsibility for what he's done... but without success. The best I've been able to achieve is that Adam has said he's "sorry for not feeling sorry". I hope God will accept that as a first step. (Sigh.)

Adam's a very hard man indeed. No-one with any sense messes with him... but then, not everyone has sense.

A year or so back a new convict arrived, a cocky young man 'full of p*** and vinegar' as they say in the classics. He wanted to build 'street cred' in the prison, and decided that beating up a Mob killer would get him a reputation. It did — as an idiot. He came up behind Adam while he was sitting with a group watching television, and hit him over the head with a chair. Adam sprang to his feet, bleeding from a cut on his scalp, and proceeded to take this thug apart at the seams. He ended up in hospital with several broken bones and serious internal injuries (not to mention speaking in a dulcet and henceforth permanent soprano). The guards broke it up (although they probably found it difficult to restrain themselves from cheering Adam on — they've had to deal with too many young thugs to have any sympathy for them). Adam did a spell in the Hole for fighting, but by all accounts was treated well by the staff there (who doubtless felt that Adam had done them a favor by dealing with the punk before they had to). He's back in general population now, his reputation not merely intact but significantly enhanced. The thug was transferred to another prison a long way away, with a note in his records to the effect that he and Adam were never again to be assigned to the same institution. If they were, the consequences (for the thug) would probably be lethal.

Tyrone's another classic thug. He's a young, strongly-built man who's always smiling, always talking, eyes flickering non-stop as he searches for something to steal or someone to manipulate. He's one of the leaders of a religious sect in the prison, but doesn't seem to have any compunction about breaking every moral law in his faith's nominally stringent code of conduct. He'll look you straight in the eye and lie through his teeth, and put on a mask of injured innocence when you call him on it. He's been in and out of the Hole more times than I can count for petty theft, trouble-making and infractions of prison regulations, but he never learns and he never changes. He's also the father of multiple children by multiple women, some of whom come to visit him from time to time. We've learned the hard way to pay particular attention to his visitors, and check them very carefully indeed. Many of them try to smuggle in contraband to him.

I speak with each batch of new inmates as part of the

induction process. In my presentation I warn them about Tyrone and others like him. I can't mention them by name, of course, but I (and others) try to give the newcomers some idea of how they can be conned, and how they should react to such approaches. Sadly, our warnings often fall on deaf ears. We can virtually guarantee that out of each group of new convicts, one or two will fall under Tyrone's spell and end up as troublemakers and agitators among his followers. Once they're in, they can't get out easily: he has 'enforcers' to make sure that those who give him their allegiance don't withdraw it. We've been able to 'rescue' a couple of his erstwhile followers by arranging for them to be transferred to other prisons and given a fresh start. That's just one of the reasons why he doesn't like me and the others involved. I'm sure you understand how deeply that upsets us.

Clem was an ordained minister until he was caught in the act of abusing a child, and collected a long prison sentence. His wife immediately divorced him and left for parts unknown, taking their children with her. His parents and siblings have disowned him. This once successful pastor is now a lonely emotional wreck. He wants to take me aside and talk whenever we meet. I think he expects me to do favors for him out of professional courtesy, as one clergyman to another. Trouble is, he's no longer a clergyman but a criminal. I treat him the same way I treat every other convict, looking and hoping for the best but on guard against the worst. I've talked and prayed with Clem on many occasions, but like so many others he blames everything and everyone except himself for his situation. Unless and until he realizes the truth, I don't see any future for him. He's due for discharge in a couple of years, and I greatly fear that he'll end up as a homeless derelict, blaming 'the system' and 'the church' and 'the others' for everything, but never accepting personal responsibility for anything.

The scary thing is that Clem flatly denies his crime, even though he was caught in *flagrante delicto*. I'm willing to bet that he's still a danger to children. The psychologist at his prison agrees with

16

me, but we can't keep Clem locked up once he's done his time. Sometimes we wish we could go to court and say bluntly, "If you let this man out, he's going to hurt or kill others. He's a permanent danger to society. He needs to stay behind bars." Very sadly, we don't have the legal right to do that, and courts in most states don't have the authority to order permanent incarceration for such offenders. Every year we're legally obliged to discharge inmates like Clem on completion of their sentences, in the sure and certain knowledge that someone out there is going to suffer, perhaps even die, because we're doing so. It tears your guts out sometimes.

Another sex offender I remember well was Wesley. He was an absolute maniac, and a very real danger to everyone around him, in prison or outside. He'd used PCP as a teenager, and it fried his brain. His judgment and capacity for logical, rational thought were impaired forever. He spent most of his long sentence going back and forth to the Hole for various infractions (including masturbating publicly in the chapel). When the time came for him to be discharged, he was escorted to the bus station by two Correctional Officers. They physically put him in his seat, then stood by the door to prevent him getting off until the bus left. They returned to the prison and told us that he was on his way out of the state, at which the staff breathed a collective sigh of relief.

Some of the staff started a betting pool as to how many days Wesley would be 'on the outside' before committing another offense and being rearrested. I didn't join the pool, but I told them their calculations were wrong. They were betting on days and weeks, but they should have been figuring in hours. I'm almost sorry I didn't take a place in the pool on that basis. I would have won.

Wesley somehow managed to get hold of hard liquor while *en route* to his destination. By the time the bus arrived there that evening, he was tight as a drum. He staggered down the steps, saw a woman waiting to meet her boyfriend and lunged at her, shouting drunkenly about the pleasure he was about to give her.

17

Unfortunately for Wesley, her boyfriend — a Marine — was coming down the steps behind him. After he'd finished 'expressing his displeasure' to Wesley, he handed over what was left of him to the local authorities, who charged him with sexual assault, public intoxication and everything else they could think of. Our staff breathed another sigh of relief. At least he'll be in that state's criminal justice system for the next few years, so we don't have to dread the prospect of him coming back here.

Dennis is a convict for whom I truly feel sympathy. If I were ever to say that an inmate was trustworthy (and yes, I know that, by definition, none of them are ever to be considered trustworthy), Dennis would be on my (very) short list. He did a few years in state prison some time ago for a youthful drug offense. Upon being released and completing his parole, he petitioned for the restoration of his civil rights, which he could do in that state, and his petition was granted. A year or two later he did something that was legitimate under state law in terms of the restoration of his civil rights, but which conflicted with Federal law (which did not recognize his state-level restoration of rights). It was a *malum prohibitum* offense rather than *malum in se* — in other words, not an act that's intrinsically evil or morally wrong in itself, merely something prohibited by law (like parking in a loading zone, to cite a low-level example). Dennis ended up with a prison sentence as a result. I don't think he belongs behind bars. He'd not committed any crime since his first brush with the law, and he'd genuinely believed that the restoration of his civil rights had included the right to do what he did. Sure, he broke Federal law, but he insists it was an unthinking and unwitting breach. He certainly didn't harm anyone in doing so. On balance, given the integrity he's demonstrated in other ways, I believe him.

Dennis works hard at his job in the prison. He's provided some very valuable information, which has helped to break up a few really nasty convict conspiracies that might have caused serious trouble and significant casualties. A senior prison executive has told

18

me to my face, "We owe that guy big-time." He's certainly been invaluable to me in more than one way. When his sentence is over, I'll be the first to help him find employment and rebuild his life on the outside. He's one of the very few convicts who's earned my respect, and has never tried to play me false or lead me astray. I only wish there were more like him.

Eddie worries me. He's from a far distant country, and is serving a very long sentence for crimes of violence. He's fanatical in his religious beliefs — so much so that he's constantly getting beaten up by others in the prison who (at least nominally) share his faith. They resent his ranting at them that they're 'false believers' who don't know the truth about God. He accuses them contemptuously of using their 'American prison version' of his faith as a means of getting protection and a few extra privileges in prison. (In my opinion, he's probably right about many of them.) However, he hasn't learned (even after many injuries) that it's not a good idea to swear at a bunch of violent criminals about their conduct and beliefs. He goes right on ranting, and they go right on hurting him — sometimes very badly.

Eddie attends the services of his faith group when he's on speaking terms with the rest of the congregation, and at other times prays alone in his cell. He often brings me pamphlets or typewritten screeds, asking me to arrange to duplicate them so that he can hand them out at services. Sometimes, if they're innocuous, I'll oblige. Other times they're so inflammatory and prejudicial that I have to turn him down. He's accused me more than once of censoring his religious speech and infringing on his rights. I've pointed out to him that in prison, the requirements of safety and security are paramount, and our courts have upheld that principle as far as freedom of speech and religion is concerned: but he doesn't want to hear that.

Pancho's another real headache. He's an older man who, in his youth, was among the founders of one of the most vicious of the criminal Hispanic gangs. It's spread across many States, and is a major problem to law enforcement. He and some of his sons are doing hard time, and his grandchildren look set to follow in their footsteps. Not long ago one of his relatives was murdered by a rival gang. It's alleged he put out a contract on the lives of the (unidentified) killers. Authorities suspect he used coded communications in letters and phone calls to do it, but to convict him of that means it has to be proved beyond a reasonable doubt.

It's very difficult to find people willing to testify against him, because many of those who've done so in the past (and/or their families) have later been murdered, very slowly, painfully and messily. The prison authorities passed a warning to law enforcement agencies in the area concerned, and for several weeks they were on high alert. We heard rumors that the murderers had been traced to a hiding-place in Mexico and 'dealt with' there by Pancho's gang, but we'll probably never learn the full truth.

Pancho's gang members (there are a couple of dozen behind bars with him) are cocky, pushy and on a hair-trigger for any perceived insult or disrespect. They've caused more than one riot in the prison system, and they're not afraid to instigate bad trouble at any moment. We watch them very carefully. They've tried to use the Chapel as a cover for illegal activities in the past. Some of them joined a small 'fringe' religious group and started to attend their weekly ceremonies. Discreet inquiries revealed that they were sitting at the rear of the chapel during the services, not paying any attention or participating, but instead conversing in low tones. Clearly they were using the religious service to organize their criminal activities in the prison. This was duly brought to the attention of those who could do something about it.

Finally, let's take Howard. He got drunk one night and began to smash the furniture and fittings in his uncle's home. His uncle tried to stop him… a fatal mistake. Howard beat him until he collapsed, then for two days and nights drank himself into a stupor, periodically getting up to kick and stomp his uncle as he lay moaning on the floor. Howard eventually passed out. He was found next morning, unconscious at the table, with his uncle dead on the floor beside him. He'd been in enough trouble with the law on previous occasions that this crime earned him a life sentence without parole. He's still a relatively young man, and still just as violent. He's been known to get bombed out of his skull on prison hooch (of which more later). When he gets that way, everyone steers clear of him, even the prison 'hard men' — all except the reaction squad, who have to subdue him and put him in the Hole to sober up. He's quite capable of killing anyone who crosses him.

Howard's eyes scare me. They're pitch-black and utterly lifeless. When one looks into them, one strives to detect a spark of life, of humanity, of the person inside the body... but it's not there. I've never looked into the bottomless pits of Hell, but I've got a good idea what they must be like after working with Howard. He's one of the few convicts who genuinely frightens me. I take care not to show it, but I also try to have support available if I've got to see him about something. He could snap at any moment (and has in the past). I want to make sure that if he does so while I'm around, I have the best possible chance of coming out of it relatively unscathed.

Well, there you are. I've introduced you to a dozen convicts. There are another hundred-plus like Frank and Mike in the camp, and well over a thousand like Rodney, Adam, Tyrone, Clem, Wesley, Eddie, Pancho and Howard in the penitentiary. There are tens of thousands more like them in prisons all across the country: and for every one behind bars, there are probably five to ten out there on the street. I've often thought that those who are uneasy at the prospect of citizens owning and carrying firearms would do well to spend a day or two observing the criminals inside the walls of a high- or maximum-security institution, and reading the details of their crimes. After that experience, they'd probably head straight for the nearest gun shop and training center to arm themselves and learn how to shoot, just in case they ever meet them or their ilk on the street or in their homes.

The frightening thing is that they're very likely to do so. According to the Youth Violence Research Bulletin, published by the Centers for Disease Control and Prevention and the US Department of Justice in February 2002, the odds of being a victim of a violent crime during adulthood in the USA are better than two to one. Readers may wish to think about that, and take appropriate (and effective) measures to protect yourself, your loved ones and your home. (I'll speak in greater detail about this in the Epilogue.) You may not have time to call the police (or even be able to, if criminals have cut the telephone line or are using a cellphone jammer). Even if law enforcement officers respond within thirty seconds (which would take a miracle), that's more than enough time for an assailant to kill or maim you, or your spouse, or your children. I work every day with those who've done just that... thousands of them every year.

Makes you think, doesn't it?

CONVICT TO CHAPLAIN I

THE TOP DOG

There ain't many in here wanna mess with me. In the early days, I had to fight for my place. I did, and the hassle stopped. Nowadays the old cons leave me alone, and I leave them alone. We know where we stand. We respect each other. Still, every now and then a new guy arrives. He's eager, he's pushy, he wants to make a name for himself. To him someone like me is a path to an instant rep. He reckons I'm older and slower, and he figures he can take me.

I watch 'em. You can tell they're screwin' themselves up to it, getting psyched and set to take me. I want 'em about two-thirds of the way there, far enough that they've bragged about what they're gonna do to me, so it's real hard for them to back down, but they're not quite ready for me yet.

Me, I'm always ready. That's how I got my rep in here. They all know, man: if you **** with me, you got nothin' coming but pain. I'm gonna hurt you real bad. No other way. I don't fight fair. I'm older now, and I don't have the strength and speed I used to have, so I fight hard and I fight dirty and I know all the tricks. I fight for keeps. I also got my buddies, an' they got my back. If the guy's got friends, they'll keep 'em off me while I take him.

So, when the guy's just about where I want him, I call him out, right in front of the convicts and the guards and God and the Devil and the whole ****ing world. I do it on the yard. I tell him straight, "I hear you got a big mouth. I hear you think I'm an old **** and you reckon you can take me. Well, here I am. Do it now, or shut the **** up, because this is the one and only chance you get. Take me now, or stay outta my face forever. I see you within twenty feet of me ever again, I'm gonna rip your **** off and make you eat it."

They freeze. They know everybody's watching 'em. They want me so bad they can taste it, but man, they just ain't ready. I am. That's my edge. They *know* I'm ready.

Nine times outta ten they crawfish. That's the end of it — and of their rep. Everyone's seen it. From then on they sing real low around me, 'cause they know what's gonna happen if they don't. The tenth time, the dumb **** will try to take me, and I'll put him down hard and fast and mean. He's bleeding and screaming on the ground and he's got some broken bones and he's missing some teeth and maybe an eye or an ear or something else, and I'm on my way to the Hole for a stretch — but every damn convict and every ****ing guard on this yard knows which one of us two's the boss. *I am, mother******.* You ain't ****. *Ever.* I'm top dog. Live with it.

Same goes for the guards. They treat me with respect, 'cause they know that if they don't, they got nothing coming on this yard. I pass the word, their lives are a living hell. Same goes for you, Chaplain. I got nothing against you, y'know? So far you seem an OK kind of guy... but you want to remember that.

FRIDAY — 12:30 P.M.

As I come out of my office and lock the door Ken's waiting in the passage.

"Hi, Ken. All set for the madding crowd?"

He groans. "Not really, but these things are sent to try us, as the Scriptures say." He hands me a clipboard with a copy of the Jumah call-out list. He carries another.

I echo his groan. "And boy, do they succeed!" We both chuckle as I check that I've got pens in my shirt pocket.

Together we go through the Main Chapel, making sure that everything's ready, then we wait in the foyer area. It's almost time for the move. Sure enough, my radio crackles at my waist and I cock my head to listen. "Operations Lieutenant to Compound Officer. Call the move."

A brief pause, then, "Compound to Control. Ten-minute move."

Another momentary hesitation before the loudspeakers all around the complex come to life. "The move is open. Ten-minute move is open."

Hundreds of inmates are waiting on the concrete walkway outside the steel door opening onto the compound from our corridor. The Corridor Officer unlocks it and steps back, steering the flood of inmates through the metal detector set up next to the

25

doorway. A couple of the teachers from the Education Department and instructors from the Recreation Department stand with him to help with crowd control.

I open the Chapel doors. Ken and I stand ready, clipboards in our hands. We'll check off the names of everyone arriving for the Jumah prayer service, then trace those who don't show up. If their names are on our call-out sheet, we're responsible for them — and a missing prisoner in a high-security institution like this is not taken lightly. We have to account for each and every one of them before we can relax.

For the next ten minutes we're overwhelmed with a solid mass of humanity as the inmates arrive for the service. Many of them are impatient, disrespectful, seeking to push past us into the Chapel without waiting to be checked off. They're supposed to present their inmate ID cards to us, but many don't and have to be reminded. The few who've forgotten to bring them are motioned to one side. It's an infringement of regulations for any inmate to be without his ID card, so we'll send them to the Operations Lieutenant for administrative action. As usual, there are a couple of inmates whose names aren't on the call-out, but who still want to come in. If they bring a note from their place of work giving them permission to attend, I write their names on the call-out list. No note means no Jumah prayer for them. I send them on their way despite their protests. They're supposed to be elsewhere at this time, and they know it.

After ten minutes the loudspeakers boom again. "The move is closed. The move is closed." My colleague hands me his clipboard, and I continue checking off names as he goes to the Chapel doors. He waits for the last few stragglers to hurry in, watches the Corridor Officer close his door, gives him a thumbs-up, and locks our door. From now until the next move the inmates who are in here will stay here. Ken comes back to me, we check off the last few names, then he calls the Corridor Officer to escort our ID-less inmates to the Lieutenant's Office while I take both clipboards to my office.

I scan rapidly down the lists, reconciling them and ensuring that everyone present has been marked off. There are nine names unchecked. As I finish, I hear the inmate muezzin chanting the call to prayer from the main chapel. I sigh and reach for the telephone to trace our missing men. I dial the first inmate's residential unit.

"Unit Charlie-Two, Officer **** speaking."

"Hi, Fred, it's Chaplain Grant. I'm trying to find Inmate Otis. He was scheduled to be here on the Jumah call-out and hasn't arrived. Is he in the unit, or do you have any idea where he might be?"

"I don't think he's here, Chaplain. Let me check the unit and his cell quickly." There's a pause while the Unit Officer scans his area and goes to Otis's cell to check it, then he comes back on the line. "No, Chaplain, no sign of him here."

"Thanks, Fred. I'll check his duty assignment."

I look up Otis' duty assignment. He's part of the Compound crew, and the Compound Officers don't have telephones — they're walking around the yards. I reach for my radio.

"Chaplain Grant to Compound Officer."

"Compound Officer, go ahead, Chaplain."

We switch to an unused channel, leaving the common channel free for more urgent calls. "Chaplain to Compound. I'm trying to trace Inmate Otis from the Jumah call-out. He's listed on your work crew. Any sign of him at his duty assignment?"

"Compound to Chaplain. Negative. I've not seen him at all this afternoon."

"Chaplain to Compound. Ten-four, thank you."

I mutter in aggravation, and mark Otis' name as untraceable at present. For the next half-hour I'm on the telephone or the radio, checking with the other missing inmates' Unit Officers and other likely places to find out where they are. I'm able to locate seven of them. Two can't be traced. That doesn't mean they've escaped — it just means we have to find them quickly, to make sure that they haven't. I pick up the phone and call the Lieutenant's Office.

"Operations Lieutenant's Office, Lieutenant **** speaking."

"Hi, Dan, it's Peter. I've got two missing from the Jumah call-out and I can't locate them. I've tried their units and work assignments — no joy." I give him their names, inmate numbers, residential units and work assignments.

"Right, Peter, I'll get on to it. Any others fail to attend call-out?" I can hear his fingers clicking on his keyboard as he enters their information and looks up their records.

"Yes, seven more. I've located them all and they're accounted for. I'll write up Incident Reports on them and the other two, and bring them to your office within the next hour."

"Thanks, Peter."

The seven who didn't bother to show up will earn a 'shot' or disciplinary write-up for failing to attend the call-out. If they do it three times, they'll be removed from future call-outs and denied the opportunity to attend Jumah prayer. The two who can't be located will receive a more stringent penalty. They know where they're supposed to be, and it's their responsibility to inform us of their whereabouts if they can't be present. Since they're now going to waste the time of the Operations Lieutenant and a number of Correctional Officers in locating them, their punishment will be correspondingly greater.

I leave Ken to keep an eye on the chapel while I quickly fill in the nine Incident Report forms. By 1:30 p.m. I'm heading down the corridor to deliver them. I come to the first slider at the main portal and press the call button, then wait. There are cameras covering all the sliders, and the Control Center officer will get around to me in my turn. He'll check his monitor to see who's waiting to come through, then press a button to open the door. Sure enough, in a few seconds the slider hums to life. I slip through the gap, and the door immediately reverses direction and closes as I walk across the portal to the other side. As soon as the first slider is closed, the second opens, and I walk through. It closes behind me.

That was fairly quick and painless, I muse. On busy days I've sometimes had to wait several minutes for the Control Center to get around to me.

Dan is at his desk in the Lieutenant's Office. As I approach I glance into the holding tank. My two missing inmates are sitting grumpily inside. One sneers at me soundlessly through the thick barred glass as I pass. I don't respond.

"Hi, Peter. I found your lost sheep," Dan greets me as I step inside and hand him the Incident Reports.

"Thanks, Dan. Where were they?"

"Otis was in Health Services, waiting to see the nurse. He says he has a bad headache. Leonard was skulking around the yard. What's their record like with your department?"

"Otis hasn't given us any trouble so far. He's new to this institution, and to the Federal prison system, and he's still learning his way around. I'm willing to cut him some slack if you are. On the other hand, Leonard's a pain in the butt. This is the third time he's skived off this call-out. I'm removing him from the Jumah roster."

"You got it. I'll talk to Otis and send him back to Health Services, but Leonard can spend the afternoon in the tank. I don't suppose he'll learn from it, though." He sighs, and we nod ruefully at one another. We both know Leonard too well.

Dan takes Otis' shot from the pile and shreds it as I turn to leave. Like me, he's willing to give a new inmate a chance. We're human.

Back at the chapel I fill out an inmate notification form, officially advising Leonard that he's been removed from the Jumah call-out, then log into the computer system and take his name off the list. He'll have to reapply to be put back on the roster. It'll be at least a month before we'll consider his request. I put his notification into my 'Out' tray, to be circulated via internal mail to his residential unit.

I head for my colleague's office. Ken's got the coffee brewing, thank Heaven! I take out a styrofoam cup, fill it with coffee, add creamer and sugar, and sigh with pleasure as I take the first sip. He and I enjoy a couple of minutes of peace and quiet as we drink our coffee, then he looks at his watch.

"Almost time for the two o'clock move. I suppose most of our Muslims will head back to work or to their units. We'll be left with thirty or forty to study here until Yard Recall."

"Guess so. Will you handle the chapel during the move? I'll go out into the passage and help the Corridor Officer."

"Done."

Within moments the loudspeakers come to life. "Ten-minute move. The move is open."

Ken goes to the foyer of the Chapel area while I exit into the corridor. From the Religious Services Department, Education Department and Recreation Department, hundreds of inmates pour out and head for the door. Several teachers and instructors join the Corridor Officer and myself as we marshal the inmates through the metal detector and out of the door. Some of the staff select inmates at random for a quick pat-down search. It's a pain to have to check them like this, but they weren't sent to a high-security institution because they cheated at tiddlywinks. They're all considered dangerous offenders. Many of them will pick up or steal any odd bit of metal they can get their hands on, and use it to make a shank — a primitive home-made knife. Primitive or not, they can be deadly. We've all watched security camera footage of assaults where inmates and staff have been severely injured or even murdered with shanks. Many of us, including myself, have been present during such incidents, or responded to the alarm they triggered. After an experience like that, you take them very seriously indeed.

A few weeks ago, one of the aluminum covers over an air-conditioning vent in the ceiling of one of the rooms in the Chapel area went missing. I was certain it had been stolen to make shanks. Sure enough, within a couple of weeks searches began to turn up weapons made from it. The vents had been thought to be made of metal that was too thin and flimsy to make an effective stabbing tool, but the inmates found that bending it double strengthened it. Sharpening the sides and ends produced a perfectly usable shank. One prison even found that the supply of plastic drinking vessels in the dining hall was being used to make shanks. The plastic was strong enough to hold an edge, and stand up to the shock of a stabbing blow. They had to buy replacements made of flimsier, more brittle plastic that couldn't be used in that way. Inmates may be criminals, but that doesn't mean they're stupid. If they can find a way to make weapons out of anything, they will. They've used toothbrushes, toilet brushes, bits of wire, ballpoint pens, rulers... anything they can get their hands on that can be sharpened at point or edge.

As the flood of departing inmates diminishes, those waiting outside begin to enter. There are only a few of them, some heading to the Education Department for a class or to use the Law Library, others going to the Recreation Department. None are coming to the Chapel. On Fridays our afternoons are reserved for Jumah prayer and a Muslim study period.

The loudspeakers hum. "The move is closed. The move is closed." We nod to the Corridor Officer as he hurries the last of the stragglers inside and locks the door. The rest of us head back to our departments to lock ourselves in for the next period. We never leave our doors unlocked. If trouble erupts in one department, it'll be confined there and not have a chance to spread before responding personnel can arrive. It's safer for everybody that way.

CRIMINAL MINDS
AND CONVICT CULTURE

*... few are mended by imprisonment ... he, whose crimes
have made confinement necessary, seldom makes any other
use of his enlargement, than to do, with greater cunning,
what he did before with less.*

— Samuel Johnson (1709-1784)

It can be very difficult for many people to understand how an inmate's mind works. Particularly in the case of hardened criminals, it's such a radically different perspective on life that there are few points of contact with general society. In this chapter I'll try to outline how they think and react. Please remember that I'll be speaking mainly about the hard core, those classified as high- or maximum-security inmates. Those at lower classifications will demonstrate many of the same attitudes, but not necessarily to such a ferocious or overriding extent. Minimum-security inmates will probably exhibit few of the nastier traits I describe here. Basically, the more hardened the criminal, the more crimes he's committed, the more often he's been incarcerated, the more these traits will be evident in his personality and actions.

Let's begin by looking at what makes a criminal a criminal. When we've done that we'll look at how such people live together in prisons, and the unwritten code of conduct they've evolved to regulate their strange society. Finally, we'll examine how this 'convict culture' affects attempts to rehabilitate and reform them, and why such efforts so often fail.

What are the elements, the factors, that make convicts different from normal people in the first place? What personality traits or attributes can be identified in what one might call the 'criminal mind'? It's vital to understand that criminals have a fundamentally different perspective on life and the world from you and I. This may sound very basic, but it's astonishing how many people simply don't 'get it'. There's been some excellent research covering this field[2], and I'll try to summarize its highlights and my own experience in this chapter.

First, let's dispose of the popular misconception that most criminal behavior stems from psychological or psychiatric problems. This is hardly ever true (apart from a few exceptions that prove the rule). Such problems may influence criminal behavior, but they generally don't cause it. Criminals know right from wrong. They can and do control themselves — just show them a potential crime scene where there's a significant risk of being caught, and watch how fast they back off! On the other hand, show them the same opportunity for crime with little risk attached, and they'll be all over it. They demonstrate judgment, cunning and selectivity in their approach to their profession. In many cases they devote much time and energy to producing amazingly complex schemes and plans to accomplish their purpose. They're certainly not insane.

Another popular fallacy is that environment and circumstances produce criminals. This is complete nonsense. I accept that these are *factors* in criminal development, and for those who never know anything but the worst circumstances, they can be extremely important factors: but they're not the root of criminal behavior. Criminals come from every level of society, every social class, every possible background. To assert that poverty, or overcrowding, or racism, or family background, or deprivation, or unemployment, or any other factor produces criminals, is to ignore the reality that precisely the same conditions produce vastly greater numbers of people who are *not* criminals. Even in an inmate's own family he might be the only convict among three or four children, all of whom grew up together in the same environment under identical conditions. If a given background is to blame for producing criminals, why isn't everyone who shares that background a criminal?

I would argue that there are several characteristics of a hardened criminal mindset. They are personality traits, attitudes or perspectives on life that, in my experience as a clergyman and prison chaplain, are almost always present in inmates to a greater or lesser extent. Some will be more dominant than others in any given individual, of course. (I admit that one or more of these traits may be observed in a great many non-criminals as well. I believe it's their *combined* presence, reinforcing each other, and their relative dominance over other personality traits, that makes someone potentially more likely to adopt a criminal lifestyle if he chooses to act on them.)

This book isn't a psychological textbook, so I won't go into exhaustive detail, but briefly these characteristics include:

1. **Selfishness.** The criminal wants what he wants, when he wants it. Instant self-gratification is the rule. Others may own what he wants, but that's irrelevant. As far as he's concerned, his desire for it overrides their right of ownership. On the other hand, what's his is *his*, and no-one else has any right or claim to it. Only he is important. No-one else has any standing. As one convict said to me contemptuously some years ago, soon after we began working together: "F*** everyone except me."

34

2. **A manipulative approach to relationships.** The criminal will seek to manipulate others to attain his ends. He'll do so by any means available: wheedling, fits of anger, emotional blackmail, coercion, intimidation, even violence. The end (self-gratification) justifies whatever means are necessary. Any relationship must be run as the criminal wishes. Family, friends, acquaintances, colleagues, even fellow criminals: all are there to be exploited to gratify and satisfy his needs. Their own needs are irrelevant. The world revolves around him — or else.

3. **Refusal to accept responsibility.** The criminal avoids or evades any acceptance or admission of guilt or responsibility. Even when he displays contrition about his actions, it's usually an outward show. In reality his only genuine regret is that he was discovered. He'll blame anything and everything, anyone and everyone except himself for the negative consequences of his crimes. Of course, this means that he'll eagerly agree with those blaming factors in his background for his crimes — it allows him to slide out of accepting any personal responsibility for his actions. It's *always* someone else's fault.

4. **A sense of superiority.** The criminal truly believes he's 'better' than those 'dopes' who endure normal living and working conditions. He's superior to their mediocrity. He's 'special'. He's not bound by the restrictions they accept like sheep. He makes his own rules, lives life on his terms, and won't accept the expectations of others, either individually or collectively, as being in any way legitimate or binding upon him.

5. **A quest for power and authority.** The criminal will usually not be satisfied with a perpetually subordinate position. He wants others to look up to him and respect him; he wants them to fear him. Whether it be in a criminal or a normal enterprise, he expects to direct others rather than be directed himself. In a large criminal organization such as a gang or the Mafia, he'll always have bosses to obey, but he'll also have lesser criminals and victims of his

crimes who in their turn will obey and fear him. This satisfies his
need for power. (This trait is particularly prevalent in sex criminals.
Rape truly is a crime of power, not passion.)

6. **A need for excitement.** The criminal 'gets a kick' out of what
he does. Even getting caught has its own thrill. Dealing with the
arresting officers (perhaps including an exciting car chase that gets
him on TV), establishing his place in the hierarchy in the jail,
dealing with the courts, trying to 'beat the rap': all have their own
emotional intensity. The same applies to life in prison. A really
hardened convict may spend more time in the Hole than in general
population, aggravate and infuriate staff, annoy other inmates...
but he doesn't care. He's getting a kick out of his 'power' to make
others react to him.

7. **Inability to feel guilt.** Mostly, a criminal doesn't feel guilty
about the crimes he commits. They're justified because they serve
his best interests. He might regard other criminals as 'guilty'
because he'd never do what they did. I mentioned Adam in
Chapter 2. I challenged him once, pointing out that he accused
others of theft because they stole from their bosses in the Mob, but
when he stole from ordinary people he was guilty of exactly the
same crime. He denied it indignantly. His victims were 'suckers'
who were 'born to be fleeced'. On the other hand, those who stole
from their criminal bosses were 'cheating' and deserved all they got.
They were guilty. He was innocent. In the same way, I've heard a
serial rapist condemn child-abusers and threaten to kill them out of
hand if he ever identified one. The physical sex crime was the
same. The choice of victim made the difference between guilt and
innocence in his eyes. Raping and sodomizing an adult was OK:
doing the same to a child was unconscionable.

8. **Compartmentalization.** Criminals have an uncanny ability to
put different parts of their lives into separate mental
compartments. While they're engaged with one they ignore the
others. There are many examples of child abusers who were loving,

caring parents to their own children, yet could inflict the most horrific atrocities on other children without a qualm. I know inmates who appear totally committed to and sincere about their religious beliefs, to the point where they can deliver an excellent summation of moral teaching… yet those same inmates can walk out of the chapel and stab another convict, or arrange a drug deal, without turning a hair. They'll indignantly deny that they're acting against the tenets of their faith by such actions: in fact, they might even be praying for Divine assistance while they do it!

9. **A state of perpetual anger.** Many criminals are always angry. Much of the time this is suppressed and controlled, but it can flare up at the slightest provocation. If he doesn't get what he wants — anger. When someone resists his attempts to control them in a relationship — anger. If he can't avoid being forced to admit (if not accept) responsibility for his actions — anger. When someone slights or 'disrespects' him, affecting his sense of superiority and need to be in charge — anger. If he gets bored and misses the stimulus of excitement — anger. Instead of reasoning about a problem and asking why something's happened, the criminal's reaction is anger at what he perceives to be the cause of the problem: and all too frequently he lashes out at it. If it's a person, so much the worse for them.

10. **A refusal to accept reality.** Reality is defined by the criminal on his terms, not by the victim of his crime or by society. A criminal convicted of check fraud will adamantly deny that he's a thief — he 'never took anything'. One who stole from a bank didn't steal from an individual, only an institution, and that's not theft by his lights. A rapist didn't do any harm to his victim — 'she enjoyed it'. A child abuser wasn't abusing the child at all: he was 'showing his love' for his victim. An armed robber who killed his victim when he resisted wasn't guilty of murder. If his victim had complied with his demands, he wouldn't have died. He 'asked for it' by resisting; therefore, his death wasn't the robber's fault. Most criminals will argue that they weren't convicted because of what

they did, but rather because 'the system' or 'the judge' or 'the prosecutor' was against them. It was personal bias that put them behind bars, not the weight of evidence. I could go on forever in this vein, but I'm sure you get the picture.

Having identified these core characteristics of the criminal mind. how do they affect life in prison? How do inmates manage to get along together when these traits would tend to suggest that any form of communal *modus vivendi* would be virtually impossible to achieve?

Fundamentally, inmates function by building an illusion of 'respect' around themselves, individually and collectively. It starts with their self-image. Although the 'system' refers to them as 'inmates', those in prison generally loathe the term. Most of them in my experience prefer to describe themselves as 'convicts'. It's a term carrying greater 'respect' in their view (after all, the inhabitants of an asylum for the insane are also referred to as 'inmates'). In particular a certain way of life has evolved among them which they describe as 'convict culture'. It's an unwritten code governing all inmates. Anyone entering prison will come to know it. Some will be told about it by other convicts. Others will learn about it the hard way when they suffer the consequences of disobeying or ignoring it. Such consequences can range from a dirty look or a talking-to all the way to a violent assault or a stabbing for a serious violation. I'll describe the main elements of the code.

A convict is expected to **be loyal to his fellow prisoners.** His primary loyalty is to the convicts, not to the prison authorities or anyone else — even his family. Everything he thinks, does and says is expected to reflect this. As an extension of this philosophy he should **mind his own business.** If he sees something going on, or becomes aware of a plan hatched by inmates, he shouldn't be inquisitive and try to find out more. If he wants to become involved he can discreetly make his interest known, but he has to wait for an invitation, not 'muscle in' — unless he's got the power, strength and authority to do so. Otherwise, overt interest might be taken as an indication that he's going to inform the authorities. That could lead to painful, even fatal consequences. A convict needs to **know his place in the 'convict hierarchy' and adhere to it.** This is very important indeed. Attributes such as education, good looks or ancestry might be important in the outside world, but they count for very little within prison walls. The nature of his crimes, the severity of his sentence, his physical strength, ability and willingness to stand up for himself, his 'connections' to criminal enterprises and gangs within and outside the prison: all these are the measure of a convict's worth, and confer 'status' upon him. Over and above this, every convict has to fight for his place in the prison hierarchy. It won't help the son of a Mafia boss if he's a wimp who cringes at shadows and hides behind his father's reputation. He may be spared the worst forms of disrespect out of fear of his father's retaliation, but he'll have no standing of his own. Those who don't, or won't, or can't stand up for themselves end up at the bottom of the heap, prey for whoever wants to pick on them — unless they ally themselves to an individual or group who'll protect them in return for whatever they have to offer. In a nutshell, you can be a predator or you can be prey. In prison there's no middle ground.

Of course, this holds dangers. If a convict fights for his place in prison society, he'll certainly have to prove himself against those who aspire to 'keep him down', or who are defending their own places in the 'pecking order'. Such conflicts will certainly get physical, and may become murderous. Anyone involved risks disciplinary sanctions from the authorities, perhaps new criminal charges, and probably a lengthy stay in the Hole. Nevertheless, any convict who doesn't fight in this way is doomed to be picked on by everyone else. His possessions will be stolen, he'll be threatened and brow-beaten constantly, and he risks becoming the target for sexual predators. On balance, if I were a convict I'd choose to fight rather than knuckle under.

Once a convict has established his place in the 'pecking order', there are a couple of rules. He may **never disrespect a convict who's his equal or his 'superior' in the system**. This is tricky. What might be regarded as normal conversation by one person may be taken as a serious insult by someone from a different racial, social or national background. I've found that convicts practice an elaborate, almost exaggerated courtesy to one another, not in the terms usually found in 'polite society', but in words and actions that are understood within their closed community. They don't enter another's cell, or sit on his bed, or touch his personal property without permission. They never make demeaning or suggestive comments about his family, either when they visit or if they see pictures of them in his cell. Unless their cultural group is dominant in a unit or cell block, they try not to ride roughshod over what others want to hear on the radio or watch on the TV. In other words, they strive not to act as if they're better than anyone else. In a sense it's an application of the 'Golden Rule': they treat other convicts as they want to be treated themselves.

However, this mutual respect is only directed at those who are considered a convict's equals, or those more powerful or more dangerous than he is. Those who are 'beneath' him — those who are new to prison and don't yet 'know the ropes', or those who are lower in the 'hierarchy', or who won't stand up for themselves or fight for their place in the 'pecking order' — are prey, to be used or abused or manipulated or deceived or exploited. It's a classic example of 'might is right'.

A convict must **support his brothers.** This works two ways. First, he supports his fellow convicts against the authorities. Second, he supports those who share his background, values and objectives. This is the root of prison gangs. One or two inmates can't stand up against an organized group, but if they band together with others like them they can meet strength with strength. In a high-security penitentiary, any individual will almost certainly have to develop at least informal ties with a gang, if not actually join one, out of sheer self-preservation. If he doesn't join a gang, he might ally with a group of other inmates who also haven't done so, but who band together on a less formal basis for mutual protection. Religious groups often serve this purpose in prison. I've seen many times how they'll rally round one or two of their number, help them get through a problem, mediate on their behalf with other 'power groups', and if necessary physically defend them. It may not be terribly spiritual, but it's eminently practical.

A convict must **'be a man'**. This expression covers a multitude of expectations. Don't snivel and whine. Be tough. Don't break your word. Pay your debts on time. Don't cut in line. Show respect. Don't show off or attract attention. Be 'cool'. In other words, a convict must act responsibly towards his fellow inmates. (Needless to say, that doesn't apply to the authorities or the staff! Convicts should disrespect, mislead and bamboozle them in any way they can. They don't count.)

A cardinal element in the 'convict code' is: **don't be a 'snitch' (an informer)**. A convict is quite literally putting his life on the line if he conveys information to the prison authorities. If his fellow convicts find out about it, or even if they only have a strong suspicion, they can and will arrange for him to be beaten, stabbed or even killed. It happens on a regular basis inside prison walls. I've personally witnessed such attacks, ranging from a simple beating to attempted murder by multiple attackers armed with shanks. A snitch is lower than the lowest form of vermin in convict eyes. They truly hate him.

The sad (and frustrating) thing about convict abhorrence of snitches and snitching is that it makes their own lives that much more dangerous and unpleasant. There are convicts who are brutal exploiters of their fellow inmates. They prey on them mercilessly. A snitch can provide information that will result in such men being locked away where they can't hurt anyone: but even so, most convicts will endure the misery they cause rather than run the risk of snitching. I suppose it's a classic case of the cure being far, far worse than the disease.

A final element of the 'convict code' is, oddly enough, endorsed by the prison authorities as well. It's simply put. **Do your time. Don't let the time do you.** This is a phrase frequently heard in prison. It doesn't have an 'official' definition. What it means is that if an inmate lets the prospect of the years ahead of him remain in his consciousness, it'll drive him nuts. The rule is: don't think of the future. Get through one day at a time, one hour at a time, one minute at a time. Live in the 'now' and do what you have to do. If you dwell on the amount of time you're going to be stuck in prison, or think too much about your loved ones outside the walls, or bemoan your lost opportunities, you're 'letting the time do you'. It's all too easy to despair at the years of confinement ahead of you. Don't fall into that trap.

We've looked at elements of the criminal mind and personality, and examined how those of that ilk have evolved a code of conduct that will allow them to coexist with a tolerable level of friction. What do these factors mean in terms of rehabilitating inmates and preparing them for their release? Can someone with this mindset ever 'go straight'? Can they reform, or be reformed, or are they condemned to live out the rest of their lives as they've done so far?

This question is complicated by the fact that many prison 'rehabilitation' programs are in reality purely general education or training courses. They're designed to address deficiencies in knowledge or employment skills, but they don't confront the inmate's personality. They don't address the traits outlined in this chapter. (There are exceptions, of course, but in the main this has been my experience.) Needless to say, without such confrontation of the issues underlying the inmate's crimes such programs can't really produce genuine reform.

There may be underlying physiological considerations as well. The new but growing field of neurocriminology has isolated certain genetic factors, and used imaging technology to identify physical deformations and abnormalities of function in the brain, that may predispose individuals to crime (or at least hamper them in reacting normally to certain stimuli). This science is in its infancy, and much remains to be done before it can give authoritative answers to questions of criminal predisposition, but I hope it succeeds in doing so. We need all the help we can get!

In order to give a concrete example of an approach that worked, I'd like to describe the process I went through with Felix. I'll discuss his family background (or lack thereof) in Chapter 10, where it fits better. Suffice it to say for now that he was the toughest case with whom I've ever dealt in such depth. He'd committed virtually every crime in the book. It took us almost two years of weekly counseling sessions to achieve real progress: but achieve it we did (or, rather, he did — ultimately it was he who had to make the life-changing decisions and stick to them). My approach was, of course, informed by my faith as well as elements of psychology and other disciplines, but in the end it boiled down to one single word: *truth*.

Before we could even begin the process of 'rebuilding', as I call it, Felix had to come to the point of accepting that he had done wrong. He did so within the context of religious faith by accepting (at least in theory) that it was God who defined right and wrong, not human beings. A law might declare a given act to be legal, but that didn't necessarily make it morally right. I had him conduct an examination of conscience over several weeks. Each week we drilled deeper into his past, examining specific sins and crimes and laying them out. Frequently he'd try to minimize their importance or their seriousness, and I'd challenge him (very carefully and compassionately — I'm a minister, after all — but nevertheless relentlessly). I'd ask him to think about what he'd just said, offer him a different perspective (sometimes playing the part of a victim describing how I'd experienced the crime in question), then ask him to re-examine the crime and the issues it raised over the coming week and be prepared to go into it in greater depth during our next session. It was very hard for him, but Felix had courage. He stuck to it.

When we'd completed the examination of conscience to the extent that he was capable of it at that time, I began to work with him on understanding why he'd done those things. I used the personality characteristics I outlined earlier in this chapter, and asked him to identify how they had influenced his actions in each specific case. Note that I didn't speak of them in general or theoretical terms, but applied them to concrete events and circumstances that showed them in operation. Felix really didn't like this part of the process. Several times I feared that he might do what so many inmates do, and shy away from any further examination. However, he slowly but surely came to the point of admitting that yes, his personality did contain these elements; and, yes, they did dominate his thinking, even now.

At this point I think I startled Felix. He'd become used to modern society's emphasis on feelings. Far too many people had tried to help him work through his *feelings*, or asked him how he *felt* about this or that, or urged him to consider the *feelings* of his victims. I've met many such 'practitioners' and have little time for their nonsense. Instead, as I said to Felix, one has to focus on *fact*. If something is true, it doesn't matter how one feels about it: its truth, its reality, is objective, not subjective. To those who claim that the way one feels about something creates a fact with which one has to deal, I again say, nonsense. An objective fact has existence independent of feeling, emotion or perception. If it's true, it's always true, no matter how one looks at it. There can be no falsehoods like the classic lie, 'what's true for you may not be true for me'. Something can only be true for me, or you, or anyone, if it really *is* true: and if this is the case, it's irrelevant whether I like it or not, feel good about it or not, accept it or not. The problem is to identify it. As Pilate said to Christ, "What is truth?" This, I explained to Felix, was the only way we could move forward. After some hesitation he agreed to try it.

I began by asking him how any individual would learn whether something was good or bad, right or wrong. I gave several examples. We learn if something tastes good by putting it in our mouths and chewing it. If our taste-buds curl up and die, we spit it out. We learn if something is edible or not by eating it. If we get sick, it's inedible: if we don't, it's edible. He agreed so far. I then moved on to right and wrong. I pointed out that in the absence of any law or moral code, he would soon find out whether something was good or bad when he experienced it. If someone stole his belongings, how would he experience it — as good or bad? Right or wrong? He agreed that he would know it to be bad and wrong. I nodded, and asked whether other people would have the same reaction if they were robbed. He agreed that they would. In that case, I continued, wouldn't it be logical to conclude that theft by anyone, committed against anyone, was always bad, always wrong? He agreed that yes, this made sense. I pointed out that we'd just identified a moral norm by moving from the particular to the general.

We then discussed objective standards for right and wrong. We looked at divine commandments, philosophical inquiry and legal codes. Each would be more or less binding depending on one's outlook and circumstances. By the time we'd finished we had established a basis for determining objectively whether something was right or wrong, independent of any feelings on the subject. Clearly, since we were interacting as chaplain and penitent, this focused primarily on God's law, but I expanded it to include the other elements I've mentioned as well. I then led him through his examination of conscience once more, and showed how each crime was a sin, an objective evil, not just a subjective one according to a given moral perspective or in the feelings of the victim. This was fairly traumatic for him, but he persisted.

I then spent several months tackling each of the elements of personality outlined above. For each one I asked him to tell me whether it was objectively true or false, right or wrong. In each case

I asked him to substantiate his answer from the Scriptures, legal and philosophical arguments, and any other supporting evidence he could muster. He slowly but surely completed a really thorough examination of his own personality — and he came to loathe what he saw. For the first time in his life he understood that the only way forward was a radical change in how he thought, how he perceived others and reacted to them. Action follows thought: behavior follows personality. Felix needed to remake his personality and reform his thoughts before he could hope to change the way he'd lived for so long. He had to follow the process from *repentance* through *reform* to *rebuilding*.

(By the way, this is where I have a huge problem with most of the psychological or sociological approaches to reform that I've encountered. All too often they ignore guilt and repentance. Without it, how can reform and rebuilding be possible? I don't see a way.)

To use an analogy, let's assume we're looking at a building. We determine that its present condition is unsatisfactory and it needs to be repaired or replaced. On further examination, it emerges that the very foundation of the building — that which supports the entire structure — is fundamentally flawed. It would make no sense for us to repair the walls and roof, or knock them down and rebuild them with better materials, if they remain standing on the existing foundation. They'll simply fall into disrepair once more. The only way to deal with the problem is first to remove the defective structure; then to fix or replace the foundations; and finally to re-erect the walls and roof on a sound footing. I'd liken *repentance* to tearing down the old structure, *reform* to fixing the foundation, and *rebuilding* to erecting the new structure. Felix had completed only the first element in this triad.

Everything we'd done up to now was, in a sense, the prelude to action. It had laid the foundations for change, but the responsibility to actually make the changes rested with Felix alone. I couldn't do that for him. It would be doubly difficult because he was surrounded by well over a thousand inmates, most of whom would have no sympathy with or understanding of what he was trying to achieve. Nevertheless, he had the guts to move forward. Over the next six months he kept a journal in which he noted his every thought, reaction to others, memory of past crimes, desire, and so on. In each case, he learned to consciously restrain any wayward ideas before they could take over his train of thought, and redirect his mind into new avenues, new approaches. Obviously, the Scriptures and the teachings of Christianity provided the framework for his approach. One could try to do the same thing on a secular basis by using a psychological foundation, I suppose, although I regard God's grace as an indispensable part of such an effort. (That's my calling, after all.)

By the end of a year of working with me, Felix had a vastly different perspective from when we began. He was well on the way to completing the second element of the triad, *reform*. His changed attitude had attracted the notice of the corrections staff at the prison. He hadn't been involved in an assault or major breach of regulations for six months, to their astonishment. Some of them even approached me to ask what I'd done to him. I took great delight in informing them that I hadn't done a thing. God's grace had helped Felix to do it himself.

Now it was crunch time. Felix and I sat down for a long talk. He'd made remarkable progress, and the change in his personality was very evident. Now he had to make a hard choice. Up until now he'd continued to observe the 'convict code' and interact with his fellow inmates in much the same way as he'd always done (although with a lot less criminal activity on his part, of course). Now he had to choose. If he really wanted this change to take root and grow — if he wanted to follow *repentance* and *reform* with *rebuilding* — he'd have to abandon the 'convict code' and live according to the standards of Christ. He could no longer participate in or even tacitly support the blatant falsehood that drove the convict mentality, or the communal way of life that had developed in prison on that basis. He would have to stand alone, and put up with the scorn and derision of his erstwhile comrades. Was he strong enough?

I'm delighted to report that he was, indeed, strong enough. It's been several years since we had that conversation. Felix is a very different man today, and he's shown continued and steady progress. He was released from prison in due course, and is today a street evangelist and youth pastor with his denomination - a very effective one, too. He works with troubled youth in the same slum where he was raised, trying to help them before they follow him down the same criminal path that he once trod.

Is Felix's case a pattern that anyone can follow? In theory, yes… but most regrettably, I have to admit that in practice it isn't. The vast majority of inmates in my experience are simply not serious about changing. They either can't or won't work hard at understanding themselves and deliberately focusing on change. It's just too much hard work, or they don't 'feel' good about it (there's that word again!) or they fear the scorn of their criminal comrades. I daresay that eight or nine out of ten inmates will have such reactions. I'd be astonished (and delighted) if more than one or two out of ten had the guts and determination to tackle this process and see it through to the end, in the absence of a more formal, structured requirement for them to do so.

Contributing to this problem is the reality that our prisons simply aren't set up to encourage or support genuine reform and rehabilitation. There are many reasons for this, and I'll examine the subject in greater detail in Chapter 16. Another problem is the refusal of so many authority structures in society (including universities, courts, professions such as psychology and sociology, etc.) to accept that truth is and must be an objective reality, not something that's subjective and variable. If there is no firm ground on which to stand, is it any wonder that so many in society, criminals and ordinary citizens alike, sink into a morass of confusion, doubt and uncertainty when it comes to making moral choices?

Of course, for 'lower-level' criminals (those who aren't repeat offenders, or who've never progressed to really serious crimes) this depth of reform may be unnecessary. They may well be 'scared straight' by their first experience of prison. Unfortunately, such individuals don't pose the danger to society and individuals that a hardened criminal does. The latter are, in my experience, overwhelmingly unlikely to either want to reform, or to succeed in reforming if they try. Analysis of released inmates tends to support this. A 1994 report from the US Department of Justice (see under 'Recidivism' in the 'Statistics' section) analyzed 272,111 persons released from prison in 15 states. These individuals had a combined total of almost 4,877,000 arrests over their criminal careers. (Bear in mind that this excludes crimes they may have committed for which they weren't arrested.) That means each of those released inmates had been arrested, on average, almost eighteen times. Given that a lot of them would have been first-time offenders with only a single arrest on their records, this implies that the worst among them would have had many more arrests than the average figure. I've known hard-core inmates with arrests totaling well into three figures.

How well did those 272,111 inmates do in reforming and reintegrating themselves into society? According to the Department of Justice, more than two-thirds of them — 67.5% — were rearrested for a felony or serious misdemeanor offense within three years. 46.9% of the total group, or more than 120,000, were convicted of these new offenses during the three-year period under review. (The apparent discrepancy between arrests and convictions may be explained by the fact that many of those rearrested had not yet come to trial during this period. Since their convictions fell outside the three-year time-frame, they didn't show up in the statistics. Plea-bargaining by prosecuting authorities also accounts for a certain proportion of more serious offenses that were reduced to petty misdemeanor charges, for which convictions were not measured.) I also note that these figures can't account for released convicts who committed more crimes, but who weren't caught or charged. You may be absolutely sure this happened, although we've no way of determining its extent or severity.

I invite readers to draw their own conclusions as to the effectiveness (or otherwise) of the 'reform' or 'rehabilitation' programs these former convicts had undergone while in prison.

CONVICT TO CHAPLAIN II

THE THUG

Yeah, you ain't seen me before 'cause I just got transferred here, Chaplain. Why am I inside? I killed two old ****s. Didn't mean to, though. It was their own stupid ****ing fault. Should never have happened.

**** it, man, I needed a car to go see my woman, and they had one. I jumped 'em as they stopped at the corner. Hadn't even locked their doors, the dumb ****s! If they'd only listened and showed sense they'd have been all right, but that old **** started acting up when I hauled his woman out in a hurry. ****, he musta bin eighty years old, a real feeble old ****er. I punched him. That's all — I just hit him. He fell down and hit his head on the curb and went real quiet. Out like a light. Then his damn fool bitch started screamin' and hollerin' that I'd killed him. I had to shut her up — people were startin' to look outta their windows. I tried to put my hand over her mouth, but I musta twisted her neck somehow. There was this funny crackin' noise, and she went limp. I didn't stop to check, man — I dropped her and jumped into that old car and burned rubber outta there. Damn thing even smelt like old ****s inside.

The cops stopped me before I got halfway to my woman's

51

place. Those ****ers were *mean*, man! They ****ed me up real good. Rights? What rights? If the cops want you, they park their cruisers so those dash cameras don't see ****, and they walk you down the road a bit so the mikes won't hear the noise, and they go ape**** on your ***, man. They took me back to town and threw my *** in a cell, still bleeding and hurting bad, and those ******s wouldn't even get me to a doctor for almost a whole day. *Mother******s!*

****in' DA charged me with murder and I drew life twice. Murder? **** no! I didn't mean to kill either of 'em. Those two old ****s were on their last legs anyway. I only did what they made me do with their damnfool hollerin'. Hell, I probably did 'em a favor! No pain, no waiting to die while their minds went crazy — just a quick, easy out, both together, no mess, no fuss. At worst I shoulda got five years for each of 'em. It's all they had left! ****in' judge an' jury didn't see it that way, of course.

I'm twenty-five years old, and they tell me I'll live another fifty years or more in here. No way, man. I'm not taking this **** for the rest of my life. I'll be outta here one way or another. Either I'll escape, or they'll kill me when I try. They'll have to, 'cause I'll sure as hell kill *them* if they try to stop me or bring me back here. No other way, man. You watch. You'll see my name on the news one night. I'll be dead, or I'll be out — and either way I'll be ****in' free.

Now, what about that phone call, Chaplain? I gotta talk to my woman. Word is she's goin' with some other ****. Can't have that, man, her dis-ree-spectin' me like that. If she don't listen to me, I'll have to get my homeys to take care of the bitch — and her new guy. I mean, you unnerstan', right? A man's gotta do what a man's gotta do. Right, Chaplain?

FRIDAY — 2:10 P.M.

I'm just finishing checking the chapels after the move when my radio crackles. *"Body alarm in Education! Body alarm in Education!"*

I race to the door of the main chapel and lock it, then the small chapel as well, my heart pounding and all my senses on high alert. The inmates in both rooms are now confined there and won't be able to join in any mayhem elsewhere. As I do that I see Ken rushing out of his office next to the Education Department. He calls, "I'll go! You take care of the Chapel area!"

"I'm on it!"

He disappears through the double doors to the Education Department, followed by several psychologists and teachers as they pour out of their offices. I instruct the inmates of our work crew to assemble in the main office area, and they obey with alacrity. In a crisis any hesitation will draw instant disciplinary action upon them, and they know it. The Corridor Officer unlocks our entrance door and sprints past me, heading for Education, followed by two or three of the Recreation Department instructors. I move to the door, but don't lock it immediately. There'll be more staff on their way.

In our prison there's no way to have a reaction squad permanently on standby. The budget's too small to allow for it. For that reason all of us — cooks, secretaries, teachers, psychologists, chaplains, whatever — have been trained as Correctional Officers. In an emergency we all respond. The only staff who don't are those few required to keep their own departments under control. Within a few moments, the Education Department is inundated with people arriving on the run from all points of the compass.

The body alarm to which they're responding is a small orange button on our radios. If pressed, it identifies the caller's radio and his or her location in the complex. There's no need to speak, or to describe exactly what or where the problem is. When the Control Center receives a body alarm, they announce its location immediately, and everyone runs like hell to get there at once if not sooner. It's a great shortcut, and it's saved lives before now, staff as well as inmates.

Fortunately, the problem today is minor. An inmate has attacked a teacher using only his fists. He's quickly subdued, and the teacher's not injured. The inmate is led out in handcuffs as the radio blurts, "Operations Lieutenant to Control and staff. Body alarm resolved. Stand down. I say again, body alarm resolved. Stand down."

I breathe a sigh of relief. The last alarm to which I responded ended up with two inmates seriously injured by shanks. Not good.

Ken comes back through the double doors, frowning. I unlock both chapels, and he helps me to check the area. He murmurs, "Come and talk." We go to his office and sink into chairs.

"There's something odd about that fight, Peter. The inmate involved was Gary."

"Gary? That's strange. He's never caused any difficulty before." We both know Gary. He's a long-term inmate who's fairly quiet and withdrawn. He's not a troublemaker.

"Yes. I think there's more to this than meets the eye. Can you hold things down here for half an hour? I want to speak to the Operations Lieutenant. I think Gary started that fight deliberately, in order to get locked up in the Hole. He didn't even hurt the teacher much — he was swinging, but not hitting very hard. I think he's afraid of something or someone on the compound, and was looking for a quick way out."

I nod. We've both seen such behavior before. "Go ahead, Ken. I'll keep an eye on the place while you're gone."

The department is quiet after the recent excitement. I walk from room to room, checking that all is in order. Nothing seems amiss. After twenty minutes Ken comes back. I follow him into his office and sit down, closing the door so that our work crew can't hear what we say. We can still observe them through the large glass panel in the door.

Ken says, "I was right. Gary seems to have gotten crossways with Ivan about something. Apparently Ivan threatened to have his gang take care of him tonight."

I wince in sympathy. Ivan's gang is one of the most violent of the hard-core groups of inmates on the compound. If they've taken a dislike to Gary, there could be serious trouble.

"What are they going to do about it?"

"Dan's called in SIS[4]. They'll collect Ivan from his cell during the count, and bring him over to the Lieutenant's Office for a little chat. Meanwhile, Gary's being put in the Hole for the rest of today while we find out more."

"Makes sense. Well done for spotting that."

Ken's phone rings. He picks it up, has a brief conversation, makes a few notes and hangs up. "Peter, there's an inmate notification of a death in the family. I'm leaving after Yard Recall so I won't be able to confirm it and give the notification. Will you handle it?"

"Of course," I reply, holding out my hand for the notes that he passes across the desk. "I'll get onto it now if you'll keep an eye on the chapel. Maybe I can confirm the details before Yard Recall."

I go back to my office. The note doesn't provide much information: the inmate's name and number, and the fact that his mother has died. There's a contact telephone number for his sister.

I note that she lives in a far distant state, so it's unlikely that she or other family members will be visiting the inmate anytime soon. I dial the number, and after a few rings it's answered. I introduce myself, explain why I'm calling and ask for more details. It emerges that her mother died early that morning in hospital, after a sudden collapse caused by a heart attack the previous night. I shake my head silently. Such swift, unexpected deaths are always the worst for the inmates — they've had no time to prepare themselves for the shock.

"Ma'am, would you please give me the details of the hospital and the funeral home?"

"Why do you want them? I've just told you all you need to know!"

"Ma'am, policy requires that we confirm all such information independently before we advise the inmate of his loss."

I don't tell her of our experience with vengeful ex-spouses or family members wanting to hurt an inmate by providing false information, or criminals trying to pass coded messages through fake death notifications. She'd only become indignant at my 'lack of trust' in her. I can't expect her to understand that, in this business, we don't trust *anybody* without verification.

She grumbles, but provides the information I've requested. "When can I speak to Phil?"

"Ma'am, as soon as I've obtained confirmation, I'll try to get hold of him. It may be an hour or two, but I should be able to have him call you later this afternoon, or at the latest this evening. Will you be at this number?"

She says she will, and we end our conversation. I look up the telephone numbers she's provided. Both check out as belonging to the institutions she's named. I call the hospital, and after some discussion with the switchboard operator I'm put through to one of the administrative staff. I identify myself and ask her to confirm the death of the inmate's mother.

"Sir, I can't provide that information. We're forbidden to

discuss such matters under HIPAA regulations[5]."

"I'm aware of that, Ma'am, but I'm not asking you to provide the information — only to confirm it. I've given you the authorization code to obtain that information as given to me by Ms. ****, the daughter of the deceased. You can also verify my telephone number through Directory Inquiries if you wish, and your caller ID should show it as the United States Penitentiary at ****. If you require further authentication, please tell me what you need and I'll do my best to provide it. I can't inform our inmate of his mother's death until you confirm that it's actually happened."

"Oh. Wait a moment." She cups her hand over her telephone mouthpiece, and I hear her having a muffled conversation with another person. A man comes on the line, identifying himself as one of the administration managers. I repeat my request for information. After verification of my credentials and institution, he confirms that a lady of that name did, indeed, die of a heart attack in the small hours of this morning.

"Sir, where is the deceased's body at this time?"

"I can't tell you that, but it's at a funeral home."

"Would that be the Blank Funeral Home at 123 Fourth Street, Sir? That's the information her daughter gave me."

"Oh. Well, if she told you that, I guess there's no harm in my confirming it."

"Thank you, Sir. I appreciate your help."

I call the funeral home, and one of the directors confirms that they have indeed received the body of the deceased. He gives me the proposed date and time of the funeral service and interment. With those confirmations, I can be pretty sure that the death notification is genuine.

I turn to my computer and call up the inmate's details, then mutter in frustration. He's in the Special Housing Unit. It's going to be a heck of a job getting in there to see him over the next couple of hours. They have the strictest security in the prison. If they're busy with a count, or it's feeding time, they normally won't allow other departments to interview one of their inmates. It's too dangerous. I sigh, and call the Duty Lieutenant's office there.

"Special Housing, Lieutenant Ross speaking." Not a man I know well.

"Hi, Lieutenant. This is Chaplain Grant. I've received a death notification for the mother of Inmate Phil." I give him his inmate number. "He's listed as being in the Hole at this time. When will it be possible for me to come down and inform him?"

"Wait one, Chaplain." There's a brief conversation in the background. "We're just getting some of the inmates in from their exercise period, and then the count's coming up. After that we're feeding the ranges. It's a bad time. Can it wait until tonight?"

"I'll be on my own in the chapel tonight. There's no other Chaplain on duty. If I wait until later, the Operations Lieutenant will have to assign one of the Compound Officers to take care of the Chapel while I'm gone, because we have outside volunteers coming in this evening. That'll leave the Compound short-handed, which they won't like. I know it's difficult for you, but would it be possible for me to come straight after the count? You could have your officers bring him down to me, then start feeding the ranges while I speak with him. When he's finished with me, you can put him back in his cell and feed him."

A sigh comes over the line. "Very well, Chaplain. I guess policy requires that we notify him, even if that means extra work for us. I suppose you'll be giving him a phone call?"

"I will. Is an office available?"

"I'll make sure one's free. Come at about 4:15. Oh — you might want to check with Psychology about him. I know he's being medicated at the moment."

"I'll do that. Thank you very much, Lieutenant. I appreciate your help."

PRISON LIFE

In durance vile here must I wake and weep,
And all my frowsy couch in sorrow steep.
— Robert Burns (1759-1796)

With convicts such as those I've described, you can imagine that communal life behind bars is a pretty tense situation. It's least so in minimum- and low-security institutions, of course. The prisoners there are mostly non-violent and non-threatening types, and if they prove otherwise, they're very rapidly transferred to more secure facilities. In medium-security prisons the problems are worse, but not unreasonably so. Things get really hairy in high- or maximum-security units, where the worst offenders in the criminal justice system are congregated together. Many of them are no more than predators looking for others on whom to prey. They try their wiles on the staff, of course, but we're trained and experienced at spotting such things. That leaves only one outlet for their predatory instincts: each other.

Our high-security prison is not unlike many others, so I'll describe it to you as an example. We have a dozen housing units in three large blocks, each unit accommodating up to 128 inmates in cells holding two occupants. An inmate isn't allowed in any unit

59

other than his own. Each cell is a fairly small room with a bare concrete floor, white concrete walls and ceiling, a double steel bunk, two small steel cupboards, a steel sink and toilet and a barred window. This is a modern prison of recent construction, so the buildings are climate-controlled. Some claim that's a luxury wasted on prisoners, but believe me, it's a vital part of our lives. It's bad enough dealing with fifteen hundred or so dangerous criminals at the best of times. If they were even more frustrated because of heat or cold, our jobs would be that much harder and more risky. We're all for it.

Each block of housing units opens onto a large grassed yard. The three yards are separated by wire fences, with sliding gates controlled from a central tower. At one side of the complex is the prison factory. In this institution mailbags and uniforms are produced. Other prisons make furniture, stationery and other items. There's a Facilities Department for general maintenance, a communal dining facility officially known as Food Services, a Health Services block, administrative offices, the Special Housing Unit (commonly known as SHU — pronounced 'Shoe' — or simply as 'the Hole'), an Education Department and library, a Recreation Department, the Chapel area and offices for support staff. The entire complex is surrounded by a solid wall, which forms the rear of most buildings and extends between them. Fifty yards or so beyond that outer wall is a triple fence, topped with razor wire. Tall towers are set at regular intervals along it. Outside the wire is an administration block, a facilities unit, a shooting range for staff qualification, the minimum-security prison camp, and the warehouse that handles all incoming and outgoing materials. (See Chapter 12 for a more detailed description of these functions.)

The daily routine is unvarying. Reveille is sounded at six. Breakfast starts at 6:30 a.m. The first move of the day is at 7:30 a.m. A 'move' is the name given to the set periods when inmates are allowed to pass from one part of the prison to another. Outside a move, all doors are locked, and any inmate traveling between areas requires either an escort or a call from a Correctional Officer to the Control Center to authorize it. There are more moves at 8:30 and 9:30 a.m., and the first Yard Recall of the day (when all inmates except those working in the prison factory are to return to their units) is at 10:30 a.m. Factory workers will then go to lunch before returning to their jobs. The general inmate population will eat following them, being called to the dining hall unit by unit to prevent overcrowding and confusion.

At 12:30 p.m. the first afternoon move is called, followed by another at 2 p.m.. At 3:30 p.m. the second Yard Recall of the day is sounded. All inmates return to their cells for a formal count, for which they must stand upright in their cells. (A 'stand-up count' ensures that no-one's left a dummy figure in a bed, to make it look like he's asleep while he makes his escape.) At about 4:30 p.m. supper is called, unit by unit. At 5:30 p.m. the first evening move is called, followed by others at 6:30 and 7:30 p.m.. At 8:30 p.m. the final Yard Recall is made, and all inmates return to their units for another count. Lights out is normally at 10 p.m..

Inmates are counted several times each day. Apart from those already mentioned, during the night unit officers will make rounds from time to time, and count those in their area of responsibility. During the day inmates who are in particular areas (such as the factory or another department) will be counted by the staff working there, and for major gatherings such as religious services, we normally operate a call-out during office hours. Inmates have to register to attend, and we check off their names on the list as they arrive. Being a high-security institution, we don't want to take any chances of an inmate escaping, so we keep tabs on them at all times. In theory, at least one member of staff should always know where any inmate happens to be at any time. It doesn't always work out that way, but in general we do a pretty good job of controlling them.

Outsiders are often surprised to see how good the food is in our prison. It's not *cordon bleu* by any means, but the menus are varied, tasty and nutritious. (I eat here myself often enough, so I should know.) There are several reasons for that. First, it's a major part of inmate health. If they're eating a balanced diet, they're much less likely to get sick. Second, there's the morale factor. Armies know all about this as well. If you feed your people good food, half your problems have just been solved. Offer them inedible or tasteless sludge and you'll have a bunch of very angry people on your hands. Ours are angry enough at being behind bars: we don't need to give them any additional cause for frustration. Finally, it's a matter of responsibility. The prison authorities (and the governing entity they serve) act *in loco parentis* to the inmates. They are legally responsible for them, including their health. If the prison doesn't care for them according to basically sound standards, it can be sued and forced to comply with generally accepted norms. It's in our own interests to make sure that we deal with our inmates as responsibly as possible. Regrettably, many state prison systems don't take as much trouble over inmate food as does the BOP (probably due to budgetary restrictions more than any other factor).

Lawsuits are a *huge* problem for all prisons. I've been informed that although prison inmates make up less than one per cent of the US population, they file over twenty per cent of all lawsuits in this country[6]. I'm not surprised. Most of their lawsuits are thrown out, of course, but the rulings of courts up and down the country over the years have created a huge tangle of legal stipulations that we have to observe in supervising our inmates. That's one reason why the BOP has so many people working in its headquarters in Washington DC and in regional headquarters around the country. They have to ensure that the BOP complies with all those requirements in managing its inmate population. Our lives would be a lot simpler (and the BOP's budget would probably be a lot smaller) if we didn't have to do so... but that's the nature of things in these litigious United States.

The Religious Services Department, which includes all chaplains, is particularly affected by such legal issues. Over the years inmates have sued for violation of religious liberties, denial of freedom to practice their particular religion, and a host of other matters. In many cases, we've been able to prevail by pointing out that certain religious practices are a direct and immediate threat to the safety and security of others in a prison environment. The courts have generally accepted that we can't allow inmates to do everything behind bars that they could do in the free world. However, we've also been forced to provide facilities for a multitude of religious groups, many of which are unknown to most of those living outside our walls. Some of them are unquestionably used as 'front organizations' by criminals and their gangs... but according to the courts, if it can be classified as a religion, we have to accommodate it in some way.

This has led to some interesting legal confrontations. One of my favorites is the so-called 'Church of the New Song'. Its initials, you'll note, spell CONS — probably not by accident! This 'church' was founded by an inmate at a maximum-security institution in the 1970's, following alleged 'visions' or 'revelations' which he claimed to be 'prophetic messages' from a divine being named 'Eclat'. He averred that he'd been declared the 'Eclatarian Nazarite' and directed to establish CONS. It apparently included as part of its 'paschal meal' the requirement to eat steak and drink wine (which is *not* about to happen in prison, I can assure you!) and, according to one source, even demanded the right to sexual intercourse with a member of the opposite sex during certain religious ceremonies. (My informant tells me that when they heard that, many of the guards at the facility wanted to join it too!)

Needless to say, recognition for this 'church' was denied, so the inmates sued. There were a number of court cases[7], but briefly, the inmates' religious beliefs were sustained. If anything is held by anyone to be a 'religion', it seems that it's to be recognized as such. However, the courts noted that there was abundant juridical precedent upholding the authority of prison administrators to designate purportedly religious organizations as security threat groups, and limit their activities within prison. This meant that steak, wine and sex were off the menu, so to speak. As you might expect, this led to a precipitous decline in CONS' would-be membership.

I've had my own problems in this area. The most recent was with an inmate who approached me to arrange services in the chapel for the 'Church Of Satan (Temple Of Set)'. He leered evilly at me as he made his request, doubtless taking great pleasure in the thought that he could force a Christian pastor to help him set up a Satanic group in prison. He had all the court decisions at his fingertips, too, and was convinced that I had no choice but to assist him.

I did, of course — precisely and exactly as the courts have ordered. I informed him that he'd have to fill out a special form requesting recognition of an unfamiliar religious denomination, complete with documentation concerning its doctrines and beliefs, the physical address of its headquarters (so we could verify its existence) and the names and contact details of its executive officers (so we could approach them to verify his information and confirm that he was, indeed, a member in good standing of this religious organization). If there was no formal organized religion of that name, he'd have to document his religious beliefs and requirements in full and exhaustive detail. (I provided him with examples of the sort of things that courts have required in the past.) We need all that information to verify that this really is a religion and not just another con game. After all, I solemnly assured him, we take such things very seriously indeed.

I also pointed out to this inmate that he was taking a very big risk in organizing such a group. We as staff chaplains certainly wouldn't do anything to stop him — we understand and respect his rights. We wouldn't dare ignore judicial precedent and BOP regulations, after all! However, there were a couple of hundred

Muslim inmates on the compound, and more than double that number belonging to various Christian groups. Many of them were dangerous criminals (often violently so), and none of them were likely to be well-disposed towards Satanists. He might find himself 'living in interesting times', as the ancient Chinese curse puts it, if he tried to proceed with his plans.

He took umbrage at that, and wanted to know how they'd find out about it. I reminded him how hard it was to keep secrets inside our walls, even for the staff, and assured him that they were bound to find out sooner or later. He then demanded that I arrange protection for him. I asked him to recall how many stabbings and assaults there had been on our compound over the past year, despite the presence of guards 24/7/365. Given that reality, how did he expect us to protect him, other than by putting him into protective custody in the Hole on a permanent basis? I also pointed out that for security reasons, no religious ceremonies are permitted in the Hole, so his application to me would be rendered pointless.

He never raised the subject again.

I wasn't joking when I warned him about the other inmates. Violence is a constant undercurrent to life in a high-security institution. Most of the inmates are predators, after all, and our rules and regulations can't change that deep-rooted reality. They're going to go on looking for prey — and in the absence of innocent victims, they'll prey on each other. Many of them are members of various gangs (of which more later), or join gangs once they're incarcerated. The gangs act like packs of predators, preying on individuals, other gangs and anyone else available.

There are also particularly dangerous individuals who hold themselves aloof from gangs. We shipped one off to Supermax after holding him in isolation in SHU for a long time. He'd murdered his cellmate, and used to boast that he was going to kill one of the staff before he left. He had nothing to lose, after all. He's going to be in prison until he dies. If he succeeded in killing a staff member, how could we punish him? Another life sentence wouldn't make any difference, and the death penalty would actually be merciful compared to the many decades he faces behind bars. You may be sure that we were *very* careful in how we handled him. He never left his cell without being shackled hand and foot, and guarded by a three-person escort under the command of a Lieutenant. We all breathed a sigh of relief when he left us — all except the crew assigned to escort him to Supermax. Their language reportedly scorched paint from the nearest wall when they were informed of their selection! (I'm pleased to report that they made it back safely.)

In every Federal penitentiary there's what's known as the 'Posted Picture File' or PPF. It used to be on paper in multiple files, kept in the Lieutenant's Office and updated frequently, but is now often online. Every member of staff is required to read it on a regular basis, and certify that they've done so. It contains a page for every inmate regarded as dangerous, with his photograph, a description of the crime(s) for which he's been incarcerated, and the reason(s) he's considered a threat. Prior to its automation, our institution's paper PPF filled two thick binders to capacity. They contained records for a very significant proportion of our inmate population. Their history of attempts (many of them successful) to suborn or seduce or assault or murder prison staff and inmates, their vicious attacks on fellow convicts, and their conspiracies with those outside prison to target others (including the families of other inmates and prison staff), made for very chilling reading indeed. We *don't* get complacent inside the walls, believe me.

Individual convicts and gangs run criminal rackets in the compound. These activities are a fact of life. Violence between them isn't unusual as they compete to control various criminal enterprises. There are many areas of criminal activity.

Some inmates or gangs will offer 'protection services': pay so much per month and you won't get beaten up. Sometimes the need for protection is very real. Inmates convicted of child molestation, for example, are hated by almost every prisoner on the compound. For their own protection, some prisons issue them with false papers (a 'fake jacket' as it's sometimes known in prison parlance), showing that they're incarcerated for other crimes that won't attract the same opprobrium or retaliation from the rest of the convict population. The inmate may even be given a false identity. If a gang finds out about such a person, they might use it as an opportunity to extort money or 'favors' from him. (Some inmates constantly scan news reports for the names and pictures of those newly convicted of such crimes. If one of them should be sent to their prison, he may be targeted in this way.)

Other 'rackets' involve drugs, tobacco and alcohol. Such things are difficult to smuggle in to an institution like ours, but not impossible. I'm not going to give many details of how it's been done, for obvious reasons, but our inmates have all the time in the world to think up new ways to get stuff inside. We in the Religious Services Department have been the targets of a number of such schemes. Rocks of crack cocaine disguised as chunks of incense; Bibles hollowed out and filled with drugs; 'leather' slip-on covers for Bibles that turned out to be made of heavily compressed tobacco or marijuana; 'special' candle molds that allowed small items to be hidden within the candle wax; an ornate crucifix that concealed a bottle containing liquid narcotics... the list is endless. As a result, we long ago prohibited the receipt of any religious item from outside the institution unless it's shipped directly from the vendor to the inmate, without passing through the hands of a private intermediary. Even then, we open every parcel and inspect the contents carefully (including X-ray examination) before we permit the inmates to receive them.

Alcohol is a never-ending problem. Inmates (and some organized gangs) steal fruit, bread, sugar, ketchup and other items from the dining hall. They put the ingredients into knotted plastic garbage bags, add water, and wait a week to ten days for them to ferment. The resulting scummy concoction goes by various names:

brew, buck, chalk, hooch, juice, jump, pruno, raisin jack, and others besides. It smells ghastly and tastes worse (this stuff would gag a maggot, believe me), but it's almost the only alcohol inside the walls. To those desperate for a drink, it's better than nothing. The Correctional Officers are constantly on the alert for hooch (it gives off a very distinctive odor while fermenting) and confiscate it almost every week, but there's always someone with a better hiding-place.

Sometimes inmates get really creative at making hooch. The story is told of a newly-built prison that was receiving its first inmates. The new arrivals found that a few buildings were still having the finishing touches put to them. Some inmates had a bright idea, and helpfully incorporated certain 'improvements' into one of the buildings. How they managed to get inside and do the work is unknown, but they succeeded. For the next year or so the staff were plagued by an epidemic of drunkenness among inmates. Tests of confiscated hooch revealed it to be of remarkably high quality and potency: *mirabile dictu*, it even tasted palatable. Only when an observant Lieutenant noticed that one of the store-rooms in a block seemed shorter than others was the secret revealed. Some inmates had walled off one end of the room with a partition, creating a three-foot space complete with electrical sockets and a basin with faucets. They'd constructed a carefully concealed entrance, and set up a semi-professional still. They'd been producing gallons of hooch every week, selling it to their fellow prisoners in exchange for commissary supplies, stamps and illicit drugs smuggled into the institution. It's said that almost the entire inmate population went into mourning when the distillery was discovered and dismantled.

For those wanting something a bit more hygienic than hooch, there are commercial products that can serve as a substitute. I know of one inmate who drank almost a gallon of a particular brand of hand sanitizer. It contained more than 70% alcohol by volume, in the form of ethanol, and doubtless gave him a great buzz (and presumably a royal hangover the next morning). I imagine it cleaned out his pipes, too... Some religious services are authorized to use tiny quantities of wine for sacramental purposes. Needless to say, those supplies are highly desirable to inmates. They're kept under very tight security to avoid problems.

Sex is also for sale — and sometimes taken without payment. All sexual activity is prohibited under our prison regulations, even masturbation, but of course it occurs. We do our very best to prevent cases of rape but, again, we're dealing with violent predators who've never learned to control their appetites. Inevitably, in the absence of anyone else to prey on, they're going to turn on the weaker members of their own society. We offer protection to those who feel at risk, and will transfer them to another prison if things get out of hand: but we can't be everywhere at once. Furthermore, the convict prejudice against 'snitching' prevents many inmates from complaining, for fear of the consequences. There's a fair amount of consensual sex, and some prostitution. It's much less prevalent in the Federal prison system than in some state systems, due to the far better security in the former.

Sometimes inmates coming into the system accept homosexual advances from another prisoner in exchange for 'protection'. This is always a bad choice, but they're scared to complain and don't see any alternative. (Let's face it, they don't make good choices anyway — if they did, they wouldn't have landed up behind bars!) Sometimes this can have tragic consequences. I remember another chaplain telling me of an inmate who was close to suicide. He'd entered a maximum-security prison and been 'taken under the wing' of a dominant inmate (including providing him with sexual favors). Over time this inmate began to 'rent out' his 'boyfriend' to others for sex, while collecting payment as his 'pimp'. The victim felt trapped and unable to resist. The last straw came when his 'pimp' turned to him one day and said casually, "Go with so-and-so over there — he gave me a candy bar." As he later said desolately to my chaplain friend, "Is that all I'm worth as a human being — a candy bar for my ***?" How do you help someone like that when they no longer have any foundation for self-respect whatsoever? We try... but it's a very hard (and sometimes a losing) battle.

Interestingly, many of those engaging in homosexual activity inside the prison will adamantly deny that they are actually homosexuals. They see it as a stopgap solution (you should pardon the expression) until they can get to a woman again. Regrettably, diseases such as AIDS or hepatitis are not uncommon behind bars, so the risk of infection is very high — and we don't make condoms available. There are those who believe we should, but others point out that if we do, we'd be effectively condoning the violation of prison regulations. It's a conundrum to which there's no easy solution.

Betting and gambling are rampant on most prison yards. It's illegal, of course, but so are many of the other things I've discussed. Criminals don't respect laws to begin with — that's why they're in jail. Why would they obey prison regulations any more than they obeyed the laws of the land? We make gambling as difficult as possible, including the banning of money on the compound. All commissary transactions are done on paper or in electronic systems, using the inmate's number to access his account. We also limit how much they can spend each month, and what they can purchase. Nevertheless, where there's a will, there's a way. Postage stamps have become a *de facto* currency on many compounds. We try to restrict this by limiting the number of stamps an inmate may have in his possession, but they find hiding-places for the excess.

One of our greatest successes came during a search, when a keen-eyed Correctional Officer noticed that the screws on a ceiling light fitting in a shower stall looked slightly worn. He called for a screwdriver and dismantled it, to find almost $3,000 worth of stamps concealed inside. The inmate who'd put them there immediately confessed, and asked to be placed in protective custody in the Hole. He was the bookmaker for a major part of the compound, and now that his 'stash' of stamps had been confiscated, he couldn't pay off his bets. He would undoubtedly have been badly hurt or even killed by disgruntled gamblers if he'd been returned to general population, as it was his responsibility to keep all bets secure until they could be paid. He was therefore transferred to another institution (as well as being sentenced to various disciplinary sanctions to punish his illegal gambling activities). The confiscated stamps were returned to the Commissary to be re-sold to inmates, with profits going to inmate welfare.

Prison life is pretty grim in many state institutions. Inmates who've experienced several different prison systems universally affirm that the Federal system is much better managed and much more humane, and I agree with them from my own experience. Still, it's no picnic. Imagine yourself in a high-security institution like ours. Previously you've been able to do whatever you liked, whenever you wanted. Now your home is a ten-by-twelve-foot concrete box with a steel bunk and a thin, not very comfortable mattress. Your life is regimented to an absurd extent, from telling you what to do and when and how to do it, to making you eat, shop and launder your clothes on a schedule. You can spend only a limited amount of money each month (no matter how much you may have available) on a very limited range of goods. You have limited telephone calls, all of which are monitored (as is all your mail). You can't actively manage your affairs outside prison. You see your family (if you're lucky enough to have relatives who care — many don't) on a fleeting basis whenever they can get to you, and there's no guarantee you'll be incarcerated near your home so that they can easily do so. You're under the authority of any and every staff member you see, many of whom may be younger and/or less educated than you are.

You're surrounded by some of the most vicious and

dangerous predators in society. Whenever a fight or a riot or other serious problem occurs (and they're not infrequent), you run the real risk of serious injury or death. Even if you're not hurt, after such an incident you and all the other inmates will be locked in your cells indefinitely, eating 'mystery meat' sandwiches. You'll be stuck in that claustrophobic concrete box with your cellmate (whom you probably didn't choose, and may loathe, or vice versa) without any respite until the lock-down's over. Even when you're not locked down, your horizon is bounded by gray concrete walls or wire fences (or both), with gun towers set at intervals to remind you that trying to cross them would *not* be a good idea. Your only unobstructed view is upwards, where the passing birds taunt you with their freedom to go where they please.

It's a pretty miserable existence.

Some can't handle it… and they decide to check out in the only way they can. Suicide is a never-ending problem in prison. We're all constantly on the alert, watching for warning signs among the inmates. There are many attempts, most of which are frustrated, but some of them succeed. Our psychologists offer mental health services to all inmates, and actively seek out those who might be having trouble, but like the chaplains, they can't be everywhere at once.

It strikes me as odd that some of the most evil, vicious people I've ever met can't handle the environment of prison. They may live in the most downtrodden and violence-ridden areas outside, and prey on other criminals and innocent victims to their heart's content, but as soon as they're incarcerated among others of their kind, they decide that this is too 'low-class' for them. That sounds weird, I know, but I've actually had inmates express it to me in precisely those terms. They see themselves as 'better' than the other murderers and felons surrounding them, even though their crimes are often identical. One man I recall spent almost ten years after his imprisonment fighting his conviction and sentence. He appealed through every court he could think of. The day he was informed that his final appeal had failed, he decided to take his own life. In his suicide note, he said that life wasn't worth living surrounded by so many crooks and thugs. He carefully prepared a length of corded material (stolen from the prison factory) and hung himself from the bars of his cell one evening. The Unit Officer spotted him within minutes and raised the alarm, but it was too late to save him.

Others attempt suicide because of the hopelessness of their lives. They may be under pressure from other inmates, or owe money to a gang and are unable to pay it, or their wives have divorced them... there are any number of reasons. I've learned to watch for signs of depression and hopelessness when I notify inmates of family emergencies. The Chaplains are usually responsible for this function. We take the report, and before we do anything else we verify that it's true. (You'd be amazed how often vindictive ex-spouses or family members send in false reports in the hope of distressing an inmate. There are also criminals outside who might want to send a coded message to their colleague in prison. If he's informed that 'Aunt Edna has died', it might be a warning that a shipment of drugs is on the way, or that his gang is now at war with another gang, or something like that.) Only when we're sure that the information is genuine do we inform the inmate. We offer him special telephone facilities to get in touch with loved ones at such times.

If someone's been in prison for many years, such incidents are always difficult. He's probably lost his spouse and children to divorce, and his parents may have died. As he gets older, his siblings and friends start to die as well. Perhaps one of his children has had a car accident, and been seriously injured or killed. He can't visit them in hospital, or go to the funeral (no high-security inmate is ever allowed out for such occasions, even escorted). He's stuck behind bars, and the receipt of such news can tip him over the edge from sanity to suicide very quickly.

Speaking of sanity, that's another major issue for us. A large proportion of the hardened criminals in high-security institutions are mentally unstable, to say the least. Some are downright psychotic. We have psychologists who constantly monitor our inmate population, treat those who need it, and advise the rest of us on problem areas. Inmates whose condition is severe are incarcerated in special medical facilities. Others who have been stabilized through medication are assigned to the general prison population. We have our fair share of them in this facility.

It's interesting that most of the inmates, even the most violent and predatory among them, generally don't bother those whom they call the 'bugs' or the 'crazies' (or less complimentary terms). If they lose control, things can get very interesting, very quickly: and since they can be as violent as any other inmate, and have few inhibitions and less self-control (including not knowing when to stop), others tend to leave them alone. Of course, as long as they're taking their meds, all is well. Unfortunately, every now and again one of them will decide that he's feeling fine, he doesn't need them and he's going to stop taking them. That's when things can go downhill in a hurry.

Sam, the self-proclaimed Sex God, is a good example. Let me tell you about him. Sam was on a cocktail of meds for a range of psychiatric and psychological issues, but had the annoying habit of stopping taking them now and again — whereupon he'd go stark staring bonkers within days. The authorities at his prison tried to avoid this by making him take them under supervision, but he learned to conceal pills in his cheeks or under his tongue, so that it only appeared as if he'd swallowed them. When the supervisor turned away, he'd spit them out and dispose of them. (That's one reason why many prisons try to give medication in liquid form whenever possible — it's harder to fake swallowing it.)

I witnessed Sam's most memorable breakdown, the one that earned him his glorious title. He left his residential unit one day with a vacant look on his face, humming and jiving to himself. His Unit Officer, nobody's fool, recognized the signs of 'bugging' and called a psychologist to investigate. Unfortunately for her, the psychologist on duty that day was a rather attractive young lady. She hurried over and confronted Sam, who decided the fact that she'd approached him must surely mean that she had the hots for his magnificent body. He reached out and tried to embrace her. She backpedaled frantically and hit her body alarm.

Next thing you know, Sam had stripped off his clothing (and I do mean *all* his clothing) and was being pursued around the yard by a reaction squad of half a dozen puffing, panting Correctional Officers. He was a fit, strong man (he'd obviously done a lot of gym work and body-building before his incarceration), and he wasn't hampered by boots, trousers and the like, so he was able to keep comfortably ahead of them. As they ran, inmates boiled out of the adjacent housing units, shouting ribald encouragement to Sam, who was screaming at the top of his lungs, "I'M A SEX GOD! ALL THE WOMEN WANT ME!"

A number of staff (including yours truly as a visiting chaplain) gathered at a nearby window to observe proceedings. The comments by some of the ladies concerning Sam's naked athleticism and his self-asserted divinely priapic status were of a nature rendering them entirely unfit for reproduction here.

Eventually Sam spotted his presumed light o' love trying to creep away down the walk, and made a sharp right-angled turn across the yard towards her. This proved to be his undoing, as the pursuing posse 'cut the corner' on him and piled on, six deep. Sam disappeared beneath a heap of heaving, thrashing bodies. Judging from his whinnying cries of excitement, he must have thought that all his wildest fantasies were being fulfilled.

At last Sam emerged from a cloud of dust, handcuffed behind his back, still naked as a jaybird. One of the Correctional Officers clearly wished to spare the blushes of the female staff, because he took a handkerchief from his pocket, unfolded it, and draped it gently over Sam's rampant maleness. As Sam was led away to the medical unit, cooing gently to himself, the handkerchief fluttered and bobbed like some sort of weird fishing lure (giving rise to even greater hilarity among his fellow inmates and other onlookers). The poor psychologist returned to her office looking a little glassy-eyed, and was *not* very polite in response to our proffered suggestions as to how she might better have handled the situation. (Then again, they may not have been the most helpful of suggestions.)

Who says prison work is always boring?

CONVICT TO CHAPLAIN III

THE RABBIT

I… I don't know where to start, Chaplain. I mean… I…

I came here three months ago. I was convicted of fraud for helping the Mob siphon off money from municipal contracts. I was the accounting manager for one of the companies involved. Everyone does it — you know that, Chaplain! — but my boss made a deal with the prosecutors. They picked on me, and the judge gave me ten years. Why am I in a place like this? Oh, I see what you mean. Yes, for financial crime I'd normally be in a lower-security institution, but I bought a pistol for one of the Mob men. He asked me to help him, and paid me more than it was worth, so I did it. That got me a weapons enhancement on the charges, and a high-security classification.

Soon after I got here, I found my first purchases from the commissary had been stolen. I didn't know what to do, so I just… well, ignored it. I didn't want trouble. You know what they're like out there. They're evil, vicious thugs! No decent man would ever associate with them! What's that? Well, yes, I associated with criminals before, but they weren't like these… these *animals!* They had standards. These scum don't know the meaning of the word!

My second purchase was stolen too, and then this… this *brute*

77

approached me. He forced me to move nearer to him, and he takes two-thirds of my commissary purchases — but that's not the worst. He calls me his 'rabbit', whatever that means. He told me I had to... I mean... he *rents me out*, Chaplain! Others pay him to *rape* me! It's been happening now for over a month, and I can't stand it! The pain, and their goatish stench, and their piggish grunts, and their coarseness — to them I'm no better than a blow-up rubber doll! I'm *nothing!* I'm just there to be used! Chaplain, I've never experienced such filth and degradation in my life!

(He takes a handful of tissues and mops his streaming eyes, hands trembling.)

Chaplain, you're my last hope. If you can't help me, I'm going to kill myself. I just can't take it any more! I... no decent man... I mean... what's that? Report the situation and ask for protective custody? *(He laughs wildly, hysterically, his voice shaking.)* Don't be a fool, Chaplain! I'd be called a snitch — and you know what happens to *them!* Besides, protective custody is in the Hole. Can you see me spending a year or more in there with those mad beasts, inhaling the reek of their unwashed bodies, hearing them scream and snarl all day and all night? I'd rather be dead! *(He takes more tissues.)* Stand up for myself? Fight back? I *can't*, Chaplain! I don't know how! I've never had so much as a fistfight since I was a little boy! I mean, I'm *educated!* You are too! Civilized people like us don't *do* things like that!

I'm not in a civilized world now, you say? Oh, I know *that!* *(He laughs bitterly.)* Death would be better than this living hell! Can you help me, Chaplain? Will you? If you can't, or won't, there's only one way out — and I'll take it. I mean that. It's not worth living like this. I won't. I *won't*, I tell you!

FRIDAY — 3:05 P.M.

As I replace the telephone after speaking with the SHU Lieutenant, the loudspeakers come to life. "Short Line is open. Short Line is open."

Short Line is an early meal for those who are on a medical diet, catering for specific nutritional requirements, and those approved for a religious diet (usually vegetarian). Those placed on such diets are always fed before the rest of the inmates to avoid complications, as other convicts would certainly try to steal their food. It's perceived as being 'better' than the regular menu.

I check my watch. It's a little after three, and they'll be announcing Yard Recall soon. I call Inmate Phil's Unit Manager to advise him of the death notification concerning the former's mother, and to tell him that I'll be seeing Phil about it within an hour or two. He promises to have one of his team go to SHU to speak with Phil tomorrow. I then call the Duty Psychologist.

"Sally, I've got a death notification for Inmate Phil. His mother's died of a sudden heart attack. Phil's in SHU at the moment, and I understand your department is working with him. Is there anything I need to know?"

Sally whistles. "That's bad. Phil's under treatment for schizophrenia. He's on a heavy dose of antipsychotic meds, and his moods are unstable. He was sent to the Hole for fighting with

79

another inmate just a few days ago, and he's not doing well there. He's got a history of violent outbursts when disturbed. This could be tricky."

"Any advice on how I should handle him? I can't delay the notification, you know that. If we don't tell him, his family will sue us up hill and down dale for violating his rights — unless you or Health Services can formally certify that he's not in a fit state to be informed."

Sally considers. "Tell you what, Peter, let me come down to the Hole with you. I'll fill you in on his background before you see him, and I'll be in the room with you when you inform him. After you've given him a phone call, I'll stay behind and talk with him for a while. I'll also contact Health Services, and ask them to prepare a booster shot of his meds in case we need it tonight."

"Thanks, Sally, I really appreciate it. Lieutenant Ross has asked me to be there at 4:15. Can you make it?"

"I'll be there."

"OK, Sally. See you later."

Sally's a good person. I know she'll stand by to talk to Phil again this evening if SHU calls and asks for her. I put my scribbled notes into a folder on my desk and leave my office, locking it behind me. We never leave our offices open unless we're inside them.

Ken's waiting in the foyer. "Did you confirm the details?"

"Yep. I'll go to SHU to give the notification after count. Yard Recall's almost due. If you'll assist the Corridor Officer, I'll get the inmates out of here."

"OK."

I get our work crew sorted out and ready to leave. They stow our department's cleaning gear in the utility room. I carefully check that everything's accounted for, then lock it.

The speaker hums. "Yard Recall. Yard Recall."

Immediately inmates start to move out of the two chapels and other rooms where they've been studying, and head for the corridor. I watch them go, checking for anything suspicious, then inspect each chapel. A couple of inmates are waiting for me. I escort them to the supply room, where they put their textbooks and materials into the steel cupboards assigned to their faith groups. I lock the cupboards, check the room for stragglers, then lock it; search both chapels to make sure that all inmates have left, switch off the lights and lock the doors; check the inmate bathroom, switch off the light and lock it; check the staff bathroom and re-lock it; check each of our offices and make sure that they're empty and locked. Outside, the flood of inmates down the passage dwindles to a trickle, and stops.

I reach for my radio. "Chaplain Grant to Corridor Officer. The Chapel is clear of all inmates."

"Ten-four, Chaplain, thank you."

Within moments similar calls are made by the Education, Psychology and Recreation Departments. The Corridor Officer informs the Compound Officer and Control Center that our corridor is now clear of all inmates, then locks the door to the compound. Our section of the prison will remain closed to inmates until the 5:30 p.m. move.

Ken returns from the corridor, and goes into his office to put on his jacket and collect his briefcase. He calls, "Should I leave the coffee on?"

"No, thanks, Ken. I'll brew a fresh pot when I get back here."

I collect the folder from my desk. Ken comes out and double-checks all the doors with me, then we lock the department behind us and head for the main portal. All down the corridor, other staff members are doing the same. Most will go home now, except for those like Sally and I who are working an evening shift. It takes us almost ten minutes to pass through the multiple sliders and come out at the Control Center.

"I'll see you tomorrow morning, Peter."

"Sure, Ken. Have a good evening. My regards to your wife."

He's been on duty since seven this morning, and is doubtless

81

looking forward to a quiet supper with his family.

Ken heads for the Control Center to return his radio and keys. I flip my name tag on the staff board, to indicate that I'm no longer in the prison, then walk out of the door and head towards the camp a little way down the hill. I'll grab a hurried meal there — we eat the same food served to the inmates — then come back to go down to the Hole and meet with Phil. I'm not looking forward to the encounter.

It's a strange feeling walking out of the penitentiary's front door. To me, it seems that the place has a dark, grim, glowering atmosphere. It falls away from me as I exit, almost like a weight coming off my shoulders. I can't comment on the psychological implications of such a feeling, but I certainly have a spiritual explanation. The penitentiary is one of the Devil's playgrounds. He has all too many willing servants inside its walls, even though many of them would scoff at the thought and deny his existence. I don't. I've known corrections staff who are avowed atheists, who'll deny the existence of God from dawn to dusk and all night long... but they won't deny the existence of the Devil for a moment. Like me, they've worked inside a penitentiary, and they've experienced the reality of evil for themselves.

I think about it as I walk down the hill towards the prison camp. It's hard to convey that reality to those who've lived a sheltered existence. Not all the inmates in the penitentiary are dedicated to evil, of course, but there are enough of them — as attested by our bulging two-binder Posted Picture File — that the oppressive miasma of their presence seems to be absorbed and radiated by the very concrete walls that keep them inside. You'll sense the same foulness if you visit the site of a major atrocity such as a Nazi extermination camp (although, admittedly, it seems to feel worse in places like that; in Auschwitz, it felt very much as if the tormented souls of the dead still screamed in and around the poison-gas 'showers'...).

What else but evil personified can explain the actions of some of the hard-core criminals inside prison walls? Take, for example, the Central American drug lord who silenced a prospective witness by ordering the kidnapping, rape, torture and murder of his six-year-old daughter. He then had her broken, bloody, naked body nailed to the front door of the witness's home, with a note thrust into her mouth promising the same treatment to his wife and their other three children unless he 'forgot' what he knew.

There's the terrorist who planted a bomb beneath a table in a fast-food restaurant. It blew off the legs of a mother and her young daughter as they sat there eating.

There's the warped intellectual with what's been described to me as a genius-level IQ. His intelligence didn't stop him mailing bombs to those expressing views with which he disagreed, killing and maiming the recipients (and sometimes their unfortunate assistants who opened the parcels) over a mere difference of opinion.

There are the prison gang bosses who couldn't kill an inmate who was about to betray their secrets to the authorities, because he'd been moved to protective custody in another institution. Furious, they instructed their associates 'on the street' to murder his ex-wife, children, parents and grandparents (none of whom had anything to do with his crimes, or the gang) in order to 'wipe out the entire treacherous bloodline' and teach him a lesson.

You may think I'm exaggerating, but I'm not. I can name every one of those individuals, and show you the prisons where they are or were incarcerated. Evil incarnate: the Devil's spawn in truth. None of them appeared to feel even the slightest shred of remorse for their actions during my encounters with them. It's in the hope that some of their ilk may yet do so, and that we may be able to help those less steeped in evil from becoming like them, that people such as myself work in places like this. Most of the time we're disappointed: but every now and again, in far too few cases for our peace of mind, we're able, by God's grace, to penetrate the walls of evil and viciousness which such people have built around themselves, and lead them out. Fortunately, many of those in prison are less hardened. Only about one-tenth of the inmates in the Federal corrections system are classified as 'high-security', and even of those, not all are such hard-core evildoers. We hope and pray that we can turn inmates away from the life of crime that leads down that slippery slope… help them to change before it's too late.

Many criticize us for even trying. They ignore the Biblical exhortation to visit the imprisoned (Matthew 25:34-46) and seem to think that we should be expending our efforts on those more 'deserving', those who haven't become criminals. They point out (quite correctly) that many who 'get religion' behind bars abandon it as soon as they're 'on the street' once more. However, not all abandon it — and our critics forget one crucially important aspect of prison ministry.

With recidivism rates as high as we're experiencing in this country, we can predict with confidence that two out of every three convicts will commit further offenses after leaving prison. (That's how many are likely to be rearrested for new crimes, statistically speaking: see the chapter on 'Statistics' for more information. There may be more who'll re-offend, but who won't be caught.) They tend to become more hardened, and their crimes to become more brutal and serious, as they gain experience. They'll make innocent men, women and children their targets. Even if they survive, their victims will be traumatized, shocked, perhaps scarred physically as well as mentally.

That's what drives us. If we can turn a criminal from his path, we've saved not only him, but also everyone who would have become his victims, had he gone on to commit more crimes. Prison ministry isn't only for the inmates — it's for all those who won't become the victims of crime because of our (admittedly few) successes. We won't know those who would have been victims, and they won't know what they've been spared — but we trust that God will. Perhaps one day we'll find out.

Have you ever tried to help a family when the wife's been murdered, leaving her husband a widower and her young children motherless? Have you ever been asked to counsel a seven-year-old boy who's been sodomized — not to mention helping his distraught parents? Have you ever had to tell a father and mother that their eleven-year-old daughter, standing in the street with her friends, has been shot in the head during a random drive-by shooting, and will be a mindless vegetable for the rest of her life? My fellow ministers and I have been in all those situations, and more... and believe me, there are no words even remotely adequate to describe them.

One understands what the apostle Paul meant when he commanded, 'weep with those who weep' (Romans 12:15). Sometimes that's all we can do. It's in the hope of preventing at least some tragedies like those that some of us become involved in prison ministry.

PRISON GANGS

We may be a minority on this compound, but if you get in our face we'll cut your throat ... Convicts ain't scared of the staff, but they're ****-scared of us. They'll do what we say, because they know for sure we'll kill them if they don't. That's what power's all about ... Killing's more intimate than ****ing. We're tighter with each other than we are with our women, because we've killed for one another, we've killed with one another. We share the blood on our hands. It makes us one ... If you cross us, no matter who you are, no matter what you do, we're going to get you. We'll get you in a unit, we'll get you on the yard, we'll even get you in protective custody in the Hole. If you won't stand up like a man and take what's coming to you, if you try to run or hide from us, we'll punish you by killing your family. You can't stop us. Sooner or later we'll own you, man.

— Remarks by members of prison gangs

Gangs say a great deal among themselves and to outsiders about race, or creed, or nationality, or other reasons for their existence. It's important to understand that those are just smokescreens. Gangs aren't just inmates banding together for mutual protection, they're not just convicts associating in a criminal enterprise — *they're predators running together in a pack.* Along with a few particularly dangerous individuals, gangs are at the top of the prison food chain. There's no other way of expressing it. Think of a pack of wolves. They may go out individually, but if any one of them encounters danger or finds prey he'll howl. The rest of the pack will rally to him. Together they'll defend one another or their territory, or attack and bring down their prey. That's how gangs behave — at least, those worthy of the name.

Gangs, whether in prison or outside, are nothing new. It seems likely that within a few years of the first major urban settlements being developed, the first gangs came into existence. Certainly, throughout the recorded history of almost every major urban area, we read of gangs being active. In ancient Rome, senators recruited their own gangs of street ruffians to intimidate their enemies and influence political sentiment. The conflict between Clodius and Milo in the first century BC (including the gangs they formed or hired) makes interesting reading, reminiscent in many ways (including its violence) of how political party 'machines' ran New York, Chicago and other US cities in the not too distant past. (Some say they still do.)

In the eastern Roman Empire during the first millennium AD, particularly in Constantinople and Alexandria, the Hippodrome factions known as the 'Blues' and the 'Greens' (from the racing colors of the charioteers they supported) were, by all accounts, street gangs in all but name. They often fought pitched battles and intervened in political struggles. They united against the Emperor Justinian during the Nika riots of January 532 in Constantinople. Some Senators tried (but failed) to use the unrest to replace Justinian with their own puppet, Hypatius. According to contemporary reports, some thirty thousand people were killed in the fighting, including most of the Blues and Greens (plus the hapless Hypatius and his brother Pompeius, whom Justinian had executed), and a large part of the city was destroyed. Carnage on this scale makes modern gangs look almost tame.

In the fifteenth century the 'Coquillards' of Paris were a feared criminal gang. The poet François Villon wrote some of his works in their criminal argot. London in the nineteenth century had gangs such as the 'Drury Lane Boys' and the 'Boys From Lambeth Walk', who arranged pitched battles with one another at mutually agreed venues. In New York during the same century we read of the 'Forty Thieves Gang' of criminals in Manhattan in the 1820's, and in mid-century the 'Dead Rabbits' and the 'Bowery Boys', Irish immigrant gangs that would engage in heated political activity, and occasionally indulge in the odd 'donnybrook' on the streets. (However, the reality of gang life in that city was not nearly so violent as depicted in the book and film *The Gangs Of New York*. For example, where the book claims that at one time a certain tenement saw a murder almost every day, police records for the period report an average of only about one murder per month in the whole of New York City. As is so often the case, the book and film are entertainment, not fact; Hollywood, not history.) Gangs in the West, such as that of Jesse James, were groups of 'outlaws' rather than city-style street gangs.

Although we have no histories that speak of it, it's highly likely that such 'street gang' affiliations spilled over into the prisons of every era. Those incarcerated would almost certainly have gravitated to others from the same social background and geographical area, and allied with them against the rest of the inmates — and the warders, as prison guards were called in earlier times. However, prisons were very different to what they are today. Most necessities were supplied from outside by families and friends, not the authorities. Many commodities forbidden in modern prisons (alcohol; drugs such as cocaine, heroin, laudanum and morphine; tobacco, and so on) were regarded as normal, everyday necessities of life. There was thus little opportunity to traffic in contraband. This continued well into the nineteenth century.

During the twentieth century, gangs in the United States

began to change. During Prohibition in the 1920's various Italian criminal gangs became dominant (most infamously Al Capone's in Chicago). They would later form the alliance that has since become known as *La Cosa Nostra* or the Mafia. They became progressively more vicious and violent, driven by the huge profits to be made. With the end of Prohibition they lost their most lucrative source of income. The beginning of large-scale illegal drug use in society has been dated to this point by some authorities — deprived of one market, the gangs simply used the enormous wealth they had amassed to create another. They also moved into labor unions, gambling, loan-sharking and other activities.

The Civil Rights movement of the 1950's and 1960's played a polarizing and radicalizing role in gang life. Many black gangs such as the Bloods and the Crips mushroomed during the 1960's and 1970's, coming to dominate crime in their areas of operation. Other, more revolutionary organizations, such as the Black Panther Party of the 1960's, were overtly militaristic and violent in their aspirations and actions. During the same period many Hispanic gangs were formed, some of which (particularly the more recently formed Mara Salvatrucha, also known as MS13) are considered among the most violent and dangerous threats to society of our time.

Imprisoned members of these organizations continued to associate behind bars, and sought to recruit other prisoners. In response to black gang activity in the California corrections system, the most feared of the white prison gangs, the Aryan Brotherhood, was established at San Quentin prison in 1967. Many others followed. Hispanic prison gangs were also formed, sometimes competing with one another (often violently), but also co-operating with those who could help them, even gangs of other races. For example, there is a long-standing alliance between the Aryan Brotherhood and the Mexican Mafia, also known as 'La EME'.

Apart from their origins behind bars, it's often difficult to distinguish between prison gangs and gangs 'on the street'. The former may have begun with an exclusively convict membership, but as their members have been released, they have often set up 'outside' branches of the gang, and continued to engage in criminal enterprises to support their comrades behind bars. Street gangs have also become some of the largest and most powerful groups in prison, as more and more of their members have been incarcerated. Gangs are now a nationwide problem, and a real headache for all law enforcement authorities and all correctional systems. The BOP prefers to call them 'security threat groups' or STG's rather than 'gangs', probably because not all STG's are gangs (as we'll see later in this chapter). For the purposes of this book, we'll concentrate on their activities within prison, and pay less attention to their external activities unless these are connected to what happens behind bars.

There are a large number of prison gangs. I'll mention only a few of them, in alphabetical order (although not all of these will necessarily be encountered in a given prison, due to deliberate segregation by the authorities, and some are more prevalent in certain States or regions than others). Many of the gangs listed here operate on a 'blood in, blood out' basis. Prospective members have to kill to gain admission, and can only leave by death (whether being murdered by another person or gang, or dying a natural death, or being killed by their own gang if they turn traitor or try to leave).

The following are considered the most dangerous gangs or STG's in most prison systems nationwide. (Allied and enemy gangs were correct at the time of writing, but such relationships can change.)

ARYAN BROTHERHOOD ('AB'): Founded in San Quentin prison in California in 1967 and has since spread nationwide. It's nominally white racist/supremacist (and certainly began that way) but in reality has become more focused on criminal activity. It's extremely violent and very dangerous, and has arranged many murders inside and outside prison. The AB constitutes less than half of one per cent of inmates in the Federal prison system, but is rumored to be responsible for at least twenty per cent of prison killings.

Allied gangs: Dirty White Boys, Mexican Mafia (EME), motorcycle or 'biker' gangs (particularly the Nazi Low Riders), Silent Brotherhood, white supremacist groups. Tolerates other regional AB 'offshoot' gangs, but there are sometimes conflicts between them, with 'real' AB members often regarding members of the latter organizations as 'wannabe AB's'. Despite its white supremacist roots the AB has been known to encourage and even help gangs made up of other races to stir up trouble in prisons, if this is to its advantage.

Enemy gangs: Black Guerilla Family, Bloods, Crips, El Rukns, other black gangs.

Distinguishing tattoos and marks: Shamrock clover leaf, initials 'AB', swastika, double lightning bolt, the number '666', old Norse or Irish symbols or runes or figures. The shamrock in particular is fiercely defended as a unique symbol, and non-AB convicts with such a tattoo (even those of Irish extraction for whom it is a national symbol) risk being killed unless they remove it or keep it covered. Symbols are often intertwined. However, some AB members avoid distinguishing tattoos to make it more difficult for corrections staff to identify them as members of the gang.

BLACK GUERILLA FAMILY ('BGF'): This gang was founded at San Quentin prison in California in 1966 by an imprisoned Black Panther Party member. It has since spread nationwide. It's the most politicized of prison gangs, with a Marxist, Maoist and Leninist philosophy. The BGF overtly advocates the overthrow of the US government as well as struggling to maintain 'black dignity' in prison and eradicate racism. It has one of the strictest 'blood in, blood out' policies, and is regarded as a very serious threat to corrections staff and law enforcement personnel in particular.

Allied gangs: Black Liberation Army, La Nuestra Familia, in times past the Symbionese Liberation Army and Weather Underground, and black street gangs such as the Black Gangster Disciples, Bloods, Crips, El Rukns, etc.

Enemy gangs: Aryan Brotherhood, Mexican Mafia (EME), Texas Aryan Brotherhood, Texas Syndicate.

Distinguishing tattoos and marks: Due to the fact that membership is restricted to black males, tattoos are not always used, as they don't show up well against this skin color. The initials BGF, crossed saber and shotgun, and a black dragon over a prison or prison tower, have been encountered on lighter-skinned members.

LA NUESTRA FAMILIA ('LNF'): An Hispanic gang founded in the 1960's in Soledad prison, California. Its roots were with the 'Nortenos' (Hispanics from northern California) and rural Hispanics. It sought to run prison criminal enterprises in order to gain influence and control over its environment and protect Hispanic inmates. It has spread nationwide, and has both prison and 'street' components, each organized separately.

Allied gangs: LNF has an uneasy working relationship with the Black Guerilla Family, driven more by mutual enemies than by common interests. It also has close ties to a group called the 'Northern Structure', which may be a LNF spinoff designed to distract prison authorities.

Enemy gangs: The most adversarial relationship is with the Mexican Mafia: these two gangs are said to have a 'kill on sight' relationship, which has led to the BOP strictly segregating their members in separate prisons. Other rivals include the Aryan Brotherhood, F-14's, Mexicanemi and Texas Syndicate.

Distinguishing tattoos and marks: Red rags, large tattoos (often covering the entire back) with an emphasis on the letters 'NF', 'LNF', 'ENE' and 'F', the number 14 (for the fourteenth letter in the alphabet, N, which stands for 'Norte' or 'Northern California'), and a sombrero with a dagger.

MEXICAN MAFIA (EME): A Hispanic gang which formed at Duel Vocational Center, California, in the late 1950's. Its roots were with the 'Surenos' (Hispanics from southern California) and with Los Angeles street gangs. It should not be confused with the Mexicanemi of Texas, although both groups work together and share many ideas and identifying marks. It concentrates on ethnic solidarity and drug trafficking, and is said to be the most disruptive STG in the BOP in terms of number of incidents caused (if not their severity).

Allied gangs: Aryan Brotherhood, Mexicanemi, New Mexico Syndicate, urban Latino street gangs.

Enemy gangs: The most adversarial relationship is with La Nuestra Familia: these two gangs are said to have a 'kill on sight' relationship, which has led to the BOP strictly segregating their members in separate prisons. Others include Arizona's New Mexican Mafia, the Black Guerilla Family and black street gangs.

Distinguishing tattoos and marks: The initials 'EME', frequently associated with symbols from the Mexican flag such as an eagle with a snake; a single black hand print; the initials 'MM' or 'M'.

NETAS or NETA ASSOCIATION: The Netas were founded in 1970 in Rio Pedras Prison in Puerto Rico. This gang was initially formed to stop fratricidal conflict among inmates, but rapidly became a fully-fledged prison and criminal enterprise in its own right, concentrating on drug activity, extortion and violence (including murders carried out under contract for other gangs). Today it recruits other Hispanics as well as Puerto Ricans. It is very patriotic and nationalistic, and associates itself with a Puerto Rican revolutionary movement known as 'Los Macheteros'. It is considered a major threat to corrections and law enforcement personnel. It is found mainly in Southern and Eastern states, but is expanding nationwide.

Allied gangs: Netas reportedly seldom enter into alliances with other gangs, and typically allow other Hispanic gangs to assume a high profile while they keep out of the limelight.

Enemy gangs: Latin Kings, Los Solidos.

Distinguishing tattoos and marks: The Netas shun publicity and exposure, and thus display far fewer tattoos and symbols than other gangs. This makes it difficult to identify their members. Their symbol is a heart pierced by two crossing Puerto Rican flags, with a shackled right hand with the middle and index fingers crossed. This is sometimes found in the form of a tattoo or on an identity card. Members wear beads of different colors, depending on their standing within the organization, and salute each other by holding the crossed fingers of their right hand over their heart. This carries the meaning 'N' in sign language, and also conveys 'togetherness' and 'unity'.

TEXAS SYNDICATE ('TS'): Despite its name, this gang was formed at Folsom Prison in California in the 1970's by Hispanic inmates from Texas and surrounding states. It was intended to protect them against predation from Californian prison gangs. It has since spread nationwide, and accepts recruits from other Latin American nations. Its criminal activities include drug trafficking, extortion and pressure rackets.

Allied gangs: Dirty White Boys, Texas Mafia.

Enemy gangs: Aryan Brotherhood, La Nuestra Familia, Mexican Mafia (EME), Mexicanemi, Mandingo Warriors.

Distinguishing tattoos or marks: Tattoos usually include the letters 'TS' somewhere in the design (often artfully concealed).

Readers will notice that apart from the Netas, all the gangs listed above began in the California prison system. For some reason they have come to dominate the national prison 'scene' as well — perhaps because they're simply more violent and more ruthless than their 'competition'. Another anomaly is the strange relationship between some gangs. For example, the Texas Syndicate is listed by authorities as being in conflict with the Aryan Brotherhood, but allied with the Dirty White Boys — a gang that is also allied with the Aryan Brotherhood. It's not just the ancient philosophy of 'The enemy of my enemy is my friend', but sometimes 'The friend of my enemy is my friend'. This has led to complications in certain prisons from time to time.

Some readers may wonder why I haven't gone into more detail about gangs such as the Bloods, the Crips or Mara Salvatrucha (MS13). The reason is simple: these are street gangs rather than prison gangs. They're represented in prison, to be sure, but that's due to the large number of their members who've been incarcerated for criminal activity. Even inmates don't consider them 'true' prison gangs. However, there are often very intimate relationships between prison gangs and street gangs. The former will offer assistance and protection (and sometimes services such as contract murder) to the latter behind bars, in exchange for criminal assistance from the latter 'on the street', or a helping hand to the families of the former's members. There are rumored to be flourishing criminal enterprises run by alliances of such gangs.

There are an enormous number of 'minor' gangs — certainly scores, probably hundreds, perhaps thousands of them. We don't have enough space to go into them here in any detail. However, for those who wish to investigate further, the names of some of the better-known minor prison gangs (and some 'street' gangs active in prisons) are (in alphabetical order): 18th Street, Arizona Aryan Brotherhood, Aryan Circle, Barrio Azteca, Black Liberation Army, Bloods, Border Brothers, Bulldog Nation, Crips, Dirty White Boys, El Rukns, F-14's, Hell's Angels, Hermanos de Pistoleros Latinas (sometimes known by only the last two words), Latin Kings, Los Solidos, Mandingo Warriors/Seed Brothers, Mara Salvatrucha ('MS13'), Mexicanemi (also known as the Mexican Mafia, although not to be confused with the 'EME' of California — the Texas-based Mexicanemi sometimes refer to themselves as the 'EMI'), Nazi Low Riders, New Mexican Mafia, New Mexico Syndicate, Old Mexican Mafia, Outlaws, PRM/Mexicles, Silent Brotherhood (also known as The Order), Skinheads, Texas Aryan Brotherhood, Texas Mafia and the Vice Lords. There are many more (some now defunct, such as the Symbionese Liberation Army or the Weather Underground). Although these gangs may be 'minor' on a national scale, in certain prisons and regions they may be more numerous and dominant (and more dangerous) than the major gangs described earlier.

For those wanting to learn more, there are many books and several television programs about prison and street gangs. Many of the latter are re-broadcast regularly or are available for purchase. An Internet search will also locate many relevant Web sites. Regrettably, some of these resources focus more on entertainment than on fact, and are more dramatized than accurate: but with careful research, one can find the information one is seeking.

What do the gangs do in prison? For a start, they operate as mutual protection societies. They protect their members, and form alliances with other gangs if they're in a numerically inferior position, so that several gangs look after their mutual interests. They also engage in criminal activities. The most frequently encountered of these is 'protection rackets'. A new arrival, particularly someone who is new to the prison system and doesn't yet 'know the ropes', might be 'persuaded' to pay a gang (or one of its members) 'protection money' to prevent other convicts from victimizing, robbing or raping him. There are well-known 'setups' where a gangster might arrange for a couple of fellow inmates to threaten a new arrival, then 'help him' or 'protect him' against them. In his terror and gratitude, the new inmate may arrange to routinely buy commissary goods for his 'protector', or for family members outside to pay a regular amount into the criminal's bank account (or to a gang representative) to ensure that such protection continues. This is a very well-known scam, but it still reaps rich rewards thanks to a never-ending supply of new inmates ('fresh fish' or simply 'fish' as they're called in prison parlance), who aren't aware of it.

As part of being a 'mutual protection society', gangs frequently take extreme care to verify the credentials of members transferred from other prisons. I've known gangsters who've had to wait six months to a year before being accepted into their fraternity in our penitentiary. The local leadership used the time to write to leaders elsewhere, to confirm that the new arrivals were, indeed, what they claimed to be. (All such communication is illegal, of course: it had to be carried out clandestinely, which accounts for the lengthy delay.) Only when confirmation was received would they allow them to participate fully in gang activities on our compound.

Sometimes a 'wannabe gangster' arrives, and tries to fool the local gang. He may even have the right tattoos on his body. Nevertheless, he's usually found out in due course — and with the more dangerous gangs, the consequences of his attempted deception may be lethal. They'll almost certainly assume that he's a 'snitch' trying to infiltrate their group, and they'll deal with him accordingly.

Gangs frequently lay claim to certain areas of the prison as their 'turf'. This can range from certain tables in the dining hall, to a part of the yard or compound, to reserving certain jobs for their members. This is much less of a problem in the BOP, where strict discipline is maintained, but in less well-funded corrections systems where the security budget is low and there aren't enough staff, sometimes the latter will actually co-operate with the gangs in making such arrangements. The staff get an easier, less stressful, more co-operative relationship with the inmates, and the gang gets what they want — their own territory.

The gang will then use such control to 'muscle in' on criminal enterprises operated by others. If you succeed in smuggling drugs into the institution, you may not be free to sell them to other inmates wherever and whenever you like. You may have to go to a gang, and make a deal with them to be allowed to sell your drugs on their portion of the yard. In return for giving you permission to do so, they'll take some of your drugs or a share of your profits, and 'protect' you from other gangs wanting a similar arrangement. Similarly, gangs might have mutually exclusive criminal activities: making hooch, gambling, bringing in drugs and so on.

A gang controlling one activity, rather than face competition for that market, might make an arrangement to exchange a certain amount or proportion of their commodity for something else produced or 'imported' by another gang. Both gangs get what they want, and each retains exclusive control of its particular prison racket. If (all too frequently *when*) greed overtakes good sense, gang conflicts may erupt over such 'exclusivity', leading to murders, assaults and a sharp increase in tension and violence on the compound. Gangs hate free enterprise, even if the enterprise isn't 'free', so to speak. They're all for a controlled economy, provided they're the ones doing the controlling.

Gangs will co-operate when it's in their mutual interest to do so. Frequently prison gangs will 'take care' of a problem in prison for members of a street gang. In return the latter will arrange to ship contraband to them, or do a favor for their family members outside prison, or something like that. There have even been instances where a major criminal enterprise has developed, with gangs on the outside smuggling large quantities of contraband into the prison, where it's sold on the compound by prison gangs. Part of the profits are 'repatriated' to the gang outside through complicit guards, or used to buy other products that the external gang wants. (However, since most criminals are, by definition, untrustworthy, there are all too often those who unwisely try to keep too much of the profits for themselves. This frequently leads to conflict and bloodshed.)

The same co-operation may be encountered in 'enforcement

operations'. A gang in prison may assault or kill inmates regarded as traitors by a street gang, or whose testimony might pose a threat to the latter. In return, the street gang will threaten or apply pressure to those who can be 'persuaded' to smuggle contraband into the prison, or turn a blind eye to gang activities there. Corrections staff and their families have frequently come under that sort of pressure to obtain 'favors', or prevent the former from testifying against inmates in assault and murder cases.

I've experienced one such threat myself. An inmate was nagging me to allow him additional telephone calls from the chapel to 'his family'. He could provide no verifiable reason for me to do so: and the telephone numbers he gave me weren't on his regular calling list, and didn't check out as belonging to any obvious relatives. I refused, and kept on refusing despite his repeated requests. In due course I was approached by a known prison gang member. He warned me that if I didn't allow this inmate a few phone calls, I might 'run into some trouble on the outside'. He refused to be more specific, saying only that I 'knew the score' and that I should co-operate to 'save everyone a lot of trouble'. I reported the incident to SIS, who took steps to deal with it. I was on the alert for a considerable time, but nothing came of it, fortunately. I assume that the gang intervened because this inmate wanted to use the phone to arrange some criminal activity to their advantage, and I was getting in the way (which, of course, I continued to do).

Gangs may also try to keep other inmate groups 'in their place'. Regional differences are a frequent source of conflict. For example, the BOP accommodates inmates from Washington DC, which (unlike the fifty states) has no prison system of its own. DC inmates have a system-wide reputation for being generally violent, anti-social and utterly untrustworthy. They're loathed as a group by many convicts from other areas. There have been occasions where prison gangs have combined forces to put them in their place, and stop them interfering with criminal activities run by other groups.

At other times, inmates from different regions (particularly in the South) have banded together to teach a lesson in manners to their DC counterparts. I've witnessed several such encounters, and they can be very violent indeed.

(Staff find the DC inmates as difficult to deal with as do other convicts. One incident in particular comes to mind. When some DC inmates initiated an assault, other convicts nearby jumped in *en masse* and handed them a severe thrashing. The CO's and staff — including myself — had to work hard to restrain our approval whilst responding to the fight alarm. Several of the DC inmates later complained that we broke up the fight far too slowly, particularly since they were losing very painfully. I really can't imagine how they got that impression, of course.)

However, as always, generalizations are tricky. I've known DC inmates for whom I had respect, and who never tried to push me around or play me false. Admittedly, they were in a minority among their fellows, but nevertheless, it demonstrates that one can't classify all individuals according to their group, or race, or gang, or any other collective criterion.

The line between gangs and other groups is frequently blurred behind bars. I can think of several religious groups who function very much like gangs in terms of mutual protection of their members, and control of certain criminal activities on the compound. One group even assigned two burly inmates to act as 'bodyguards' for their elected religious leader, to make sure he was kept safe on the compound and wasn't bothered by others. (We regarded this development with a jaundiced eye, because that particular leader had been in the Hole for violence on the compound on several occasions before his election to office. He was an extremely powerful man, very well developed physically, and was demonstrably more than capable of looking after himself. This made us wonder what he and his two 'bodyguards' were up to in reality... because we were convinced it was far from religious.)

In another case, the link between a religious group and

external criminal activity was very clear indeed. This faith group actually approached the BOP some years ago, to request that its incarcerated members be permitted to take part in elections for its leadership. Upon investigation, it emerged that well over half of the entire male membership of that faith group was behind bars! Needless to say, their request was refused. Other 'religious' groups are even more dubious in orientation.

This illustrates a serious problem for prison authorities. The cloak of 'religious belief' can be used very liberally, thanks to rulings by the US courts. As a result, many gang members deliberately set up their groups as religious organizations, or try to 'muscle in' on otherwise legitimate faith groups to use them as cover. One example would be Pancho's gang, mentioned in Chapter 2. Another is the Asatru religious group. Outside prison this faith follows the ancient Norse religious tradition, and seems to have few or no overtly racist teachings or tendencies. (The Nazis tried to incorporate certain Asatru teachings into their warped philosophy, but this can hardly be blamed on the religion itself, or its adherents.) Behind bars, however, the group is known throughout the BOP and other prison systems as a haven for white supremacist gang-bangers, particularly Skinheads of various kinds. This means we have to be careful in scheduling Asatru meetings, to make sure they don't coincide with those of other groups who are aware of the racist leanings of some of their members, and might take umbrage. (The really dangerous white supremacists, such as the AB, scorn such pretensions. They neither want nor need to disguise their activities, regarding this as a tacit admission of weakness. Those who do so are 'lesser beings', as one of them put it to me.)

Other legal decisions can also favor gang operations. Courts may rule to eliminate discrimination on racial or other grounds, or provide certain rights to inmates, which sounds fine in theory: but in practice their rulings may have the side effect of making a gang's activities easier. For example, the landmark case of *Guajuardo v.*

Estelle (580 F. 2d. 748 [5th Cir. 1978]) allowed inmates in Texas prisons to correspond with one another. This led to that state's corrections system being unable to conceal the identities of many informers, as other inmates could more easily report their activities and locations to those wishing to trace and 'deal with' them. It also allowed gangs to communicate more freely with their members. The result was increased gang recruiting, greater violence, and an outbreak of threats and extortion against other inmates and their families. All this came from a simple decision to allow inmates to communicate more easily through the mails… a classic demonstration of unintended consequences when dealing with such hardened criminals. They'll use our society's emphasis on rights and privileges against us, any and every chance they get.

I must say, though, that from my perspective as a Chaplain the stronger gangs (and the religious groups that are gangs in all but name) do have one positive aspect. There are many gang members who'll try to take advantage of Chaplains to wheedle extra privileges to which they're not entitled, or try to pressure them in other ways, or perhaps behave inappropriately towards them or in the Chapel area. Under such circumstances, a quiet word with one of the leaders of their gang can work wonders. There are no concessions made, no nonsense involved, certainly no violence requested or implied: but the leaders know full well that Chaplains provide special assistance in family emergencies and similar circumstances. They don't want that to stop, so if they're informed that one of their members is causing trouble, it's been my experience that he rapidly becomes a model citizen (at least around me). I don't think violence is involved. Someone will have a quiet word with him, and usually he'll get the message. If he's too dumb or full of himself to take heed, we have disciplinary measures we can use to enforce good behavior. We prefer not to do so (we're Chaplains, after all) but sometimes there's no other way.

Some may wonder why I've not mentioned Asian gangs: Chinese, Japanese, Korean and Thai criminals. They're certainly active in the USA, but they appear to restrict their activities largely to their own communities. They can be at least as violent and brutal as any other gang, though. The police in Hong Kong have some very gruesome footage of gangland victims, and they and other Far Eastern authorities have provided useful intelligence to Western law enforcement agencies. The battle against such gangs goes on, but largely in the shadows, usually unnoticed by the media.

Gangs are an ever-present menace on many prison yards, and the way things are going, they're likely to remain a menace for years or even decades to come. The 'first generation' of prison gangsters are older men now, but they've recruited younger followers, who are taking the baton (or the shank) from their hands and continuing their work. We have to remain on constant alert to prevent them becoming even more of a threat to the safety of our prisons.

CONVICT TO CHAPLAIN IV

THE PREDATOR

Sure, he's my rabbit, Chaplain. God made him that way. He's *always* gonna be *someone's* rabbit. On the street he'd be working for the Man, for whatever they felt like paying him. In here, he works for me. Makes me sort of an employer, don't it? *(Laughter.)* Damn, I got class now!

I knew he was a rabbit the first time I saw him. Pale guy, office type, trying to look tough but way out of his depth. I couldn't figure out why they put him in a place like this on just a fraud charge, until I found out he'd also bought a gun for a wise guy. If you got a weapons charge, they always put you in a higher risk category. Dumb ****s! Him? *Dangerous?* Fat chance!

I stole his first commissary order when he was away from his locker for a bit. The others in his area didn't squeal — I squared 'em. The rabbit didn't complain to anyone. I waited till I was sure of that, then stole his next order as well. By now he was getting desperate. I waited a bit longer, till I was sure he hadn't reported that either, then I talked to him.

I gave him a choice. He requests a transfer nearer to me where I can keep an eye on him. I get two-thirds of his commissary, he gets to keep a third. If he don't like it, he can report me — and I'll pass the word that he's a snitch. On this compound, with that rep, he won't last a week. He'll have to go into protective custody in the Hole, and since he was in there for a spell when he arrived while they processed him, he knows what it's like in there. If he wants to fight me instead, that's fine with me. Let's settle this like men right now. Why not?

Of course, he didn't do that. Rabbits never do. I've owned his *** ever since that day. Even had to fight for him, would you believe it? Couple of other guys wanted him for their own rabbit. I had to put my mark on 'em before they'd accept he was already taken.

Sex? *Hell,* no! I got standards, Chaplain! I don't screw guys. I take care of my own needs when I feel the urge. Others? Sure. They pay me, I let them have him for a while. A few smokes, a joint, a bottle of hooch, whatever. It's OK — I make sure they don't hurt him too much. That'd be bad for business. What? Well, of *course* he don't like it, but who gives a **** what he likes? He's a rabbit. I own him. He'll do what I ****in' tell him to do — or else! Hell, I'm probably doin' him a favor. Man's gotta get some ****in' relaxation in here. *Ha!* That's a good one! "****in' relaxation", get it? *(Raucous, sneering laughter.)* I oughta be on one of them TV comedy shows!

You want to help him, Chaplain? Here's how. *Tell him to ****in' learn to ****in' like it.* You want to make a case about this and lock me up, you go right ahead. It won't do him no good. My buddies will look after him for me while I'm in the Hole, and I'll be out again soon enough. You know it. Even if you transfer him to another prison, it won't help him none. He'll only land in a deeper hole at his new place. That's where rabbits live — in holes. It's their nature. It's just my good luck, and his bad, that he landed up in *my* hole... an' that's where he's gonna stay.

FRIDAY — 3:45 P.M.

I arrive at the camp. This place is entirely different from the penitentiary. The hundred-odd inmates here are classified as minimum-security, not considered a risk to themselves or the community. The atmosphere is very different, much lighter, almost cheerful. There isn't even a wall or a fence around the place, and only one Correctional Officer works down here. They're assigned in rotation from the penitentiary staff, and many of them seem to regard it as the equivalent of a paid holiday. In fact, the tougher guards prefer to avoid this assignment. There's never any excitement in the camp, in their opinion. (For that, the camp inmates are devoutly grateful.)

I enter the dining hall. Taking a cash card from my pocket, I pay for a meal ticket at the automated dispenser next to the door. Staff are required to pay for any meals eaten in the prison, but the prices are very reasonable — just high enough to cover costs. I go to the serving counter, where the Food Services administrator is supervising a few inmates as they put trays of food in the heating unit. The inmates will eat after the four o'clock count, but a few staff from the penitentiary are already here. We'll get a quick meal while the count's in progress, so that we can get on with our work as soon as it's cleared.

We take plastic serving trays and plastic knives, forks and

spoons, and are served heaping portions of sausages and gravy. The food's simple, but nutritious and well-cooked. A central self-service island carries a small selection of salads on a bed of ice, a heated section with trays of mashed potatoes and vegetables, and a gooey dessert. Sodas and water are available from a dispenser at one side of the room. We sit together at a table, two recreation specialists, a teacher and myself, and eat our meal whilst exchanging casual conversation about the events of the day.

I ask the teacher about the assault in the Education Department earlier that afternoon. He shrugs. "Strange sort of assault. The inmate wasn't really trying. We all think he did it deliberately, so as to be arrested and locked in the hole. There's got to be something behind this."

The two recreation specialists nod, as do I. I don't share Ken's comments with them — they'll hear about it soon enough, once Ivan's been dealt with. The inmates will probably learn of it even sooner. The speed, efficiency and accuracy of the 'inmate grapevine' never ceases to amaze me. It's almost impossible to keep something secret for long, unless it's very tightly held and controlled: and even then, it's best never to speak of it within the perimeter wall. There may be listening ears anywhere. (Of course, the grapevine can be very helpful too. Many of us have learned of an inmate's difficulty in dealing with a personal problem, or a looming conflict, or a clash of personalities, in time to intervene and sort matters out before they exploded.)

I finish my meal and glance at my watch. It's already 4:05. I need to be at SHU in ten minutes. I bid a hasty farewell to my colleagues, and hurry back up the hill to the penitentiary.

As I pass the Lieutenant's Office on my way to the Hole, I look out of the window. Two Correctional Officers are escorting Ivan across the yard towards the office. I smile with grim satisfaction. He can now explain his threats against Gary to the Operations Lieutenant and representatives from the SIS office. With luck, he'll be in the Hole later this afternoon, and a major source of difficulty on the compound will be removed... at least for a time.

At the slider ahead of me, Sally is waiting. "Hi, Peter," she greets me. "All set for Phil's notification?"

"As set as I'll ever be," I reply, fingering the folder in my hand.

We wait until the Control Center responds to our press on the call button and opens the slider, then walk through. We pass the Receiving and Dispatch area, where new arrivals are entered into the prison's systems and departing inmates are processed out. Another slider brings us to the door leading to the rear yard, where buses load and unload inmates. We walk past it, down the passage, until we come to the slider separating us from the entrance portal to the Hole.

I reach for my radio and set it to the Hole's communications channel. "Chaplain Grant to Special Housing Unit. A psychologist and myself are at your door." There's no acknowledgment, but we know the staff within will have heard my call. As soon as one of them is free he'll come to the portal, check our identity through the windows, then radio the Control Center to admit us. I glance at my watch. It's 4:15 p.m. precisely, and we're right on time.

Sally and I enter SHU to a cacophony of noise. The inmates incarcerated here tend to be unruly, uncooperative and unfazed by authority. They yell back and forth, scream insults at passing Correctional Officers, and make disgustingly rude and suggestive remarks to any unfortunate lady (nurse, psychologist or Correctional Officer) who happens to wander into their field of vision. In another prison where I've worked, the cells in the Hole had barred doors rather than solid units. Some of the inmates would masturbate, and try to time their ejaculations so as to spray any passing woman with semen. If they couldn't manage that, they'd hurl urine and feces at anyone within range. That's one of the reasons why our SHU has solid doors with inset glass windows. It's a whole lot more sanitary for those working here.

The Hole is always a stressful place to visit, and I have the deepest sympathy for the staff here. It's probably the least desirable duty station in the prison. SHU staff tend to be selected from amongst the toughest and most unflappable CO's we've got. They'll need those attributes in spades if they're to stay sane here. We Chaplains visit it at least once per week, logging our attendance as per regulations, and go to every cell to give all those in here a chance to make their concerns known. Our visits usually attract half-a-dozen requests for assistance, plus a superfluity of oaths, threats and profanities. Most of those in the Hole seem to fear neither God nor the Devil.

Sally and I enter our names in the SHU Log and sign it, then go to the Lieutenant's Office. Lieutenant Ross is waiting for us.

"Hi, Sally, Chaplain. I'll have Phil brought out. Sally, are any special precautions required?"

"I'll be here during the notification. After Chaplain Grant's finished, I'll stay on for a while and talk to Phil. I've got Health Services standing by with a booster shot of his meds if I think he needs them."

"Sounds good. We've got him in one of the isolation cells, so we should be able to manage him." He looks at me. "Chaplain, I know that sometimes SHU staff have handcuffed inmates with their hands in front of them in situations like this, so that they can hold a telephone more easily. Not this time. Phil's too damn dangerous, and I'm not prepared to take any chances with him. He'll be in leg-irons and handcuffed behind his back, and I'll fasten his handcuffs to a waist chain. You'll have to hold the phone to his head. Also, if he gives any trouble I'm putting him straight back in his cell, no matter what." I can tell he's not happy.

"Fair enough, Lieutenant. You know him better than I do."

"OK, let's get this thing moving."

The Lieutenant goes out and calls for some of his officers to go to Phil's cell with him. I look at Sally, raising my eyebrows in surprise, and she nods grimly to show her agreement with the

Lieutenant. She briefs me on Phil's background, diagnosis and treatment, and I take due note to be extremely careful with this man. He's dangerous and unpredictable — and I'm going to be the only one standing within range if he decides to get violent.

After about five minutes I hear the clanking of chains approaching. The door opens and the Lieutenant backs in, holding on to Phil's waist chain. The leg-irons' chain is short enough that he can only move in a slow shuffle. He's wearing a white jumpsuit and flimsy paper slippers. Behind him two CO's are holding an arm each, watching him narrowly. The three lead him to a chair in front of the desk and sit him down. Sally and I are behind the desk, she standing back against the wall while I sit by the telephone.

The Lieutenant looks at me. "A CO will be outside the door at all times. Call if you need anything." I nod at his unspoken message, and the three of them exit, leaving the door ajar.

"Phil," I begin, "I'm afraid I have some bad news for you." As gently as possible I break the news to him of his mother's death. He just looks at me, saying nothing.

"Did you understand me, Phil?"

"Yeah, I unnerstan'. The ****ing bitch is dead. So what? She ain't bin ta see me in years. She didn't give a flying **** for me, so why the **** should I care about her? Good riddance is what I say!"

Inwardly I sigh. So much for filial loyalty and concern.

"Your sister called to give us the news. Would you like to speak to her?"

"Yeah, why not? I'm entitled, aren't I?"

"Yes, you're entitled to a call under such circumstances. I'll call her now, and hold the telephone for you while you talk with her."

I pick up the phone and dial the Control Center. No telephone in SHU can make a long-distance call directly — we don't take any chances that one of these particularly hardened criminals might get hold of a phone. All such calls are made by the

Control Center staff, and then connected to an extension here. I identify myself, give them the area code and phone number I want, and replace the receiver. Within seconds it rings, and I pick it up again.

"Chaplain Grant here."

"You're through, Chaplain." There's a click on the line.

"Hello, this is Chaplain Grant."

"Hi, Chaplain, this is Phil's sister."

"Hello, Ma'am. I have Phil with me. I'll put him on the line."

I stand up, walk around the desk and hold the telephone next to Phil's head. For several minutes he and his sister talk, conversation on his part being largely limited to grunts and profanities. My hand and arm grow cramped holding the phone in one position, and I change hands, earning a scowl and a muttered complaint from Phil as he glares at me. I can't make out his words, which is probably just as well.

At last Phil grunts something and looks up at me. "She wants ta talk ta ya, Chaplain."

I nod, go back around the desk, sit down and lift the receiver to my ear. I speak with his sister for a few moments, explaining that no, Phil won't be permitted to attend the funeral. While I'm doing that, I'm aware of Sally talking with Phil in a low voice, but I can't concentrate on two conversations at once. I conclude my conversation with Phil's sister and replace the receiver.

Sally looks at me. "I'll stay and talk with Phil for a while, Peter. Will you please pass the word for me on your way back?"

"Sure, Sally." I understand immediately that she wants me to drop in at Health Services, and send one of their staff down to give Phil his booster shot. I get up from behind the desk and she slides into the chair, keeping the desk between herself and Phil. I open the door and nod to the CO waiting there. He wedges the door open with his foot so that he can keep a watchful eye on Phil. If he makes trouble for Sally, the CO can be at her side in seconds. With someone like Phil, that might well become necessary.

I turn to the Lieutenant, who's waiting nearby. "I'm through with Phil, thanks, Lieutenant. Sally wants me to pass the word to Health Services for his booster shot. She'll be talking with him until it arrives."

"OK. I'll have a team standing by to secure him while they administer the shot. He probably won't feel like co-operating."

Most of his staff are now taking food trays up to the ranges, where they insert them through slots in the cell doors. He'll have to take one or two of them off that duty to handle Phil. I've certainly inconvenienced him and his crew by coming down at this time, but he understands that sometimes these things happen. We're on the same team, and he knows I won't abuse his time or his staff if my business can wait until later. I've demonstrated that in the past. That's why he was willing to help me today, despite the inconvenience.

I enter my time of departure in the SHU Log, while the Lieutenant calls the Control Center on his radio to have them let me out. No-one simply buzzes for attention in SHU: one of the staff here has to personally authorize every entry and exit. It's time-consuming and inconvenient, but necessary... just one more precaution, based on the danger posed by many of those locked away here.

FAMILIES

Families are like fudge: mostly sweet, with a few nuts.

— Anonymous

Family life is critical for almost every human being. In every society, on every continent, families have been the foundation of civilization for millennia. It should therefore come as no surprise to learn that a frequent factor in personal problems — including criminal behavior — is the absence of a normal family background. Furthermore, the consequences of criminal behavior frequently include the complete destruction of any remaining family ties.

There have been many studies about the relationship between criminal behavior and a dysfunctional family background, although some 'experts' disagree with others. I'm willing to bet that of the inmates with whom I've worked in eight prisons on Federal, state and local level, well over eighty per cent came from dysfunctional family backgrounds. Single-parent families, families with one or more divorces in recent history, families where drug and/or alcohol abuse was rampant, families where violence and damaged relationships were the order of the day: they've all done their damage. Individuals who already have elements of a criminal personality, and in addition come from such backgrounds, tend (in

113

my experience, at least) to be more susceptible to the lure of the criminal lifestyle. However, this has to be balanced with a reality check. Many who come from such backgrounds don't become criminals. It's not the background that produces the criminal — the former can only be a contributing factor to the latter, not the deciding factor.

Our behavior is a matter of personal choice, personal responsibility. Each and every one of us must make his or her own choices about how we're going to live, and we can't blame others for what we've chosen. We may be influenced by environmental factors to select certain paths, but that doesn't mean we can't choose to turn away from them once we know they're wrong. This is where I differ profoundly from those who blame criminal conduct solely on background and environment. They're quite correct that such factors may be a more or less significant element in the equation, but such factors can't eliminate personal responsibility. In any and every aspect of life, there comes a time for each of us to willingly and knowingly choose to act in a certain way. That's an adult responsibility which can't be avoided or evaded. Remember what I said earlier, about inmates blaming anything and anyone but themselves for their plight? They're trying to evade that responsibility — and the courts (quite rightly) won't let them get away with it.

Nevertheless, it's very difficult to make responsible choices when the only examples you've ever known are of outrageous irresponsibility. Even when the examples have been good, there are many kids who've turned out badly. I've had to deal with good parents whose son or daughter has chosen a criminal path. In some cases they've committed the most horrific and despicable acts, including rape, torture and murder. I've sat with their parents as they wept openly, and their feelings of guilt have been heartbreaking. They've asked me through their tears, "Where did we go wrong with our child? What did we do that we shouldn't have done? What did we fail to do that we should have done?" In

114

the vast majority of cases, once I've learned more about the criminal's background, I've had to say to such parents that they did little wrong, and almost everything right. They truly did their best for their child. He decided, on his own initiative, to make really bad choices. He now has to live with the consequences of those choices: and one of the consequences is that he's almost destroyed his parents.

(In a few cases he really *has* destroyed them. I know of several instances where one or both parents died, suddenly and without any rational explanation, soon after their child was convicted of a particularly sickening crime. I've no doubt that they died of a broken heart — although that's hardly a medical diagnosis, of course. I believe that they simply couldn't face life any longer, knowing what their child had done. Others have committed suicide under similar circumstances, adding to the tragic burden of the surviving spouse.)

Sometimes inmates come from surprisingly well-educated and affluent families. I know one who's worth a significant amount in his own right — in fact, even while incarcerated he inherited a six-figure sum from the estate of a relative. He lacked for nothing in his life outside prison, but turned to crime because of the 'thrill' involved. He's now serving a very long sentence. All his money does for him now is to make the correctional system view him as a potential escape risk (because he can afford to hire professionals to 'spring' him from prison, if he wishes to do so). As a result, he's condemned to serve out his sentence in high-security prisons that are protected against such attempts. He's a man of considerable intelligence, with a not unattractive personality... a tragic waste of a promising life. I can only hope and pray that when he eventually gets out, he'll be able to make the most of the years left to him.

There are those who claim that the proportionately greater representation of certain races among the incarcerated is *prima facie* evidence of racism. In the past this might have been true, but I doubt that it's nearly as much of a factor today. I submit that this disparity is more a reflection of two factors. The first is that those who can afford good lawyers, and a strong support system, get better results in court than those who can't. Race is far less important than cold hard cash. Money talks. It's true that certain races are proportionately less wealthy than others, but again, this isn't necessarily a reflection of racism: instead, I believe it leads into the second factor. I strongly suspect that the breakdown of family structures, and a 'welfare culture' of reliance on government hand-outs and 'entitlements', has as much to do with the problem as anything else. Once people surrender the need and responsibility to take care of themselves and earn their own living, it's all too easy to grow used to a less affluent lifestyle, and vegetate in it rather than bestir oneself and work hard. This applies to people of all races and cultures.

I blame politicians on every level, local, state and national, for this situation. For decades, many such individuals have proclaimed the doctrine of government support for the 'underprivileged', and accused all who oppose them of being 'uncaring' or 'unfeeling' — even 'racist'. They've had great success with such tactics. No-one in his or her right mind would begrudge support and assistance to those who need it for a short period, or even in the long term for those who are genuinely unable to support themselves. However, in far too many cases the 'welfare' system has been corrupted into a permanent 'freebie', where those who are fully capable of supporting themselves are instead living for years on end at state expense, drawing weekly or monthly stipends which are more than enough to obviate the need for them to provide for themselves.

I've seen this in operation all too graphically. One of the most striking examples comes from a city where I was asked to speak to a group of high school students. Among them I met a young woman. She was pregnant at the time, and I asked a few questions. It turned out that she was only seventeen — and this was her fourth child. She'd become pregnant for the first time at the age of twelve. All four of her children had different fathers: and her own mother had encouraged her to have the children, because the state would pay her child support every month for each of them. She and her mother were drawing over $2,000 per month in cash allowances and food stamps to support these kids, as well as welfare payments for themselves.

Dear reader, put yourself in the position of one of those children. How would you feel about yourself as you grow up, once you learned that the only reason for your existence was to serve as a source of income for your mother and grandmother? You'd know that you had no value to them except as a 'cash cow'. Would that give you any self-esteem, any sense of self-worth, any feeling that you were treasured for yourself at all? I doubt it very much...

This is a good example of something I mentioned a few paragraphs ago: the catastrophic breakdown of family structures among certain groups. Their youth thus have no role models to follow, and must grow up without domestic stability, proper guidance or adequate mentoring. The greatest tragedy, in my opinion, is that this breakdown was identified and predicted many decades ago by numerous sociologists and anthropologists. One of the most important and seminal documents in this regard was the so-called Moynihan Report[8] of 1965. I hasten to add that although it addressed the then-current situation in many black communities, its recommendations can be applied to any community of any race experiencing similar problems. I highly recommend that you read it in full — it's available on the Internet, and a link is provided in the Notes.

The overall conclusion of the Moynihan Report was nothing less than prophetic for many race groups. The Introduction bluntly stated:

> "The fundamental problem ... is that of family structure ... for vast numbers of the unskilled, poorly educated city working class the fabric of conventional social relationships has all but disintegrated ... So long as this situation persists, the cycle of poverty and disadvantage will continue to repeat itself."

Today, almost half a century after the Moynihan Report was released, inner-city areas all across the nation bear grim testimony to the truth of these statements. They have proven to be true for all communities and races facing similar problems. The facts speak all too clearly for themselves. Groups demonstrating the greatest breakdown of family structures are disproportionately represented among prison inmates, gang members, welfare recipients, and those classified as living below the 'poverty line'. The groups' language, skin color, etc. are irrelevant.

Tragically, the Moynihan Report was pilloried by the 'politically correct'. Some denounced it as racist because of its focus on the black community, ignoring the fact that it spoke nothing more than the truth about conditions in that group. Others either denied or tried to minimize the problems it identified, or insisted that its emphasis on the family was outmoded and irrelevant. Such rejection did much to ensure the perpetuation of the problems identified in the Report, and has forced two subsequent generations to endure the very disadvantages it sought to address. Those same factors have spread to other races and communities, and there is no end in sight even now.

Many local, state and Federal government agencies offer social services to address some of these problems. Most regrettably, such efforts are frequently driven by political considerations rather than cold, hard realism. They are also often underfunded and over-extended. To cite just one example, the General Accounting Office has said of child protective services[9]:

> "The CPS system is in crisis, plagued by difficult problems, such as growing caseloads, increasingly complex social problems underlying child maltreatment, and ongoing systemic weaknesses in day-to-day operations. The states we visited have experienced large increases in maltreatment reports in recent years, thus increasing the CPS caseload to an overwhelming level. In addition, states report that families are entering the system with multiple problems, among the

most common of which is an increase in substance abuse. Experts consider this increase to be a significant factor in maltreatment, which has caught all parts of the CPS system unprepared. Moreover, CPS units have been plagued by long-standing systemic weaknesses in day-to-day operations…"

Clearly, such problems have a direct and immediate impact on many of those destined to enter the criminal justice system. I could cite many examples, but I'll give you just one so that I can go into detail. Felix (whom we discussed in the chapter on 'Criminal Minds and Convict Culture') is a dangerously impressive man, about 5' 10" tall and seemingly almost the same across the shoulders. None of it is fat. He has bulging muscles, and a glowering face that would be enough to give anybody pause. He's definitely not the kind of person you want to meet in a dark alley late at night.

I came to know Felix very well. He was born to a prostitute in the inner-city 'ghetto' of a major American city. He never knew the name of his father (probably she didn't either). The first words he can recall his mother speaking to him were, "Who do you think you are, you worthless piece of ****?" His infant years were spent in the kitchen as a never-ending succession of 'uncles' came to visit his mother in her bedroom, leaving money on the table as they left. By the age of five he was roaming the streets with others in the same situation.

There were child welfare workers, school inspectors and the like, who were supposed to take care of people like Felix and make sure they got an education. However, to go into the area where he lived was difficult and dangerous, and the number of problem cases there was overwhelming: so they simply didn't bother. They appear to have concentrated their efforts and limited resources on those cases they regarded as having a greater hope of success (and which were safer, from their point of view). As a result, Felix went to school for only a few months, then 'dropped out' and disappeared from the system. His mother certainly didn't care where he was, or what he was doing. He wandered the streets with a gang, battling other gangs, learning that if he wanted anything at all, he was going to have to fight for it and take it from others by force.

By the age of ten Felix was serving as a look-out for drug dealers, hovering on street corners, directing potential customers to them, whistling a warning if a suspicious vehicle showed up that might contain cops. (He became very good at spotting them.) He spent several terms in juvenile detention facilities, but they merely served to teach him more advanced criminal tricks: and once again, the case workers who should have tried to help him neglected their responsibilities. By the age of fifteen, he'd killed his first man and raped his first woman. Both were the first of many to come. By now his mother was dead of a drug overdose, so there wasn't even that minimal domestic restraint on his appetites.

Given such a 'Lord Of The Flies'[10] type of existence during his formative years, allied to a personality susceptible to criminal tendencies (see Chapter 4), it should come as no surprise that Felix ended up doing hard time — a lot of it. I met him when he was in his early thirties. He'd raped and killed a young woman, and was very fortunate to have escaped life imprisonment or the death penalty. I was given to understand that threats and bribes to witnesses and jurors had produced a situation where the prosecution had to settle for a ten-year sentence. Be that as it may, he was four years into that sentence when I met him. For almost a year he merely sneered at me, contemptuous of all 'Jesus freaks' and 'holy moleys', as he called pastors. That changed after one of his friends had a death in the family. I notified him about it, arranged for a local church to sponsor a visit by his family, and was generally supportive. His friend said to him that I seemed different from the other ministers they'd encountered, and that maybe he should talk to me. After a few months, he did.

It took me almost a year to penetrate Felix's defenses. He gradually opened up to me, and let me in to the ghastly morass of pain, darkness and hatred that filled his memories of his formative environment. When I finally managed to persuade him that, no matter what his origins and no matter what he'd done, God still felt love and compassion for him, he broke down and wept for over half an hour. It was a surreal experience, having this monumentally dangerous man crying on my shoulder like a baby. Over the next few weeks I led him through a detailed examination of conscience, laying out all his sins and asking for forgiveness. It was sometimes all I could do not to turn aside and vomit as the filth and evil of so many years spewed from him, but by God's grace I was able to remain outwardly calm. That's why people such as myself work in prisons, after all. We're not there as ministers of justice, but of mercy. We're there to show by our lived example that God hasn't given up on these folks.

Felix had to accept a number of hard truths. He had to stop blaming his mother and his environment for everything, and realize that from an early age he had chosen his way of life. Others born under similar circumstances had made different choices, and led very different lives. He had to accept personal responsibility for his choices and lay the blame where it belonged — on his own shoulders. Once he'd done that, he could begin to reassess and rebuild (his journey is described in more detail in Chapter 4). Of course, from a religious perspective, I'd say that God's grace could begin to work on him at that point. Prior to that, he'd painted himself into a corner. (I like to compare grace to the water in a tap in one corner of your room. You're desperately thirsty, but you refuse to go to the tap. Instead you insist that the tap has to come to you. I'm afraid it doesn't work like that. The water's there, but you have to move to reach it and slake your thirst. By acknowledging his guilt and his need for redemption, Felix put himself in a place where grace could operate.)

Felix became a changed man. He earned his GED, and read the Bible daily. Where he was getting written up for infractions of prison regulations on a monotonously regular basis, and spending several months each year in the Hole, he suddenly ceased such infringements. He became a powerful force for good among the most criminal of his peers. (I mean 'powerful' literally. On one occasion, he brought a notorious skeptic to our weekly sessions by frogmarching him down the walk, with his arm locked firmly behind his back. Apparently this gentleman had been overly rude in his comments about what we were doing, so Felix decided to 'invite' him to discuss the matter with me. I had great difficulty persuading Felix that people had the right to disagree with me, and that the Lord really wouldn't want him to make converts by the 'Charlemagne technique' of evangelization[11]. (I'm not sure that he agrees with me on the latter point, even now.)

After his release from prison, Felix attended a Bible college run by his denomination. I made arrangements with a number of pastors for their congregations to support him during his studies. After he graduated, he went back to the inner-city slum where he grew up, to work with kids and youths who are living as he did. He wants to help them make better choices, accept personal responsibility for their lives, and break out of the cycle of poverty, violence and crime before it entraps them as it did him. I hear from both church and police sources that he's a powerful force for good in that neighborhood. (I had to laugh at reports of what happened to the first gang-bangers who tried to 'get in his face'. Felix is as muscular and strong as ever, and he's never quite become reconciled to the 'turn the other cheek' school of Christianity — as they learned to their cost. In a place like that, when having to deal with people like that, I daresay the Lord understands...)

Without minimizing the fundamental importance of personal responsibility, I accept that family background contributes to the behavior that gets many criminals locked up. What about their families once they're behind bars? I don't know the official statistics (if they even exist) for the proportion of inmates whose spouses divorce them before or during their incarceration, but judging by my experience, it's at least eighty per cent, probably well over ninety per cent for the hard core of convicts in high- and maximum-security prisons. One of the most frequent subjects raised during counseling sessions with inmates is that their wives have divorced and remarried, or have taken the kids and 'disappeared', leaving no forwarding address, or have obtained restraining orders prohibiting the inmate from having any contact with his children. Sometimes they don't bother with the restraining order, but simply refuse to allow the children to speak with their father if and when he calls, or tear up his letters to them. This is almost invariably the case where the inmate has been convicted of sex crimes.

This frequently drives inmates to tears, despair, and sometimes violent breakdowns, but it's entirely understandable on the part of their spouses. Some of them go so far as to tell their young children that their father has died, and move with them to a far distant part of the country. More than once I've had to deal with the resulting mess; because the children inevitably find out, when they grow up, that their mother lied to them, and that their father's still alive and has been in prison all these years. I've been asked to arrange a few reunions. They're usually very emotional on both sides. What's worse is that the children will never again trust their mother, after discovering that she's lied to them for so long about something so fundamental. Her attempt to protect her children by breaking their ties with their father all too often ends up damaging or even destroying their ties with her instead.

It's even more difficult when both spouses have been engaging in criminal activity, and both get locked up. I've had to deal with several such cases (for example, I mentioned Laura in Chapter 2). Their children are invariably taken from them by Child Protective Services, and distributed among foster parents. CPS will try to locate relatives to take care of the kids, but if the former also have criminal tendencies or records, or can't provide a stable home environment, the courts usually refuse to allow this option. In many cases the children will be adopted and taken out of state. It's heartbreaking for their parents to come to terms with the realization that they'll never see them again — unless, perhaps, the children decide, in adulthood, that they'd like to trace their biological parents and meet them. Very often, once they find out that their parents were (and perhaps still are) criminals, the children abandon their efforts at that point.

Given that so few marriages survive incarceration, that leaves many inmates with only their parents (and possibly siblings) to visit them. Very often their families aren't wealthy, and can't provide much in the way of financial support. They may also live far away (particularly in the Federal prison system, where there's no guarantee that an inmate will be sent to a facility near his loved ones). This means that their visits will be few and far between. Generally, the longer an inmate spends behind bars, the fewer become the visits from his family. It's not unusual to find that inmates who've spent a decade or more in prison have no visitors at all.

I know one man who's been in prison for thirty-seven years at the time of writing. He'd had no visitors for twenty-four years since his father died. He had no-one to telephone, no-one on the outside who knew or cared if he lived or died. I was able to recruit a few pen-friends to correspond with him, and a prison visitor volunteer group arranged for a couple to visit him. Groups like this seek out inmates such as this man, and try to provide at least some outside human contact for them. It's a vital service, but those providing it are tragically few.

Of course, the reason so few are willing to serve in this way is that they find out very quickly the perils of such work. Far too many inmates will seek to 'con' them, in the same way that they try to use, manipulate and deceive corrections staff and each other. For that reason, we have to caution such volunteers never to give their address or telephone number to an inmate. They are advised to use a central office or a post office box for contact purposes. The BOP does a pretty good job in educating volunteer ministers and visitors about the dangers involved, but some state systems don't make the same effort.

If volunteers aren't constantly on their guard, they'll be used and/or abused by inmates in one way or another, and they'll frequently become disillusioned and stop coming. This is very sad for those of us who need their help to help others, but it's completely understandable. One has to be tough and resilient to serve in this environment. If one's motivation is more of a 'touchy-feely' or 'warm-and-fuzzy' delusion, instead of the hard-nosed practicality and realism that should prevail, one won't last in prison ministry.

Working with inmates' families is made all the more difficult by the fact that so many of them aid and abet their incarcerated relative's criminal tendencies. We've had to institute rigorous background checks of those wishing to visit, and very often find that they have criminal records of their own. We search their belongings, and restrict what they can bring to visitation, but all too often they'll try to smuggle contraband and deliver it to their inmate relatives. That's one reason why non-contact visits are the norm in certain prisons. The inmates can speak with their visitors over a telephone while viewing them through a pane of glass, but can never touch them. The risk of something being passed to and fro is too great. Even where contact visits are allowed, the risk remains. We have staff permanently on duty in the visiting room, and cameras monitoring everyone there. Even so, there's seldom a visiting day without at least one attempt being made to pass something illegal to an inmate.

The methods of smuggling contraband are legion. Very often a female visitor will conceal a small packet of drugs in her vagina. Some with small children will conceal such items in diapers, feeding bottles or toys. Once in the visitation room, the woman will go to the bathroom, retrieve the package from her person or her children, and conceal it. If it's small, she might put it in her mouth. During a kiss she can pass it to her inmate spouse or boyfriend, who swallows it. He'll retrieve it from his stools after a bowel movement over the next couple of days. Larger packages might be surreptitiously exchanged and hidden on the inmate's person. (This is why all inmates are searched after visitation, before they go back to their units: but in the rush of dealing with many inmates at the end of the visiting period, there's always a chance that something might be overlooked, or passed from one inmate to another and smuggled past the guards while their attention is elsewhere.)

The tragedy of such attempts is that families don't think of how it might affect their children. I recall one incident vividly. A woman had come to visit her boyfriend, bringing her three small children of 6, 4 and 3 years of age. (Only the youngest was the child of the inmate concerned.) She brought in a condom-wrapped packet of drugs, and passed it to the inmate in a kiss, but they were detected. He swallowed the package, but was immediately placed in a dry cell, where the package was retrieved in due course with the help of hefty doses of laxatives. (To illustrate his desperation, the first time it came out, he seized it before the guards could stop him and swallowed it again, even covered in his own feces as it was. They got it the second time it came out.)

His girlfriend was immediately detained — whereupon she threw a fit, screaming, shouting and resisting for all she was worth. We had her cold, of course, with the evidence of our cameras and the recovered narcotics to take to court. We called law enforcement authorities to arrest her, and Child Protection Services to take her children into protective custody. Those poor kids stood there, crying and screaming for their mommy, as they watched big uniformed men putting her in handcuffs and taking her away. What sort of impression did they get of police and authority figures? They were far too young to understand that their mother was responsible for what was happening, not the law enforcement officers involved. They're going to grow up with that trauma permanently imprinted on their psyches.

I mentioned that the inmate was the father of only one of this visitor's children. That's a distressingly common problem behind bars. There's a national program, run by an association of churches, that seeks to provide Christmas presents for inmates' children, working through local congregations. The inmates have to fill in a separate form for each child. I've sat at my desk in stunned amazement as the convicts brought in their paperwork. The record so far, in my experience (which has been exceeded by other chaplains) is a convict who had nine children by seven different women. He wasn't concerned about them, and wasn't paying a cent in child support — but he was extraordinarily proud of his 'prowess'. It seems that the more children an inmate has fathered upon the greatest number of women, the higher his status in certain circles. As you can imagine, those children have virtually no prospect of a normal family life.

Prison gangs try to use family members to smuggle in drugs and other contraband. They're constantly on the lookout for new inmates who are expecting visits from their family, and put pressure on them to have their visitors bring in such items. The pressure starts out in a friendly way, and might even involve the payment of a bribe to the inmate: but if he won't cooperate, very often things turn ugly. The inmate might be threatened with harm if his visitors won't do as they want, or the gang might have outside associates take a picture of his family. They'll show it to the inmate as proof that they can get to them if he or they won't 'play along'. (They sometimes use the same approach to target staff members whom they regard as potentially vulnerable to such threats.) If the inmate has any sense, he'll report the threats, whereupon we can do something about them, including providing protection for his family and transferring him to another facility. Unfortunately, very often they don't do so for fear of being branded a 'snitch', and they and their family end up in all sorts of trouble as a result.

Another frequently-used technique is to have gang members pose as family or friends of inmates and come to visit them. The BOP investigates visitors (requiring them to sign a form giving permission for a background check), and this helps to catch such attempts much of the time: but many state and local prisons are less rigorous. Such attempts can even go so far as arranging marriages between an inmate and a 'mule' or drug carrier.

One particularly blatant attempt happened when one of our inmates was sent to another state to testify in a court case. He returned claiming to have married while he was there, and requested permission for his 'wife' to visit him. We investigated, and found that the prison where he'd been incarcerated while giving evidence had no record of his having married there. Further inquiry revealed the name of the minister on the marriage certificate. I telephoned him, only to be informed that he'd conducted the marriage by proxy, had never met the inmate concerned, and knew nothing about the backgrounds of either party. He'd simply accepted a fat fee to perform the ceremony and submit the license to the authorities, duly endorsed by himself as the 'marriage officer'.

We took care to report to the authorities in that state the way in which the minister had misused his official position, and asked the FBI to look into the background of the 'lady' concerned. She turned out to have been married several times in this manner (and was still technically 'married' to two other inmates in that state's prison system). It was almost certain, based on our experience of such situations, that she was using this technique to smuggle contraband. She ended up facing bigamy charges. Our inmate languished unvisited (and, in due course, unmarried, because we had the 'wedding' annulled on the grounds of bigamy).

The reason inmates and gangs will go to such lengths to smuggle drugs into the prison is, of course, their extremely high value within the walls. The difficulty of bringing them in, and their consequent scarcity, makes them vastly more expensive than they would be 'on the street'. A rock of crack, or packet of marijuana, that sells for ten to twenty dollars in a street transaction will be worth eighty to a hundred dollars in a penitentiary. With profits like that at stake, the pressure to bring them in is immense: and criminals don't care at all about the jeopardy in which they place innocent persons by doing so. After all, selfishness is a way of life for them.

Not all marriages are drug-related, of course. There seems to be a type of personality that's fascinated by criminals, to the extent that some people will marry inmates even though they know they'll have to wait years for their spouses to complete their sentences. Some may be genuine love matches, but I suspect most are driven by other factors. I simply don't understand the psychology involved, and I've always refused to conduct such ceremonies. Most chaplains do the same. Usually, we make those wanting to get married use the services of a Justice of the Peace or minister from outside the prison. There are, of course, more legitimate marriages. For example, a partner of long standing might decide to marry the inmate in order to legitimize their children, or gain access to benefits legally available only to a spouse. We make the necessary arrangements. A sentence of confinement doesn't nullify an inmate's right to marry.

In a few cases (mostly involving inmates with shorter sentences), their marriages survive their incarceration. However, their release frequently gives rise to serious problems, often so severe that their marriages eventually break up. After all, the inmate's spouse has had to care for their children and raise them without their partner's assistance (sometimes even without their co-operation, if they was in a facility far away, where visits were difficult or impossible). They've had to earn money for their family, build a home life without their spouses, and deal with the very real problems caused by conviction and incarceration (which might have included the forfeiture or seizure of some or all of the family's assets). When the spouse comes home, the family must adjust to their presence once more. Former prisoners often find it very difficult at first to get anything more than a menial job, paying minimum wage, and must also adjust to children who are older and more mature than their memories of them. The relationship between the spouses must also find a new foundation. It's not surprising that many of the relatively few marriages that have endured through one partner's incarceration fracture under the strain of such adjustments, and end up in a divorce court.

The problems encountered with family background, and the break-up of families after incarceration, are, in my opinion, a major reason for the strength and persistence of prison gangs. For many inmates, their gang *is* their family. This is also why many gangs continue their relationship with their members once they leave prison. The association may be criminal, but it's all they have. It fills the social need for family and community that they can't fill any other way. They may not be able to find a wife in the normal way of things, as many women will understandably turn away from a man whose past history and present associations are overtly criminal: but the women who hang around with gangs have no such scruples. They may marry someone from this group, or simply use them for sex and companionship in the medium to long term, rather than look for a permanent relationship.

The gangs may also interfere in existing marriages. I've had some experience with this. They'll offer to 'look after' the inmate's spouse and children, but in reality this is often used as an excuse to try to exploit them. I've heard examples of gang members trying to 'shack up' with an inmate's wife, or force her into prostitution, or try to make her children serve the gang as lookouts or couriers. (They think — erroneously — that cops are less suspicious of kids than of adults). They might also try overt coercion to make them smuggle contraband into prison. All in all, it's a nightmarish situation for many families.

It also affects our work as chaplains. As a full-time prison chaplain, I'd never visit the families of inmates for fear of complications. I'd ask local ministers to do so if an inmate requested it (after warning them of what might be involved, of course, and advising them to take a witness with them). However, in part-time ministry at other prisons, I and other pastors frequently made such visits, particularly to try to mediate in cases where divorce was on the table. It wasn't easy.

One minister engaged in such a mission had an interesting encounter. He was sitting with the inmate's wife and her two young children when one of her husband's 'homeys' entered the house (without an invitation). He was carrying a sealed envelope, which he handed to the minister, telling him that he was to deliver it to the inmate without it being inspected by the guards. It felt as if it contained pills of some sort, probably illegal narcotics. The minister, of course, refused to co-operate, whereupon this gang-banger started raving that he was going to 'kick his ***' and 'he had a black belt'.

Fortunately this pastor had learned the hard way about the hazards of prison ministry, and carried a gun on such occasions. As he drew his pistol, he remarked that 'he had a black gun'. This seemed to adequately trump the black belt, as the gang-banger exited at high speed and made himself scarce. The pastor handed the envelope to the local Sheriff's Office, which had the contents analyzed and confirmed that they were, indeed, illegal drugs. The inmate didn't get his envelope — and yes, his wife did end up divorcing him. After that experience, I suppose the pastor couldn't really blame her...

(For those surprised that a minister of religion should carry a gun, think again. We're called to be shepherds of the flock, after all. Shepherds sometimes have to deal with the wolves that threaten their sheep. I'd say the majority of ministers of my acquaintance who have in-depth experience with prison ministry have neither moral qualms nor compunction of conscience about arming themselves — rightly so, in my opinion.)

CONVICT TO CHAPLAIN V

THE KILLER

Hi, Chaplain. What's up?... *You're *****ing me!* You want me to do *WHAT?*...

So lemme get this straight. This rabbit comes in, and Les puts his brand on him? Happens all the time. ****, Chaplain, if a rabbit ain't got the guts to stand up for himself, of *course* he's gonna be food for everyone else! That's the way it is in here!...

You're serious. You really ain't *****ing me. You want me to take over this rabbit from Les and help him to grow a pair? Teach him to fight, to stand up for himself? Why me, Chaplain?... Yeah, I'm a killer, I got that rep. I'm one of the toughest mother******s on the yard, and they all know that — but why should a wise guy like me put that on the line for a rabbit, or for you? I'm not one of your *holy* guys! *(Sneer)*...

Yeah, I was with the Mob in Anytown... Yeah, if he was workin' for 'em, too, I guess they might appreciate my helping him. They might even do something nice for my girl. She's at university there. Smart kid — gonna be a doctor. *(His face falls.)* Ain't seen or heard from her for five, six years, o' course, 'cause her ma turned her against me... but *damn*, I'm proud of her!

Oh, sure, I can take Les any day, with one hand tied behind my back. He knows it, too. If I tell him I want his rabbit, he'll crawfish. Be easier if I can offer him something, though — show I don't disrespect him, know what I mean? Man holds a grudge in a place like this, it's gonna fester an' turn septic sooner or later. When it blows, someone's gonna get hurt bad... Yeah, that might work. Les gets a third of the rabbit's commissary for the next year — and I get another third for teaching him? Damn, Chaplain, you shoulda been in business! *(He laughs.)* Les can brag he's getting as much as me. Boosts his rep a bit, and it don't bother me none.

You got your head on straight, Chaplain, I'll give you that. You know when to go by the book, and when to put it aside. Still, ain't no way you figured out all this on your own. It breaks too many rules. You must have got the go-ahead from someone high up. Who was it?... Yeah, I guess you can't say anything about that, but we both know the score...

Uh-huh. I guess they listened when you put it like that. This way *is* better than havin' a dead or buggy convict — and you're right: even if you got him a transfer, he'd end up in the same sort of **** at his new place.

I want something more, Chaplain. I got this shot pending. If the Man feels like it, I'm going to the Hole for another stretch, and I've had enough of that place for a while. Besides, I can't help you from in there. Will you talk to him for me?... Yeah, I know it's his call, but if you, and whoever gave you the go-ahead to talk to me, both tell him I'm helping you, I reckon he'll listen... OK, we'll see.

Can you get the rabbit transferred to my unit, real quick? I'll need him where I can keep an eye on him. The other guys there will leave him alone if they know he's mine. You'll find out today? Great. If that works, and if the Man's green about that shot, we got a deal, Chaplain. *(Handshake.)* Tonight the rabbit will have a new daddy. He won't need to worry about his *** no more.

(Thoughtfully) Damn, this might even be fun, y'know? Never heard of anyone turning a rabbit into a wolf before. There's prob'ly a law against it! *(Mutual laughter.)* Yeah, I'll teach him. He'll grow a pair if it kills him, or my name ain't Adam!

FRIDAY — 4:40 P.M.

As I walk down the passage after leaving SHU, my radio crackles. "Control to all units and staff. We have a clear institutional count with 1,512 inmates present. The count is clear. Attention Unit Officers. Food Services workers are to report to Food Services immediately."

I can imagine the relief of the Unit Officers. If there's any discrepancy in the count it has to be done all over again, as many times as necessary until it's right or the missing inmates have been located. On a bad day it can take well over an hour. Today's been relatively painless.

I come to Health Services, and convey Sally's message to the nurse at the dispensary window. She nods, and turns to call the doctor on duty. He'll go down to SHU and administer Phil's injection. I head for Food Services, where the first workers are already arriving. The food was prepared before the count, and only needs dishing up to the hungry inmates.

As I arrive, the loudspeakers blare, "Main Line is open. Main Line is open." The inmates will now be released from their units to have supper. The Activities Lieutenant will call them down unit by unit, according to weekly hygiene inspection scores, the cleanest unit first, the dirtiest last. As usual, those administrative and support staff on duty who can be spared will 'stand Main Line', as we put it, to be available to any inmate who wants to ask a question or discuss something. During lunch the senior executives of the prison, including the Warden, do likewise.

I enter the dining hall, and stand against the corridor windows in full view of all the inmates, so that they can approach me if they want to. Slowly the large hall fills up with several hundred inmates, taking their trays of food from the serving line and sitting at tables. The inmates segregate themselves, with blacks in one area, Hispanics in another, Native Americans in another place, and white inmates gathered in a fourth. Some gangs have 'claimed' certain tables as their own. This is technically illegal, but we can't prove they're doing it, and any inmate unwise enough to complain about it would suffer painful consequences as soon as our backs were turned. There's not much we can do about it in reality.

A few inmates approach me with questions, and I do my best to answer them. Where I can't deal with their queries immediately, I make notes and promise that I'll get back to them as soon as possible. I'll make a point of doing precisely that. If one doesn't keep one's promise to an inmate, before long one loses all credibility with them. They're too used to broken promises to be willing to forgive those who break them.

One inmate wants to know if I'll let him make a phone call to his family that evening, on compassionate grounds. He's received a letter from them with bad news, but has used up all his telephone minutes for this month, and can't wait ten days until the new month begins. I tell him to bring the letter and envelope to the Chapel tonight. I'll read it, then see about helping him. His face falls. He and I both know that he wrote the letter himself — and he knows that I'll spot it, because he won't have a stamped envelope from its sender. If he brings any other envelope, its handwriting won't match his own on the letter. He promises to see me tonight, and turns away, but we both know that he won't come at all. Just one more attempted con game.

The Activities Lieutenant comes over. There are always three

135

Lieutenants on duty during day shifts: the Operations Lieutenant in command of overall operations, the Activities Lieutenant in charge of programs and scheduled activities, and the SHU Lieutenant in charge of that highly volatile area. Bob's the Activities Lieutenant this evening. He and I are friends.

"Hi, Peter. Anything I need to take into account in the Chapel this evening?"

"Hi, Bob. Yes, I'm the only Chaplain on duty and I've got three teams of volunteers coming in, two at about six and one at seven. I'll have to collect them from the Control Center and escort them in, and take out one team after the 7:30 move. I'll need to borrow one of the CO's to supervise the Chapel while I do that. I can use the Corridor Officer, if you're not going to take him for something else."

"That'll be fine. I'll give him a heads-up to co-ordinate with you on the times involved. If you need anyone else, call me on the radio."

"Will do. Thanks, Bob."

Our conversation is cut short by an urgent call on the radio. "Alpha-Three to Operations Lieutenant and Control. Medical emergency in Alpha-Three! Immediate medical assistance required in Unit Alpha-Three!"

Without a word Bob sprints from the dining hall. The rest of us won't respond to such a call, which is of a different nature to a body alarm. Bob will escort a stretcher and staff from Health Services to the unit in question, and a couple of CO's from the Compound Officer's team will head for the unit on the double, to help with any crowd control that may be necessary.

I wait in the dining hall until I hear another radio call. "Activities Lieutenant to Control and Health Services. Inmate Andrew is en route from Unit Alpha-Three to Health Services on a stretcher. Request that the doctor be standing by. Possible heart attack."

I go down the corridor to Health Services and wait. Within

minutes the wheeled stretcher arrives on the run, pushed by panting, sweating CO's. The doctor comes back from SHU at the double, and they all go into Health Services together. I start to follow them, but a glance at my watch shows me that it's almost 5:30 p.m.. The first move of the evening is almost due. I'm going to have to hurry back to the Chapel to open it up for my early customers. If I'm needed at Health Services, they'll call me.

I meet the Corridor Officer at the main portal sliders, and we walk down the corridor together. "What's going on in your area tonight, Chaplain?" he asks. "The Activities Lieutenant said you'll need some help."

"Yes, thanks, Harry, there's a lot on the go — three sets of volunteers and five different religious groups. I'll need you to cover the Chapel area at a little after six, again after seven, and after the seven-thirty move, so that I can bring volunteers in and out."

"I'll do that," Harry nods. "If I'm not in the corridor, I'll be doing rounds in Recreation or Education. Call me on the radio if you can't see me."

I go into the Chapel while he continues to the door. I check the schedule on our notice-board. It's one of our busier evenings. The Jewish group meets for their Sabbath celebration in a small conference room in the Psychology area. The Asatru group meets in a classroom in Education, just beyond the swing doors separating our departments, as does the Jehovah's Witnesses group. There are two consecutive Protestant Christian meetings in the main chapel, and a Native American contingent in the small chapel. Over and above the organized groups, we'll have a meeting of the leaders of the Wiccan group to plan their upcoming festivities, and there'll be the usual trickle of inmates wanting to make a telephone call for some reason or other. There may also be one or two inmates needing to talk about something. I'm going to be kept busy tonight, for sure!

I unlock the various rooms and prepare for the evening rush. As I finish switching on all the lights, the speakers come to life.

"Ten-minute move. The move is open."

I don't go out into the corridor this time. As the only member of staff in the Chapel area, my primary responsibility is to keep it and those in it under control. Teachers from Education and instructors from Recreation move out to help with traffic control. Within a few minutes, the first arrivals come through the Chapel doors. I open the cabinets for their faith groups in the supply room, and make sure that only those authorized to use each cupboard are taking out their books and equipment. As soon as they've done so, I re-lock each cupboard. We've learned from bitter experience that, even though most of the materials in each cupboard are of no value to anyone except the religious group concerned, inmates will try to steal them on principle: so each cupboard has been fitted with a padlock and hasp. It makes for annoying extra work, but it's the only way to keep our supplies secure.

As I'm finishing up, my radio crackles. "Operations Lieutenant to Chaplain Grant."

I pick up the radio. "Chaplain Grant, go ahead."

"Phone twenty, Chaplain?" (Are you near a telephone, and if so, what's the extension?)

"Negative. Can I call you in five?"

"Ten-four. I'll be in my office."

Something's up, and Dan wants to speak to me about it without risking any inmates overhearing our radio conversation. However, I have to get the inmate groups settled down before I can get to a phone. I close and lock the supply room, and check each of the rooms in use tonight. Most of the inmates are still eating supper, and will arrive with the 6:30 move, but the early arrivals will settle down to read and enjoy a little peace and quiet. The Chapel area is one of the very few places in the prison where that's possible.

The Jewish group has set up their ritual gear in the conference room, and are waiting for me to issue them with the authorized quantity of grape juice for their celebrations. The Asatru group are waiting to speak with me. I ask them all to hold on for a moment, shut the door to my office, and call the Operations Lieutenant.

"Dan, Peter here. What's up?"

"We're sending Inmate Andrew out to the hospital. Looks like a heart attack. The ambulance is on its way. He's registered as a member of your faith group. He's unconscious, so I guess there won't be much you can do, but he may need the Last Rites — he's in a bad way."

"Thanks for the heads-up, Dan. I'll try to get down there as quickly as possible."

I mutter in aggravation. I really should give Andrew the Last Rites before he leaves, just in case: but in a prison environment, I can't leave the Chapel unsupervised. At once I notice Sally walking past my window. I knock on the window, and she jumps, looking around at me. I mouth, "Wait a moment!", and hurry out.

"Sally, there's an inmate about to go out to the hospital. He's seriously ill, and needs the Last Rites. Would you please keep an eye on the chapel for a few minutes, while I go to Health Services?"

"Sure, Peter, go ahead." The psychologists' offices are in an annex off the Religious Services Department, so she'll be able to look after both areas without difficulty.

I turn to the inmates. "Guys, I'm sorry, but you heard me. There's an inmate going out to the hospital who needs me urgently. Please wait a few minutes until I get back."

One of the Asatru group gives me a surly look. "You're delaying our scheduled meeting! I'm gonna write you up for this!"

I sigh in exasperation. "Go ahead and file a complaint if you want to — but think about this. One day *you* might be on your way to hospital, and need a chaplain yourself. On that day, do you want a chaplain who won't come to you, because he's afraid of being written up by someone else? Or do you want one who'll drop everything and get his *** over there?"

Another member of his group nods sharply. "Don't worry, Chaplain, we'll wait. Go do your thing." He turns to his colleague. As I hurry to my office to grab what I need for the Last Rites, I hear him telling him — not exactly *sotto voce,* and in words of approximately one syllable — a few things to his advantage. I can't help grinning as I unlock my door. There won't be any complaint lodged tonight, that's clear — at least, not by this inmate.

I radio ahead to the Control Center, and ask them to give me priority passage through the sliders as I hurry down the corridor. They oblige, and I'm through the portal in seconds. I reach Health Services within five minutes of my conversation with Dan, and find them about to take Andrew out to the rear entrance to meet the ambulance. Hurriedly I administer the Last Rites. He's unconscious and can't participate, but I've done what I can — and if this proves to be the end for him, there may be someone on the outside who'll appreciate knowing that he received them. He never comes to our services, and I've no idea of his standing with God, but I hope the Rites might help him there, too. Judging from what I know of his record (he's listed in our Posted Picture File), without sincere repentance, he'll need all the help he can get.

They wheel the stretcher out into the corridor as I turn and head back to the Chapel. I stop at the Lieutenant's Office to thank Dan for the heads-up, and advise him that I've administered the Last Rites. He'll note it in his log of the day's activities.

BEHIND THE SCENES

No-one can whistle a symphony. It takes a whole orchestra
to play it.

— Halford E. Luccock (1885-1961)

Everyone's familiar with the image of prisons as glamorized
by Hollywood in movies such as 'The Longest Yard', 'The
Shawshank Redemption' or 'The Green Mile'. The reality doesn't
live up to the screenplays. There are a great many elements of
prison life that are vital to our day-to-day operations, but which are
virtually unknown to outsiders. Let me use this chapter to walk you
through some of them.

Let's begin in the prison factory. In the Federal prison system,
these factories are run by a company operating under the trade
name of UNICOR. Its official name is Federal Prison Industries
Inc. It was established shortly after the formation of the BOP in
the 1930's. It produces goods for government departments, and
doesn't compete with the private sector in other markets. It
provides employment to several hundred inmates at each facility
where it operates. In our prison it produces mailbags for the US
Postal Service, items of uniform such as exercise apparel for the US
military, and a few other items of clothing. Factories in other

prisons manufacture furniture and other institutional requirements. We enter the factory through a metal detector leading to a secure doorway. A lobby separates us from the factory floor behind a second secure door. Inside there are long rows of tables and workstations, with sewing machines, cutters, fabric rolls and the like. I visit UNICOR regularly to walk down the rows, speak with the inmates in passing, and give them an opportunity to approach me and ask for a more lengthy appointment if they wish to talk about something.

The workers here have the best-paid jobs in the prison. A skilled worker can earn over a dollar an hour — slave labor wages outside the prison, but excellent remuneration within the walls. Prisoners have no real incentive to work hard. They're not going anywhere, after all. Most of the workers dawdle through their shifts, producing a bare minimum. Those newcomers who set to work eagerly, and produce a lot, are usually warned by the others to slow down — or else. The foremen and managers fume at this, but there's nothing they can do about it. What are they going to do, fire their inmate workers? They can only replace them with more inmates. Send them to jail? They're already there!

Security is very tight here. There are tools that would make superb weapons with a little tinkering by an enthusiastic inmate, so they're very carefully controlled, and counted multiple times every day. If one goes missing, the whole place grinds to a halt until it's found. There's also the risk of escape. An inmate got out of one institution by hiding in a pallet of goods being shipped out. His comrades shrink-wrapped it for delivery after he crawled into a prepared hiding-place inside. Once it arrived at the prison warehouse outside the walls, he cut his way out and disappeared. Security's been stricter than ever since then at all Federal prisons with factory facilities, including very careful inspection of all outgoing pallets.

UNICOR can only accommodate so many workers. The BOP takes seriously the maxim that 'the Devil finds work for idle hands to do', and tries to ensure that every inmate has a job of some sort. It's been accurately described as a 'make-work' system. Many of the jobs are boring, monotonous and repetitive, but they're nonetheless important to occupy the inmates' time. Salaries are extremely low, starting at a few cents per hour. For many inmates, this is the only money they receive, as their families are either unable or unwilling to support them behind bars. They have to pay for whatever they want to buy from the commissary (of which more later), telephone calls, private stationery and other items, so such jobs are very necessary for them. Those inmates who can't find a job in a specific department will be put to work cutting grass on the yards (using unpowered push mowers), or cleaning corridors and residential units. It's startling to enter a prison for the first time and see gray concrete floors polished to gleaming brightness, but we have to find *something* for the inmates to do.

Next to UNICOR we find the Facilities Department. This division looks after the infrastructure and services of the prison. Down a long corridor we come to a large open room, segmented by chain-link fencing into large storage compartments on one side, and lined with offices and workrooms on the other. One storage compartment contains plumbing supplies, another electrical, another carpentry, and so on. There's a secure tool room, containing various toolboxes packed with various items of equipment. Inmates form the labor force under the supervision of specialist staff, who wear gray uniforms to distinguish them from the Correctional Officers. Facilities is normally a fun place to visit, with a loud clamor of voices, the whirr and whine of tools and machines, and a constant bustle as day-to-day maintenance work is performed.

Facilities, like UNICOR, is filled with tools that can be used as (or to make) weapons. They're very strictly controlled, and only inmates who've proved reliable and (reasonably) trustworthy are allowed to take them out to a work site. They have to have a special pass to walk around with a toolbox. It's signed by the supervisor at their destination when they arrive, and again when they depart, with both times noted. If there's an unreasonable delay between their leaving one department and arriving at the next work site, a lot of questions will be asked. At any time, they can be stopped and their toolboxes inspected by any member of staff. A laminated card attached to the handle lists the contents. If anything's missing, they're subject to immediate detention, and will probably end up in the Hole. Those working with the fixed equipment in the Department are also very carefully supervised. The grinders, cutters and other tools can be misused to manufacture weapons, so access to them is severely restricted.

Next to Facilities we find the Commissary. This is the shop where inmates can buy items from a fairly limited selection. Goods cost rather more than they would in a supermarket outside the walls. Any profits earned are used to subsidize the Commissary's operations, with any excess being allocated to inmate welfare. Those inmates who are indigent, and can't earn enough in a prison job to buy the basic necessities (over and above what they're issued, of course), can ask for assistance from these funds. The Commissary opens most weekday evenings, and is staffed by inmates under supervision. Units are allocated one evening a week when they can come and do their shopping. The inmates prepare lists of what they want, and hand them in for processing each morning. Workers take the lists, put the items into bags, then take them to a checkout window. Here the inmates queue each evening to collect their orders. The prices are totaled, and the inmate's commissary account debited with the amount. There are frequent arguments when an inmate's miscalculated the total, and doesn't have enough in his account to pay for all he wants. When that happens, he has to make a very rapid decision as to what to leave out of his purchases — or risk having the annoyed clerk disallow the entire order, and force him to leave empty-handed.

Staff keep a very careful eye on the line of inmates waiting for service and those leaving with their purchases. It's not uncommon for predatory inmates to try to bully others into giving them some of the goodies they've bought, and gambling debts are frequently settled with commissary purchases. There are limits as to how much of a given item an inmate may have in his cell, and he must have commissary invoices proving that he bought them. If an inmate has more than the allowed limit, it may be an indication that he's been gambling, or that he's stolen or strong-armed goods from other inmates. The lack of purchase documentation will help to confirm this. Staff confiscate the excess whenever they find it, which tends to produce a certain amount of resentment. The authorities don't care. Any inmate with a large supply of what are, effectively, luxuries inside a prison is highly likely to be targeted by thieves in his unit, and/or predatory gangs out to take whatever they can get. That can lead to violence, retaliation, and all sorts of complications. The easiest way to prevent this is to strictly limit quantities of such items. It's much safer for everyone that way — particularly for the staff, who'll otherwise have to break up the fights.

One of the most sought-after items from the Commissary during summer is ice cream. It sells various flavors (nothing exotic or expensive, and usually only the cheapest brands). It's not unusual to find inmates buying up to six pints at a time. They'll share them with their friends (or those to whom they owe something), and eat them right away on the yard. (Of course, they have no freezer facilities in their units to keep them cold.) Staff have found that some inmates will do almost anything for a pint of really high-quality premium-brand ice cream. If an inmate has done something for which a member of staff is particularly grateful, he or she might bring in a couple of tubs of the 'good stuff', and allow the prisoner to eat them in the privacy of an office.

(Needless to say, such largesse is against regulations, but it happens nonetheless. I know of a prison where an inmate reported a plan to attack a staff member. His information was confirmed, and those responsible were thwarted. As a heartfelt 'thank you' gesture, the staff member brought in a complete steak-and-shrimp supper, with all the trimmings, from a local restaurant. It was heated up in a microwave oven, and the inmate enjoyed the best meal he'd had for years. I can't think of a more worthy cause, quite frankly. As Douglas Bader reminded us, 'Rules exist for the guidance of the wise and the blind obedience of fools'. Words to live by, even if hidebound bureaucrats hate such sentiments. I've known senior prison executives turn a blandly Nelsonian blind eye to such gestures. They're human, after all.)

Moving on from the Commissary, we come to the Safety Department. Here staff and inmate workers ensure that the prison complies with all laws and regulations concerning safe operation, from procedures, to documentation of chemicals, to dealing with on-the-job injuries. It's a particularly important department because of inmate lawsuits. As previously noted, they'll seize on any excuse to file one, and safety issues are one of the 'risk areas'. By ensuring compliance with standards, and documenting it in detail, we nip in the bud most such spurious cases. This Department regularly inspects all others in the prison to ensure compliance, leading to much muttering and moaning as the latter scurry to fix any problems, and get into line with the stringent requirements governing our operations. I've found the Safety Department staff very helpful in many areas.

Next is the Laundry. This is run by inmates. On a regular schedule, each inmate places his dirty laundry in a mesh bag and ties it securely. The bags are brought to the laundry, where the clothes are washed and dried in industrial-size machines. With about fifteen hundred inmates, there's a lot of dirty clothing. Heavier items like sheets and blankets are exchanged and laundered at set intervals.

(One of the strange things about prison life is the number of inmates who prefer to live in dirty clothes, sleep in dirty beds, and avoid taking showers. There's a surprisingly high proportion who appear to pay little or no attention to personal hygiene.

Occasionally Unit Officers will have to deal with this, but most of the time it's a self-correcting problem. If they get too smelly, their fellow convicts will 'discuss' the matter with them — sometimes using, shall we say, 'non-verbal communication'. This tends to resolve the situation, at least in the short term. Sometimes repeat 'lessons' are required to make the point clear.)

Next we come to the dining-hall and Food Services. It's worth taking a closer look at this department. As you can imagine, preparing three meals a day for about fifteen hundred inmates (plus feeding several hundred staff on weekdays) is no picnic. A large contingent of inmates work in the kitchen under the supervision of specialist staff. They're divided into groups. One opens giant cans of vegetables, and prepares fresh produce. Another mixes food in giant cooking vats, and stirs it. A few very carefully selected inmates will be locked into a chain-link wire cage, where they're issued knives and tools to cut meat and vegetables. All such equipment is stored in a special security enclosure, and signed out individually each day. It's returned and signed in before the inmate using it is allowed to leave. Another group of inmates operates the dishwasher. Others scrub the floors and clean up as needed.

It's hot, hard, unpleasant work, and most inmates will do almost anything rather than work here. As a result, most new inmates are automatically assigned to Food Service for at least three months before they can apply for jobs elsewhere. After all, *someone* has to prepare the food! The downside to using inmates in the kitchen, of course, is that they do their best to steal food. Some will make hamburgers and other items to sell in their units. Others will steal ingredients to make hooch. They're all searched for contraband at the end of their shift, but in the hustle and bustle they frequently manage to smuggle out their loot.

There are a few inmates who don't mind working here. Some have culinary skills acquired before they were incarcerated, while others take courses on food preparation and learn the trade of a restaurant cook. They'll act as 'chefs', preparing the meals with the assistance of the less skilled inmates. They may also prepare and serve meals for the staff. I'm told that at a certain prison, one such inmate earned a significant reduction in his sentence by protecting a female cook-supervisor during an incident of violence in the kitchen. He was badly hurt defending her, but survived. In recognition of his gallantry, the remainder of his sentence was commuted to parole, and he received a cash award as well.

The inmates locked in the Hole can't come to Food Services to eat, so their meals are prepared and placed in containers. These are loaded into heated electrical units on wheels, which are pushed down the corridor to SHU and brought in through the entrance portal, then plugged in to electrical sockets to keep the food warm. SHU inmates in protective custody act as orderlies, dishing up individual portions into plastic serving boxes with lids. The boxes are passed through slots in the cell doors, and collected when the meal is over. The electrical units are then loaded with the empty containers and boxes and returned to Food Services, where everything's cleaned and prepared for the next meal.

We can't trust penitentiary inmates with knives, forks and spoons, in case they make weapons out of them. Even plastic utensils can be sharpened by rubbing them against concrete. For that reason we issue 'sporks' — a flimsy plastic spoon (too brittle to take an edge) with fork-like projections set into the front of the spoon. If food is too tough to be cut into bite-size portions with the spork, it's either cut up before serving, or the inmates use their fingers. For the same reason, we don't use metal or ceramic plates or cups. Plastic trays divided into compartments are used for the food, and plastic 'glasses' for water, soda or coffee. We specify when we order them that the plastic is to be too brittle and fragile to take an edge, so that it can't be used to make weapons. This means they're more easily damaged, and have to be replaced more often, but safety is our paramount concern. (The minimum-security camp outside the walls uses plastic knives, forks and spoons, because of the much lower risk of violence there.)

The Religious Services Department has a fairly close interaction with Food Services. Each religious group is allowed one ceremonial meal every year, to coincide with its major festival day. Muslims observing the fast of Ramadan will skip meals during the day. They'll be served a large meal after sunset each evening, and given a bagged breakfast to take back to their units for consumption before sunrise. (It's a constant headache to monitor the inmates on the Ramadan list, to make sure that they don't sneak into the dining hall during normal meals, then come back for 'seconds' that evening. If we catch one of them doing that, he's immediately removed from the Ramadan list, and refused permission to eat with the rest of the Muslim inmates at night.) Inmates from the faith groups concerned will normally assist with preparing the food for such occasions, and are also responsible for cleaning up the kitchen afterward.

Chaplains arrange religious meals in advance. One of us is always present in Food Services to supervise the event, along with one or two CO's to maintain order. The month of Ramadan is a real headache for us, because we have to reorganize our shifts to have a chaplain present at the institution every single evening. This means that our regular schedule is severely disrupted. There are also the usual complications of inmates trying to steal food, or ingredients for hooch, and take it back to their units. Since the Ramadan meal occurs after normal Food Service hours, we don't have the regular search team stationed outside the exit. We have to arrange a special group of guards to do this, which puts additional strain on the evening shift and causes a certain amount of friction.

Next we come to Health Services. Our physicians and some of our nurses are provided by the US Public Health Service. Other nurses are employed locally. They have a difficult and often thankless job in the BOP. Inmates will try to use Health Services to obtain drugs (particularly painkillers that can provide a short-term 'high'), get out of work details, and as an excuse for anything else they can think of. Sexual predators among them may also target the

149

nurses. Nevertheless, the professionals of the US Public Health Service do a superb job under very trying circumstances. I have a lot of respect for them.

Our facility can handle most minor medical and surgical problems, including small operations under local anesthetic, and dental procedures. For more serious conditions our inmates are sent to the local charity hospital, where they're guarded by a three-person team 24/7 until they can be returned to us. (The CO's compete for such assignments — it's an opportunity to rack up a lot of overtime.) Inmates with chronic or long-term conditions are usually transferred to a prison specializing in medical treatment, where they can receive appropriate care.

State prisons and local jails often have very inferior health services. I've been outraged by the neglect and indifference I've encountered in certain facilities. I wouldn't treat an animal — not even an insect! — the way some of them treat their prisoners. It's all a question of money, of course: health services are expensive, and when a prison has a very limited budget to begin with, it's usually prioritized towards security requirements. Prisons operated by private companies under contract to the state are frequently the worst offenders in this regard, in my experience. It's one of the reasons why many professionals in the corrections field are adamantly opposed to privately-run prisons. The profit motive is paramount, which means that urgent and pressing needs in any department may well go unmet for far too long. This certainly has a detrimental effect on the inmates, and may pose serious risks to surrounding communities as well.

Next to Health Services we have R&D, the Receiving and Dispatch department. Here all newcomers to the prison are entered into the system, searched, and issued uniforms and basic requirements. New arrivals typically spend up to a week or two in the Hole, while they're classified and prepared for integration into the general prison population. This is necessary because those sent to us are considered high-risk inmates. We need to take great care

150

in analyzing their suitability for placement, and assigning them to an appropriate residential unit. For example, if an avowed white supremacist comes in, it really wouldn't be a good idea to assign him to a unit (or a cell) already occupied by a black supremacist. The same applies to members of competing gangs. In each case, the result would be short, painful and 'interesting'.

Some inmates may have psychological or psychiatric problems, and may have come to us from a medical facility, where their condition was stabilized using a cocktail of various medications. Our psychologists will assess their current status, liaise with Health Services concerning their ongoing treatment, prepare individual plans for rehabilitation, and attend to a host of other issues before we put them into general population.

Also in this section are our mail sorting facilities. All inmate mail is opened and searched for contraband. Some inmates who are considered high-risk have their mail monitored. It will be read, and perhaps photocopied, before they get it. Parcels will be opened and searched, and if the contents are in any way suspicious they may be X-rayed. In the same way, outgoing mail is read and checked before dispatch. There have been cases where 'hits' — contract murders — have been set up by inmates using coded communications. Gangs may try to communicate with their members in other prisons; some inmates may be running schemes to blackmail, extort or pressure others; there may be covert arrangements to smuggle contraband into the prison. In order to prevent such things, our inmates' outgoing letters are very carefully scrutinized.

A favorite inmate trick is to try to use the mails to communicate with those incarcerated elsewhere, without alerting the authorities to what they're doing. Gangs, in particular, do this. One of their members will write a letter to a fictitious address that doesn't exist, or to someone who will know to mark it 'Return To Sender', then put it back in the post box. Instead of putting his own return address on the envelope, the inmate will put the name and address of the person (in another prison) who is the intended recipient of the letter. When the Post Office returns it to the 'sender', it'll go to that person instead. We check return addresses very carefully to catch this. When we find one, we single out that inmate for special mail monitoring precautions.

Another tactic might be for several inmates to write to different persons, all of whom use the same mailing address. When we detect this, we're immediately suspicious. Very often that address will be a gang 'clearing house' for information. Each inmate might include one or two snippets of idle 'gossip'. When they're all put together, they'll form a detailed report of the gang's activities at our institution. Some gangs use surprisingly sophisticated codes and ciphers to convey messages. Recipients of such letters will gather information in this way, and either pass it to gang bosses on the outside, or circulate it to inmates in other prisons. There have been cases where the recipient or another person has arranged to visit a gang's 'big boss' in his prison, verbally relayed the collected information to him, received his orders, and then forwarded them to his subordinates in other institutions.

One of the most fascinating examples of this sort of communication occurred in a South American country. An individual received news from inmates in various prisons through the mail, collated it, and reported to a gang boss in another institution. He, in turn, made decisions (allegedly including instructions to murder certain individuals), and verbally conveyed them to his visitor. She went home and, with the help of several colleagues, placed a large number of advertisements in a particular newspaper. Not by coincidence, the gang under-bosses in various prisons all subscribed to this newspaper. Each advertisement was carefully phrased, with key words to identify it, and certain numerals (component part numbers, telephone numbers, postal codes and so on) that appeared innocuous, but in reality designated a word on a specific page in a known edition of the Bible. All the under-bosses owned a copy of that Bible.

When the inmates received the next issue of this newspaper, they sat down with their Bibles and went through the classified advertisements. By checking each one for a key word or phrase, they identified those meant for them, then used the numbers they contained to select words in the Bible and arrange them in the correct sequence. When they were all put together, they formed detailed instructions from their boss. It was an expensive and time-consuming way to convey information, but virtually foolproof, and very reliable. In this case, one of the under-bosses turned informer and alerted the authorities, who were able to decipher the messages and deal with those involved. Since this incident, I'm told that prisons in that country (and, I daresay, in ours) watch carefully for similar schemes.

Special arrangements are made for legal mail and other sensitive items. It has to be marked in a special way by the sender. Such incoming mail is opened in the presence of the inmate and searched for contraband (although the documents themselves are not read — the inmate is entitled to confidentiality under lawyer-client privilege). In the same way, outgoing 'special mail' is searched for contraband, but not read. If an inmate wishes to see his lawyer, special arrangements are made. They use separate offices in the visiting area, and apart from being searched before and after his interview, the inmate is guaranteed privacy. Sometimes this is abused, of course. A few years ago a prominent lawyer was found guilty of passing communications between a convicted terrorist and his organization in the Middle East, thereby abusing the privilege of lawyer-client confidentiality. We took due note of this, but we still can't interfere in the process.

The Education Department probably sees more inmate traffic each day than any other department except Food Service. It has three components: a series of classrooms for instruction, a general library, and a Law Library. The general library has a reasonable selection of books, many obtained from the local library service on rotating loan, plus many paperbacks donated by inmates. Prisoners are restricted to a maximum of five books in their personal property by the BOP, so if their family and friends arrange to have more sent in to them, they have to get rid of the surplus. (Educational and religious materials, if duly authorized, are exempt from this restriction). The Law Library is equipped with typewriters, and a very comprehensive selection of reference works and case records from the Federal courts. It's expensive to maintain it, but by judicial *fiat* we have to provide it. Every day it's jammed with inmates working on their appeals, filing motions, or initiating lawsuits against anyone they can think of. Most will be rejected, but they've got plenty of time on their hands to file them, and nothing better to do.

The classrooms are busy with many courses, day and night. A computer laboratory teaches personal computer operation, using the most common office productivity software (although, of course, there's no Internet access, or anything that might present a security risk). All inmates in the Federal system who haven't graduated high school are required to earn their GED (or put at least 240 hours of study towards it). Other courses are offered in Spanish and English, mathematics and various subjects of interest. Teachers are employed by the BOP, and inmates with specific skills and certification in certain subjects may be given jobs as auxiliary instructors. Regrettably, most education is academic in orientation, not necessarily geared towards practical application in the commercial world. The only place in our prison to learn such hands-on skills is at UNICOR or in Food Services or Facilities.

(I still chuckle as I recall a conversation with one of the teachers. I showed him an article from an Australian newspaper, discussing the vocational training available to inmates at a prison in that country. It cited one inmate who'd received a certificate of competency in chainsaw operation. The teacher and I looked at each other dumbfounded, then burst out laughing. The thought of giving our high-security inmates access to *chainsaws*... well, let's just say that the title of a popular horror movie set in Texas came to mind!)

Some state correctional systems do far less than the BOP to educate and train their inmates. Their limited budgets are often stretched to breaking point merely to provide adequate security, never mind 'luxuries' such as health care or education. The same goes for training for job opportunities in the outside world. I'm afraid politicians and administrators may speak of education and training for rehabilitation in oratorical flights of fancy, but it's not as widely available, or as suitable to the purpose, as it should be in most prisons. Inmates in the Federal system may complain, but they're very well off compared to their counterparts in many state and local facilities. I'll have more to say about this later.

The Religious Services Department is discussed in the chapters describing a typical duty shift, so I won't address it here. Beyond it is the Recreation Department. This is a very large room, with exercise mats and a couple of basketball hoops. There are smaller rooms on two sides. Some are used for music practice by inmate bands. Many, including myself, would assert emphatically that the term 'cacophony' was specifically invented to describe most of their efforts! Another room is devoted to crafts. Those who have the skill and the inclination can engage in painting, leather-working and other hobbies. Recreation staff organize inter-unit sports tournaments (softball in summer, football in winter, and other competitions as space and time allows), and also arrange for 'variety concerts' put on by the inmates from time to time. (See my comment above about 'cacophony'!)

It's time to leave the prison compound. On the way out, let's look at the administration building. Apart from the Control Center, this houses various administrative departments such as Training, Human Resources and Finance, a locksmith's workshop, an armory, and offices for the Warden, Executive Assistant and various managers. There's a large conference room for regular meetings of managers and heads of department. The SIS department is also housed here. Their work concerns our inmates, but security requirements for the information they handle (sometimes highly sensitive or confidential) dictate that their offices be more secure than could be arranged inside the compound. This is also more convenient for their frequent liaison work with the FBI, US Marshals Service, and other law enforcement agencies.

Most of those in the administration building don't work inside the walls, but if a body alarm sounds, they also respond to it, and are trained like the rest of us. It adds to the camaraderie of prison work to know that if you run into serious trouble, *everybody* will be coming on the run to help you. At such times you really appreciate your fellow workers!

Moving outside the penitentiary, the inmates at the minimum-security camp do a great deal to keep our institution running. Some of them work in the warehouse. This is where all supplies and materials are received and dispatched. Since these inmates are non-violent, and not considered a threat to the community, the more trusted among them may even drive trucks into the city to collect and deliver goods. All incoming items are carefully checked against expected orders. Anything arriving without proper documentation is regarded with suspicion, and frequently rejected. Parcels and boxes are X-rayed to detect any contraband they may contain.

It's quite a process to bring in goods for the Religious Services Department. After they're received and X-rayed, they're racked, and we're notified that they're ready for collection. One of us has to go down to the warehouse with all relevant documentation, check it against that provided with the shipment, sign that everything is in order, then bring the goods up to the prison and ferry them in through the sliders. Larger items come through the rear gate to the loading dock, from where we arrange to collect them.

Once a week, one of us goes down to the warehouse and collects an electric cart loaded with firewood and rocks for the

Native American Sweat Lodge ceremony. We drive this up to the rear gate, have it inspected there, then travel around the perimeter track between the fence and the wall to the compound entrance. When the Compound Officers have time, and the yards are secure (usually when inmate traffic is at a minimum, such as between moves), they'll radio the Control Center, which will open a double-slider portal. This admits us to a secured corner of the compound, and the Compound Officers then unlock it to let us onto the yards. We drive the cart to the outdoor worship area. Our inmate orderlies unload it there, then we laboriously retrace our steps.

(I once had a dispute about the right of way along the perimeter track with an itinerant skunk, who'd obviously made his way through the wire from the woods surrounding the prison. I returned the electric cart to the warehouse, parked it a long way from the door, and beat a hasty retreat, before the staff realized that its — and my — fragrance did *not* resemble the odor of sanctity! I'm sure the inmate who subsequently washed it had a few profoundly irreligious things to say about its driver, who by then had excused himself to go home, shower and change before returning to continue his shift!)

The warehouse also has a vehicle maintenance facility. All cleaning and minor maintenance on prison vehicles is performed there. The institution has a large bus for inmate transport, similar to those traveling commercial routes between the states (although the latter are not — at least in my experience — equipped with shotgun cages and chains for the passengers); several police-type cars, to serve as escort vehicles and general-purpose personnel transports; a few pickup trucks with gun racks, for local patrols of the grounds; several trucks and light commercial vehicles, to collect and deliver supplies and personnel; and specialized vehicles for gardening and maintenance. Looking after them all is a big job.

Other camp inmates look after the extensive grounds surrounding the penitentiary and the camp. On any day from spring through fall, work crews will be driving large lawnmowers to and fro, trimming bushes, planting flowers, washing windows, and generally keeping the place in top condition. They do a great job. Some crews go out to the highway to keep brush cut back from the road, so that the turnoff to the prison is clearly visible. They also maintain a hundred-foot clear space for a couple of miles along each side of the road, so that any escaping inmates will be clearly visible if they approach the highway. Patrol vehicles and helicopters will thus be able to spot them more easily if necessary.

I'm informed that one inmate in another camp was particularly enterprising. He took advantage of his job on a road crew to carve out a well-concealed niche in the thick woods surrounding his camp. Since it didn't have a wall or fence around it, inmates could (if they were careful) sneak out for an hour or two during the evening without being missed. Our budding entrepreneur made arrangements with a couple of the local ladies of the night. On certain prearranged evenings, they brought air mattresses and blankets out to the woods, and set up an *al fresco* bordello in the clearing he'd made. He found customers for them among the camp inmates, who paid in commissary goods that the ladies could resell. The prostitutes paid him a kickback percentage of their earnings.

This went on for several months, until a guard spotted an inmate returning from the woods one evening, looking altogether too happy. He investigated, and the racket was exposed and shut down. The inmate who'd thought up the scheme was 'promoted' to a medium-security prison as punishment. (I hope they employed him in prison industry there… with a business sense like that, he'd probably have made a fortune for them!) The ladies of negotiable virtue were given their marching orders. So far, nothing of the kind has been discovered at our camp… but you never know.

Our camp inmates also provide a very important service during lock-downs at the penitentiary. If a major incident occurs there, all the inmates are locked in their cells for days or weeks on end while it's investigated. During that period, their food has to be prepared and taken to them. Camp inmates don bright yellow overalls (to visually distinguish them from penitentiary inmates), and form work crews in Food Services, preparing thousands upon thousands of sandwiches and other food that's easy to put into brown paper bags.

Those of us who are support staff rather than Correctional Officers join them in preparing these bags, and loading them onto trays in wheeled carts. Three times a day we form long processions, taking the food to the units, distributing it, and returning the carts to Food Services for the next meal. You'd think staff would object to such menial work, but in reality we're not too upset. After all, the only time we can be sure we won't have a major incident, or run the risk of attack, is when all the inmates are locked in their cells! The penitentiary becomes a remarkably peaceful place during such times. All of us, even those working regular office hours, switch to a special shift rotation to cater for the different requirements of a lock-down period.

The camp inmates don't like going into the penitentiary. Since they're all non-violent offenders, they're genuinely afraid of the far more dangerous inmates inside the wall. Apart from lock-downs, they're delighted to steer clear of the place. The only time they'll end up inside is if they commit a major breach of regulations. When that happens, they have to be locked up — and the camp doesn't have its own SHU. Instead, they're escorted to the Hole in the penitentiary. This can drive them to tears (literally), as they simply can't handle the foul language, violence and generally unspeakable attitude of hard-line penitentiary inmates in the Hole. The mere threat of confinement there is usually enough to produce a drastic improvement in their behavior. Those few who've experienced it, if they're not shipped out to a higher-security institution in due course, come back and tell the others about it, with hushed voices and terrible expressions on their face. This very effectively dissuades most of their colleagues from any desire to sample the delights of the Hole for themselves.

I've tried to show you most of the support services and activities that allow a penitentiary to function. As you've seen, the highly visible and publicized areas of our activities — the walls and the wire and the bars, the guards and the guns and the towers — are only the 'surface layer' of what is in reality a labyrinthine organization.

A penitentiary such as ours is equivalent to any medium-sized business in complexity (and in the size of its budget). Those who run it have to be good managers and executives. The difference between their jobs and those of commercial managers is that if the latter make a mistake, it usually costs only money. If our bosses make a mistake, it may cost injuries, perhaps even lives. They take that responsibility very seriously indeed.

As you enter the lobby of our institution, you'll see a memorial to BOP officers who've been killed in the line of duty. It's our heartfelt ambition to ensure that none of our names are ever added to that memorial. So far, we've succeeded.

CONVICT TO CHAPLAIN VI

THE WOLF

Hi, Chaplain. Thanks for taking the time to see me privately like this.

I... I wanted to thank you for saving me. I guess I haven't done that properly before. If I'd had to stay with Les for another week, I'd have killed myself for sure. Getting me out of that mess saved my life. Even giving up two-thirds of my commissary for a year was cheap at the price. Adam told me you'd considered asking for me to be transferred to another prison, but I'd have had the same problem there. I'd have ended up either dead, or insane. No question about it. Your way was better, even though I'd never have thought of it.

I... I guess I really hated you for a while, until I began to understand. Adam wouldn't let up on me. He made me do push-ups, and sit-ups, and pull-ups, and weight work in Recreation, and circuits of the yard, until I thought I was going to die! I'd never been active, and I was very unfit. A year later, I'm thirty pounds lighter and much more muscular. I've had to get a new issue of clothing - I dropped two whole trouser sizes! *(Happy grin.)*

Learning to fight? It hurt! *(Wince.)* Adam was really brutal with me. He made it clear that unless I was willing to stand up for myself, I'd be somebody's 'bitch' all my time behind bars. He trained me hard. Didn't pull his punches. He said unless I learned to fight through the pain, I'd never be able to hold my own. He was right, I know that now — but it didn't make it any less painful! *(Grimace.)*

It was an eye-opener to learn how many ways there are to hurt or kill someone. Adam's the hardest, most dangerous man I've ever known — but I guess that's why you chose him, right? I never thought I'd say this about a murderer, but he's not all bad, in his own strange way. *(Smile.)*

Yes, I was in the Hole for a few days while they investigated. I got out last week. I never thought I'd thank you for getting me into a position where I'd have to go to the Hole, Chaplain, but I do. *(Deep breath.)* I *had* to stop that guy. If I hadn't, I'd have been a rabbit again. Adam made it clear that I was on my own now. He protected me for a year, but that was all. From then on, I had to stand on my own two feet.

Yes, it worked. The guy's still in the Hole. The Man reckoned the fight was his fault — and it was — so he drew thirty days. He's not happy about that, but he won't make trouble. He lost the fight *big*-time! *(Satisfied smile.)* I've got a rep of my own now. Adam says I won't be bothered much from now on, as long as I carry on standing tall. He seems oddly proud of me, almost like a father with his son. Heck, even the CO's are more respectful!

Yes, I promise. I'll watch for others coming into the prison as I did, and I'll try to help them, the way you and Adam helped me. That's the least I can do to repay what I owe both of you. I might have to discuss that with Les, of course. *(Feral grin. Teeth. Wolf. Poor Les.)*

I'd always been too ashamed to tell my wife everything: but I know she guessed something was badly wrong, a year ago. I told her the whole story last weekend, after I got out of the Hole. She asked me to thank you for her — Adam, too. When I get out, we're going to start over. She's worth it — and thank God, she thinks I am too! She and the children will be visiting again next month. I can't wait to see them again!

FRIDAY — 5:50 P.M.

I get back to the chapel after administering the Last Rites to Andrew, put away my equipment, issue their grape juice and *matzot* to the Jewish group, and turn to the Asatru contingent.

"Thanks for your patience, guys. Now, what were you needing?"

"Chaplain, can we watch a movie tonight?"

"I see no reason why not."

Our TV's are mounted on wheeled stands, with integrated players, so that they can easily be moved from room to room. I get one out of storage for them, while they look through the Chapel library and select a couple of titles. They thank me, and head to their allotted classroom for the evening. Watching them go, I shake my head sadly. The Asatru group in this prison is comprised largely of Skinhead gangsters. Most of them can't be here tonight, because they're locked up in the Hole for various offenses. That's a pretty normal state of affairs for them.

I chuckle as I recall a recent incident. A group of Asatru inmates were nagging a chaplain in a certain institution to find them materials about the Norse gods. Keeping an absolutely straight face, he asked if they'd ever heard of Wagner's 'Nibelungen' or 'Ring cycle'? They shook their heads. He found them some material describing it, and they were wildly excited at the references

163

to pagan gods. They insisted he spend some of the Chapel budget — the part allocated to their faith group — on buying a set of CD's of the entire Ring cycle. When they arrived, the group took them into a room to listen avidly... and were dumbfounded at the sounds of Wagnerian opera floating from the speakers (in the original German, of course). Furious, they accused him of having tricked them, but he pointed out in injured innocence that they were the ones who'd insisted he buy the CD's. He had their signed requests and Special Purchase Order on file to prove it, too. The CD's have been sitting unused in the Asatru cupboard of that institution's chapel ever since. I suppose they were just too much of a change from gangsta rap and heavy metal...

I check my watch. It's almost six already. I brew a pot of coffee, and call the Corridor Officer, who arrives within a few minutes. We pour ourselves some coffee, and spend a couple of minutes enjoying it and passing the time.

My radio blurts, "Control to Chaplain Grant."

"Chaplain Grant, go."

"Five volunteers ready for you, Chaplain."

"Thanks, Control, I'm on my way."

I leave Harry to keep an eye on the Chapel area, and make my way out to the Control Center. Three volunteers from the Jehovah's Witnesses, and two for the Protestant Christian group, are waiting for me. One of the latter is an attractive lady, and I wince internally (although I don't show any outward sign). We have more than our fair share of sex offenders, perverts and moral degenerates in this institution. Some of them are likely to try to attend the service if they know a woman will be present — and they'll know as soon as she walks down the corridor. She'll be visible from the yard outside. Such inmates are more than capable of masturbating in her presence, hiding in a back row and indulging their sick fantasies. If we catch them, we'll lock them in the Hole, of course, but that won't necessarily deter them. There's also the risk that more devout inmates might take umbrage at their 'disrespect', and show their displeasure physically. That might spark a full-scale brawl. I resolve to watch carefully tonight, and 'discourage' known troublemakers from attending.

The Lobby Officer has already had the volunteers sign their special register, checked their belongings, put them through the metal detector, and stamped their hands with ink that's only visible under ultraviolet light. As they go in, the Control Center will check their hands for today's mark (it changes every day), and as they come out they'll be checked again. Anyone leaving without the correct mark will be stopped. Just another precaution to make sure our inmates don't try to escape disguised as religious volunteers. I grin as I recall one volunteer who disregarded our warnings and instructions, and washed his hands several times while inside. I wasn't on duty that night, but I was told it took him a long time to convince the Control Center not to lock him in the Hole for the night. The other volunteers were said to be highly amused. His wife, reportedly, was not.

I usher the volunteers through the first slider, then wait as each of them passes a hand beneath the ultra-violet light fitting, while one of the Control Center staff peers through the window to make sure that today's security mark is clearly visible. When he's satisfied, he notifies the officer at the console, who opens the inner slider. We walk through, and head for the buildings. I notice a slight shiver from a couple of the volunteers. It's an unnerving thing for many visitors to realize that armed guards in the towers are watching their every move — just in case.

We pass through the main portal, and head down the corridor towards the Chapel. One of the volunteers, new to this work, asks me, "Chaplain, what are all those men doing in there?" He nods to the Law Library on our left. Inside a couple of dozen inmates are seated at typewriters, thick volumes of legal reference books at their sides.

"That's the Law Library. By order of the courts, we have to provide our inmates with all the reference materials they need to file motions and appeals. Those inmates are working on their cases."

The volunteer is shocked. "But it must cost a fortune to keep current subscriptions to all the laws and legal records of the Federal Government and courts, not to mention those typewriters and everything else!"

"It does indeed: but the courts have mandated it, so we have to provide it."

I don't add that this is one reason why inmates flood the judicial system with countless irritating and ultimately futile cases. They do it simply because they can. We've even had inmates file liens against the property of BOP staff on a technicality. It's cost the individuals concerned a great deal of time, money and aggravation to have them lifted. The inmates concerned have actually had the nerve to be indignant when punished for such actions — but what else did they expect?

We reach the Chapel, and I thank Harry for looking after the place in my absence. I take him aside, and mention the problem of the female volunteer. He suggests asking a couple of the steadier and more devout inmates to help me screen those attending tonight. I can't officially exclude anyone wishing to attend an open service like this, but a 'suggestion' from the inmates (backed up by the implicit threat of more direct measures if the 'suggestion' is disregarded) may well have the desired effect. Harry and I grin at one another. There's always a way, if one uses one's head.

Harry goes back to his post in the corridor, and I settle the volunteers into their rooms. The three Jehovah's Witnesses volunteers sit down with a dozen or so inmates in a classroom, while the two Protestant ministers tune their guitars, preparing for an hour of praise and worship in the main chapel. A few of their congregation are already here, but most will arrive with the 6:30 move. I check those already present. Sure enough, there are three inmates who are regulars at this service, and whom I regard as 'steady'. I call them outside and explain the problem of the female volunteer. They immediately agree to stand unobtrusively in the lobby, to assist me in weeding out 'undesirables' during the move. Their smiles are... well, 'nasty' just about describes it. They don't intend to have their service disrupted. I feel more at peace about it now. I'll do them a favor sometime, as a 'thank you' for their assistance tonight.

I take a moment to check all the rooms in the Chapel complex. The inmates are busy with studying, watching movies, listening to tapes, or discussing issues. There don't seem to be any problems... not so far, at any rate. Let's hope the rest of the evening passes without incident.

The loudspeakers come to life. "The move is open. The move is open."

Once again the hustle and bustle of a move interrupts the evening. Inmates stream into the Chapel area, about fifty or sixty going to the main chapel for the Protestant service, twenty or so Native Americans heading for the small chapel for an evening of study and discussion, a few more Jehovah's Witnesses and Asatru to join their groups, and some wanting to see me to discuss problems or ask for a telephone call. I keep an eye on my three inmate 'screeners' as they carefully scrutinize those heading for the main chapel. Several times one of them moves forward to have a few quiet words with someone, who generally looks sullen, but turns and leaves the chapel area. I nod approvingly as the three glance at me. When the move closes, they re-enter the main chapel. I issue supplies from the faith group cupboards and re-lock them, settle everyone down, and as the music starts from the Protestant service I return to my office.

I pause to greet three of our Wiccan group leaders. They're sitting around the desk of an inmate orderly in the lobby outside my office. We don't have any outside volunteers to assist their group, but one of our inmates is a duly and properly instituted Wiccan priest, and he leads their services. August is almost over, and the next of the eight Wiccan holy days — Mabon, the Autumn

Equinox on September 21 — is drawing nearer. They're preparing a special celebration for the occasion, and tonight they'll be planning their ceremony. They're a good bunch, generally peaceful and co-operative (unlike many others inside these walls). Regrettably, many people mistakenly believe that Wiccans are, in fact, Satanists. Nothing could be further from the truth. A true Wiccan will have nothing to do with those who serve the Evil One.

The Asatru group also celebrate that date as the Feast of Winterfinding, and may want to organize something special. They're rather less realistic and co-operative than the Wiccans. Last time they had a ceremonial meal, they asked for elk steak and mead! In prison, no less! We offered cheeseburgers and soda — not exactly traditional Norse fare, but they didn't have much alternative. Grumbling, they accepted.

There are half a dozen inmates waiting to see me. "How many of you need telephone calls?" I ask. Four hands are raised. "Guys, you know the rules. If I'm satisfied that you have a genuine need, and it's an emergency, I'll give you a call: but if I think you're trying to con me, or I give you a call and there turns out to be no emergency — don't forget, I'll be listening, and recording every word — you'll be taking a trip to the Lieutenant's Office, and perhaps from there to the Hole later tonight. Are you sure you want a call?"

Two of the inmates lower their hands, shuffling their feet in embarrassed disappointment. There are always some who'll try it on. Two others keep their hands in the air. "Very well. What about the rest of you? You need to talk to me?" The two remaining inmates nod. "Very well. I'll take the two callers first, then each of you as I have time. You may have to wait while I bring in volunteers before the next move." They again nod their understanding.

The first inmate produces a letter from his ex-wife. Their daughter is ill, and he's worried about her. I check our call log. He hasn't asked for an emergency call in months, and he has the envelope for his letter. The handwriting on the former matches that of the latter. I decide that this is probably a genuine case, and place a call to his home number. He spends ten minutes talking with his former wife, who takes the phone through to his daughter's bedroom so that she can speak with her father. There are tears in his eyes when he finishes. It's tough being so far from your loved ones. He thanks me, and leaves as I enter the call in our log book.

The second inmate comes in and closes the door. "Chaplain," he says softly, "I need to speak to the Duty Officer." I raise my eyebrows, but ask no questions. This man's an informer. He occasionally comes to the chapel on the pretext of calling his family, but in reality we put him through to someone who can take his information and act on it. He and others like him don't abuse our good offices. They only come to us if they have urgent information that they can't pass on any other way. That means this is likely to be important.

STAFF

The Warders strutted up and down,
And kept their herd of brutes,
Their uniforms were spick and span,
And they wore their Sunday suits.
— Oscar Wilde (1854-1900)

What sort of person chooses to work in a prison? The answer varies, depending on the prison system in question. The BOP requires that its Correctional Officer candidates possess a Bachelors degree, or at least three years of appropriate and relevant experience. State prison systems are less onerous in their requirements, while local jails are frequently run by area law enforcement agencies, which use them as an entry path for those who wish to progress to full law enforcement status as police officers or sheriff's deputies. All agencies typically attract a large proportion of military veterans (particularly those with a Military Police background).

Some States, and the BOP, strive to locate new prisons in economically depressed areas, so as to provide employment opportunities there. This appears to have been very successful. It also has the not insignificant advantages that land, housing and other facilities in such localities tend to be substantially cheaper than in more developed areas, and the locals are usually eager to welcome the prison because of the economic benefits it brings to the region. Potential downsides are that large enterprises — supermarkets, etc. — may follow the prison, putting pressure on local businesses. Over time, the prison may come to dominate the area's economy to such an extent that if it later downsizes or closes, the impact may be very severe.

Requirements for Correctional Officer training vary from agency to agency. Local prisons often train their jailers in-house as they work towards full P.O.S.T. (Peace Officer Standards and Training) certification, according to their state's requirements State corrections agencies usually have their own specialized training curricula and facilities, and may recognize the training offered by other States as more or less equivalent to their own. The BOP probably offers the most comprehensive training. New recruits undergo ten days to two weeks' initial orientation at their institution, and will then be sent to the Federal Law Enforcement Training Academy (FLETC) at Glynco in Georgia. This is the size of many small universities or colleges, a campus of 1,500 acres used by scores of Federal law enforcement agencies. Here BOP recruits spend three weeks undergoing a very thorough training program, including the use of vehicles, firearms and restraining devices, strength and fitness evaluation, and an in-depth academic and practical grounding. This is required for all prison staff, not only Correctional Officers. In the event of an emergency, we're *all* Correctional Officers, and we *all* respond. During the first year of service, additional on-the-job mentoring and guidance is provided.

Following initial training, every year each BOP institution provides a week of annual refresher training for all its staff, during which the latest threats, gang activity and other important matters are discussed. Every staff member will also be sent to ongoing professional training in his or her field of activity as they gain seniority and promotions. There are self-study courses available for those wishing to improve their professional skills, and opportunities to transfer to other career paths within the BOP, as well as other law enforcement agencies within the US Department of Justice. This emphasis on professionalism and ongoing training costs the BOP tens of millions of dollars every year, but it's the only way to keep its staff operating with the desired degree of competence. I'm very grateful to the BOP for the truly excellent training they gave me. It's world-class.

Thanks in part to this rigorous training, the BOP is one of the few corrections agencies whose staff are recognized as law enforcement officers by the US Department of Justice. It's a constant source of frustration to many in the corrections field that they are denied this status in many States and local jurisdictions. It's been the experience of many (including myself) that 'real cops' (as police officers and sheriff's deputies have been known to refer to themselves) tend to look down on corrections staff as 'wannabe cops', and act somewhat condescendingly towards them. In my view, this is ridiculous. Officers 'on the street' carry guns to defend themselves. They make arrests, and then hand over the criminals to custodians. They don't have to put up with the criminals for more than an hour or two — and they're armed to help control them, if necessary. Correctional Officers have to live cheek-by-jowl with those same criminals for years on end, unarmed, vulnerable to assault, manipulation and coercion. From that perspective, prison staff have a more dangerous and more demanding job than that of a 'street cop'.

Let's examine the career paths open to a newly recruited Correctional Officer. I'll discuss the BOP model, but most state-level corrections agencies will be roughly similar (although they may use different job titles and descriptions). A Correctional Officer can progress through the ranks to Lieutenant, controlling a shift or an area of operations during a shift, and then to Captain, the person in charge of all Correctional Officers and the security of the installation. It'll typically take ten to fifteen years to become a

Lieutenant, and fifteen to twenty to become a Captain (although top performers may take less time to achieve these ranks). A Correctional Officer may be assigned to a number of different duties. Some will be Unit Officers, controlling a housing unit containing scores or even hundreds of inmates. Some will be Tower Officers, occupying a gun tower on the perimeter (and, in some facilities for high-security inmates, in the center of the compound as well). Some will be assigned to SHU, to control the particularly troublesome inmates confined there. Some will be Compound Officers, walking the open yards inside the prison and controlling inmate movement. Some will be Corridor Officers, supervising access to the institution's buildings. Some will be on outer perimeter patrol, usually in vehicles, circling the institution and watching for any breach of security. Some may be assigned periodically to escort prisoners to and from the institution, or take inmates to hospital for medical treatment and guard them during their stay there. All Correctional Officers can expect to work in all of these situations, usually rotating between them on a quarterly basis. As they gain seniority, they'll be able to request the assignments they prefer, and have a better chance of getting them.

If a Correctional Officer wishes to pursue a different route to higher rank, there are a number of possible career paths (which are also open to recruits applying directly for such positions, although preference is given to internal transfers and promotions whenever possible). Each inmate residential unit (or a cluster of smaller units) will have certain staff assigned to it. The Unit Counselor will provide counseling and advice to inmates concerning institution discipline and problems they may be encountering. He assists the Case Manager, who prepares and supervises a program of education and other interventions for each convict, monitors his progress, and draws up parole and release programs as appropriate. The Unit Manager is in overall charge of all these officials, and is responsible for all aspects of unit management and operation. Many Correctional Officers choose these career paths, rather than continuing through Lieutenant's rank to the Captaincy of an institution.

There are a large variety of other opportunities in the BOP. UNICOR hires factory foremen and supervisors to control the inmate work force. The Facilities Department needs qualified plumbers, electricians and other skilled tradespeople for institution maintenance. The Food Services Department requires cook-supervisors, dieticians and others to purchase food, supervise its preparation, plan menus, and ensure that a balanced and nutritious diet is provided (including provision for special dietary requirements). Receiving & Dispatch may draw staff from Correctional Officers, or may employ its own staff, to deal with inmate processing, mail handling and other functions. Health Services needs medical and support personnel. The Education Department hires teachers and specialist instructors. Ministers of religion of numerous faiths and denominations are recruited as Chaplains. The Recreation Department wants specialists to supervise sporting events, inmate fitness and institutional activities related to those fields. The Safety Department seeks specialists to ensure that all aspects of the institution's operations conform to legal and regulatory requirements. In addition, they assist staff who suffer work-related injuries, helping them deal with the Workers Compensation process. There are also administrative positions such as clerks, secretaries, Human Resources officers, bookkeepers and accountants, computer specialists, warehouse and supply staff and the like, just as in any corporation.

Once staff reach the level of a department manager, they are eligible for consideration for executive management positions in the BOP. Executives will usually (but not always) have at least some experience as a Correctional Officer, or in a closely related field. They are normally not hired from outside the BOP unless they have extensive corrections experience. Each institution will have multiple Associate Wardens, in charge of areas such as programs, prison industry, and other major activities. A Warden is in charge of each prison. At regional offices and BOP headquarters in Washington DC, there are senior management and executive positions of various types. Certainly, anyone entering the BOP who's willing to work hard can rise as high as he or she wishes in its service.

I've given you the official staff structures found in a prison, but they can't convey the day-to-day reality of life within the walls. It's a stressful and frequently dangerous job that makes huge demands on those working there. Let's look at some of those stresses as experienced by a Unit Officer in a high-security penitentiary such as ours. There are twelve units, each accommodating up to 128 inmates in double cells. They're shaped roughly like a long, narrow triangle, with communal shower facilities, a games room, a sitting-room, three communal TV sets (to which inmates listen via headsets to keep the noise down, and request a change of channel from the Unit Officer), microwave ovens in a separate area, to allow inmates to prepare food purchased from the Commissary, and a steel door at the entrance, opening onto a portal secured by a slider.

The Unit Officer has a small office with a desk, telephone and computer terminal. He serves an eight-hour shift, which in our institution runs from 6 a.m. to 2 p.m., 2 p.m. to 10 p.m., or 10 p.m. to 6 a.m. At night inmates are locked in their cells, so it's relatively peaceful most of the time. The other two shifts are much busier — and sometimes significantly more dangerous. There may be dozens or scores of inmates moving around the unit. Some will undoubtedly be planning to steal other inmates' belongings. Others may be preparing to attack someone in retaliation for some slight, or to force them to comply with their demands, or to establish or defend their place in the convict 'pecking order'. The Unit Officer must learn the likely trouble-makers in his unit, and watch them very carefully. He must also ensure that only inmates assigned to his unit are within it. It's against regulations for any other inmate to enter it — but, as usual, most inmates don't care a hoot what the regulations say.

The Unit Officer is responsible for keeping good order and discipline. He'll open the outer door during moves, and lock it afterwards (unless it's a time of free movement, such as during the evening, when inmates are permitted to go out to the yard if they wish). He has to search inmates and/or their cells at random, to detect and confiscate contraband. He must manage access to inmate telephones, and ensure they're not monopolized by individuals or gangs (who might try to 'charge' other inmates for their use if they could get away with it). He may have certain individuals in his unit who have been designated a security threat, and require more intensive monitoring. If this is covert, he'll have to watch them without their realizing that they're under increased surveillance. Under such circumstances the Unit Counselor, who may have an office in the unit or in an adjacent structure, will sometimes assist the Unit Officer.

Inmates will watch the Unit Officers very carefully indeed, looking for any carelessness or weak points they can exploit. Male Unit Officers may be subject to advances from inmates with homosexual proclivities, while women may be stalked or attacked by sex offenders. I've responded to several body alarms caused by the latter. (Some Correctional Officers and their supervisors, both male and female, fume with anger and frustration at employment policies that require the BOP to implement a gender-neutral assignment of officers to their tasks. They believe — and to a certain extent I'm forced to agree with them — that when you have known sexual predators in a unit, it's grossly irresponsible to put a female officer in charge there, particularly when she'll work on her own most of the time. It's like a red rag to a bull. Regrettably, court decisions and Federal law make it impossible to change the situation at this time. Due to the requirements of gender neutrality in employment and promotion, any Correctional Officer must be able to do, and may be assigned to, any job that such employment normally entails. Anything else is regarded as discrimination.)

A Unit Officer will undoubtedly face intimidation and abuse. This can range from muttered curses and passive resistance by those to whom he gives orders, all the way to physical attacks or threats to his family. A colleague told me of a classic example which reportedly occurred in an institution in another state. A senior Mafia figure was incarcerated there, and was suspected of trying to control his criminal empire beyond the walls through letters, phone calls and visitor communication. In an attempt to limit this, he was subject to frequent searches of his person and his cell. One Unit Officer was particularly zealous about this, and the inmate became annoyed by what he regarded as harassment. No-one was able to figure out how he made the arrangements, but he probably conveyed his orders verbally to one of his visitors. Be that as it may, one day this Unit Officer conducted a routine shakedown of his cell. The Mafia boss waited patiently outside the door until the search was concluded, then came back inside and handed a photograph to the Unit Officer. It showed the latter's daughter waiting for her school bus. It had obviously been taken by one of the Mafia man's 'associates', who'd sent it to him in the mail. He said very quietly to the Unit Officer, "You see how easily it can be done?"

No other words or threats were necessary. His meaning couldn't have been clearer.

The Unit Officer had the good sense to retain the photograph and hand it in, along with a full report on the incident. I'm told he was transferred out of state to another institution at his agency's expense. The Mafia boss did some time in the Hole, and the officer's daughter was assigned an armed driver to take her to and from her new school for a while. Even so, her parents will never feel the same about her safety — or her father's job.

There are other ways of 'getting to' Unit Officers. Mike's experience with an inmate's wife, described earlier, isn't an isolated case by any means. Inmates will try anything and everything to con, deceive and bend correctional staff to their will. It's a never-ending process. All of us are trained to spot such approaches, but inmates have all the time in the world to think up new angles and try out different tricks. We can never be sure. That's one reason why it's important for those in the corrections field to constantly update one another on their experiences. One of us might not recognize a particular approach as being potentially risky, but it's very likely that another person will have encountered or heard of something similar. Every year during annual refresher training, particularly egregious cases are discussed so that all staff are aware of them. It's the ultimate 'con game', and it'll continue as long as there are convicts in prison.

Such attempts are by no means restricted to Correctional Officers. Anyone and everyone working in a prison is fair game. Intimidation, bribery, coercion, offers of sexual favors, attempts at blackmail — we've all experienced them. Chaplains come in for our fair share of them, because we're able to provide special privileges to inmates (extra phone calls to their families, approval to bring in personal religious property, arrangements for special visits at times of family crisis, and so on). I've been offered bribes, promised information, threatened... you name it.

One of the funnier incidents happened in another prison, several years ago. It involved a self-proclaimed Satanist and 'warlock'. He tried to wheedle me into arranging a number of special privileges for him. I refused, of course — there were no circumstances under which I could justify them. He wouldn't take no for an answer, and tried threats. Those didn't work either. (When you've been threatened by experts, you get used to it very quickly — and he was no expert!) Frustrated, he finally promised he was going to see to it that I was 'sorted out'. I took this to mean that he would arrange for some inmates to assault me when I was on the compound. I discussed it with the authorities, who tightened up surveillance, and we waited.

It didn't take long for word to reach us through informers. He'd bragged to others on the compound that he'd cast a 'death spell' upon me. He confidently prophesied that I'd be dead within thirty days. I grinned, and carried on as normal. As time passed, his predictions grew louder (and more desperate) as I continued to portray the picture of good health whenever I came to the prison. (I took care to walk around openly, to demonstrate the fact.) As the deadline approached he became frantic, and tried to bribe a prison gang to attack me. Unfortunately for him, gang leaders knew all too well that visiting Chaplains such as myself were their lifeline in the event of family problems. Some of them had needed such assistance in the past. They passed the word that any attack on any Chaplain, visitor or otherwise, would meet with their vigorous and extreme displeasure. The inmates got the message loud and clear. The attempt fizzled, the deadline passed, and I was still alive.

This curse-casting cretin now had problems of his own. Not only had his credibility been shattered by my selfish refusal to fall down dead, but certain over-credulous inmates had taken his boasting seriously. They had paid him considerable sums to cast 'death spells' on other convicts and staff whom they regarded as enemies. Since his curse against me hadn't worked, they were now wondering whether their investment had been well-advised. Sure enough, the deadline for those deaths also passed without so much as a head cold among his intended victims. He ended up requesting protective custody in the Hole, and was eventually transferred to another institution. There were too many angry inmates wanting their money back for him to dare show his face on the compound ever again.

(I hope the Lord will forgive my less-than-pastoral pleasure at his predicament...)

Another favorite technique of inmates is to use the prison's regulations as a weapon. The BOP has been obliged to develop very detailed regulations governing convict administration and its requirements. These implement Federal law and the decisions of the courts. Because they're official Government documents, they're in the public domain, and can't be withheld from inmates except for a few that are highly classified. Canny convicts study them very carefully. If they find that any clause, section or paragraph has been neglected in any way, they'll use that to file complaints, have disciplinary actions against them dismissed or overturned, and generally make life difficult for the staff. It's a well-known tactic that's very frustrating.

I've had it used against me many times, although it's only once led to a formal complaint being filed by an inmate (which was quickly dismissed). The only defense is to ensure that one's conduct is in conformity with the regulations at all times. (There are exceptions to this rule, of course, as you've read, but not many.) Unfortunately, this means that one must be highly bureaucratic in one's approach to inmate requests: but there's really no alternative. Prison executives are particularly targeted by inmates in this way. Some of them have had liens imposed on their property by inmates, who've asked the courts to do so as 'security' for any judgment for damages they may win against them. Such damages are very, very seldom awarded, but the inconvenience of responding to such lawsuits (and removing the liens) is a constant headache. The BOP is forced to maintain a large legal department for this purpose, at considerable expense.

Let me give you an example of how a litigious convict may try to use this process. I was called to SHU one afternoon to see a newly-arrived inmate. He claimed to be a member of a very old and respectable religion, and demanded to be allowed to observe its religious holy day (which was fast approaching). To do so, he required special items of ritual clothing, food and drink. Needless to say, none of them could be provided in the Hole for security reasons. I told him he'd have to wait until he was assigned to a unit in general population before he could conduct his religious exercises. These would have to take place in the Chapel area. (The courts have repeatedly ruled that such restrictions are acceptable in the light of the need for institutional security).

He then complained that the religious diet provided to him (in accordance with the requirements of his faith group) was not properly in compliance with their standards. I informed him that, on the contrary, it conformed to his faith group's dietary requirements in terms of BOP regulations (which that faith had officially approved), and had been certified to comply with those regulations by our dietary specialists in the institution. He demanded that a dietician provide written certification with every meal that it conformed to religious and regulatory requirements. I refused to arrange this, pointing out that nothing required us to provide such certification to individual inmates. It was sufficient for the dietician to certify it to the Food Services Manager on a regular basis. Chaplains would ratify her certification during our routine inspections of the special preparation area for religious meals.

The inmate lost his temper at this point, began swearing at me, and threatened to write up all his complaints in a formal application for redress to the BOP. He shouted that he'd 'take it all the way to Washington' and if he wasn't satisfied with the response, he'd proceed with a Federal lawsuit and 'sue me until I bled'. He sneered nastily at me and waited for me to capitulate. Unfortunately for him, I wasn't about to do so. I invited him to proceed with his complaints if he wished, and offered to bring him the necessary forms to begin the process. I also pointed out that the courts had previously (and repeatedly) accepted the certification of his faith group's leadership concerning our meals, so I didn't think he had much hope of prevailing.

Finally, I pointed out that the moral code of his faith was at least as strict as its dietary laws. I asked mildly whether his actions during the crime of which he'd been convicted (which was particularly unsavory and despicable) had been as observant of that moral code as his dietary demands were of the latter. I offered to ask senior representatives of his faith group to discuss the matter with the court, if his threatened lawsuit got that far (which I assured him was most unlikely).

The inmate was infuriated by my response, and shouted through the grille in his door, "You're no minister of God — you're the spawn of Satan!" I looked at the Correctional Officer standing next to me, whose eyes were wide at this revelation of my demotion. We both burst out laughing, and walked on down the passage. From the language pursuing us, we gathered that the inmate didn't approve of our merriment; but inmates in nearby cells (who'd heard the exchange) were laughing as hard as we were. A little light relief is always welcome in the Hole.

All these tactics by inmates are bad enough, but they pale into insignificance when real trouble erupts. If a fight breaks out, it can quickly spread to involve other inmates, and before you know it there can be a mass brawl or riot going on. This is particularly dangerous when inter-racial or regional conflicts are behind the disturbance. I've been in both types of situation, and believe me, it's not fun. On one occasion, a group of particularly vicious and incorrigible inmates from a central Eastern US city tried to 'muscle in' on criminal activities run by convicts from a couple of Southern states. The latter banded together for mutual protection, and called upon inmates from other Southern states to stand with them against the aggressors. The resulting tension on the compound was electric, and it didn't take long before it exploded into violence. Staff had to break up three separate fights one day, the last threatening to develop into a full-scale riot, and the institution was locked down for several weeks to let tempers cool.

I was very proud of our Correctional Officers that day. All three fights involved shanks, and our staff are unarmed within the walls (for fear that an inmate might overpower a guard and get hold of a weapon). Nevertheless, they went in like gangbusters to break up the fights, with the rest of us rushing to their assistance. One Correctional Officer in particular earned our heartfelt gratitude by charging into a struggling mob at full speed, heedless of his own safety, and performing an absolutely beautiful full-body tackle on a shank-wielding inmate who was about to stab another convict in the back. The impact smashed him back ten feet or more into the wall of a unit block. His head bounced hard against the wall, and he collapsed, knocked silly (well, sillier than usual, at any rate). It took the heart out of his faction, and broke things up before they could get even further out of hand.

I was later told that the Correctional Officer had been nominated for an award for his courage. I think he richly deserved it. His bravery saved a lot of us from injury that day. The security camera footage of his tackle was played and replayed in subsequent weeks, to everyone's huge enjoyment, and was circulated to staff at other institutions (who sent back some very admiring comments, albeit a little too profane to reproduce here).

Working in such an environment has an inevitable effect on the staff — not just the Correctional Officers, but all of us. It's very hard to maintain a cool, professional approach when you know that many of the inmates are out to get you in any way they can. After a while, the constant lies, evasions, attempts at manipulation, lack of co-operation, and just plain nastiness start to wear you down. Stress levels among prison staff are understandably very high, with inevitable negative consequences for their domestic life. The incidence of divorce and suicide amongst all peace officers is considerably above average, and corrections staff aren't exempt. It's very hard to leave your work behind at the gates of the prison, after a day such as I described in the previous paragraph.

This is very troubling from three perspectives. The first is that of inmates who genuinely want to change, to reform, and seek help in doing so. Their approach will be automatically regarded with suspicion by prison staff. We've all been 'conned' so many times that it's all too easy to regard any such approach as more of the same. The inmates, hurt and frustrated, then blame the staff for being unfeeling and inhuman. In a sense, of course, they're right — but they refuse to acknowledge the inevitability of such a reaction, given the staff's constant exposure to less-well-motivated inmates. As a result, some convicts who really *are* sincere, and *should* receive extra help, aren't given what they need. Some of them will turn away, frustrated and angry, and decide that if the system is going to treat them like dirt then they're going to behave that way, just like everybody else behind bars. Others will sink into apathy and disillusionment, perhaps giving up hope of any meaningful life behind bars. Some of them may turn to drugs: others may become suicidal.

The second perspective is that of the staff themselves. They can very easily become hardened to anything any inmate says, and discount even reasonable excuses or explanations. I've known cases where a minor infraction by an inmate new to the system (probably committed through ignorance of regulations), has resulted in extremely heavy punishment, most likely because the officer or manager concerned was tired and frustrated from dealing with far too many similar cases, and wasn't in the mood to make allowances or cut a new inmate some slack. It's all too easy to say to oneself, "If they're going to treat me like dirt, then I'm going to dish out dirt to them. Let's see how they like it!" When I trained at FLETC, an instructor commented to me in private conversation, "During his first year in the BOP, a new officer can't do enough *for* the inmate. During his second year, he can't do enough *to* the inmate. The third and subsequent years, he just doesn't give a damn any more." Sadly, I've seen this cynical observation borne out in practice many times — although there are honorable exceptions, thank heaven.

The third perspective is that of the families of prison staff. It's hard to maintain a normal home environment when one's spouse is bringing home so much stress and tension. Children feel it too. A disproportionately large percentage of 'corrections marriages' fail, and the effects on spouse and children are long-lasting. Second and subsequent marriages often go the same way. It's extremely difficult for those who haven't personally experienced the stress of the corrections environment to understand its effect on those who live in it every day. It's even harder for those who come home from it to share it with their spouses, who consequently feel 'shut out' of their partner's work life. After all, what can a Correctional Officer tell his wife about the reality of his job? If he says, "Honey, today I charged down a man with a knife, while armed only with my bare hands," her instant (and understandable) reaction will probably be to scream at him for being a fool by exposing himself to such danger. She might understand intellectually that he did something heroic and praiseworthy, but all she can see in her mind's eye is herself and her children at his funeral.

The prison environment has another unfortunate effect on staff and their families. The staff member is surrounded, all day, every day, by those he cannot and dare not trust. Every time they approach him, he has to wonder about their ulterior motives and hidden purposes, suspecting a trap or an attempt to deceive. When he gets home, it's sometimes very hard not to let this perspective affect his attitudes towards his loved ones. What might be normal behavior in a child (lies, evasions, excuses, etc.) may attract a much stronger reaction than normal parental disapproval and correction, because he's too used to exercising discipline (sometimes very physically) over real evildoers who do the same things. This leads to a great deal of stress and tension in families.

The common difficulty in all these perspectives, of course, is how to ensure that communication in both directions is truthful and sincere. There are no easy answers — I certainly don't have any. The question is, how can things be improved? Is there any way to manage the corrections environment in a more productive, more wholesome, more humane way, to the benefit of all concerned?

To answer that question we'll have to look at how prisons have evolved from their earliest days to the present. Thereafter, we'll have to ask some tough questions about what we want to achieve, and see whether there are ways to 'get there from here'.

CONVICT TO CHAPLAIN VII

THE PEDOPHILE

I hate myself. I wonder how the hell I ended up with this curse on me. It's foul. I wish I was dead... but I can't kill myself. If I did, I'd go to hell, wouldn't I, Chaplain? At least, if I do my time, maybe God will figure I've paid enough for what I've done, and give me a break. That's the only hope I've got. I've asked him for forgiveness, but I don't know if he hears me.

Why do kids turn me on? How the hell should I know? I've never understood it. All I know is, they did, ever since my balls started working. I thought I'd grow out of it, you know? I never did anything about it then, of course. Dad would have killed me. Big on discipline, he was. He used to quote the Bible. 'Spare the rod and spoil the child', you know? He said it like it was in capital letters made of solid gold. All us kids got the tar whaled out of us with his belt often enough that we were real scared of him. Mom couldn't do a thing to stop him, either. She was a saint, but if she got out of line, he whaled her too. *Bastard!* I hope he's burning in Hell!

The first kid was when I was in my early twenties. I just couldn't help myself any more. I got this boy to come inside for candy, and one thing led to another. He was hollering and bleeding and begging me to stop... but I couldn't. When I'd finished, I cleaned him up and gave him more candy. I'd read about what others had done, so I warned him that if he told anyone, I'd hurt his mommy. That shut him up. As far as I know, he never talked.

I was sick that whole night. I vomited up everything in my stomach, and then dry-heaved the rest of the time. I knew I was damned... but I couldn't stop myself. I *couldn't!* You've got to believe me, Chaplain — I couldn't help myself!

At least, in here, I can't hurt another kid... but I'm scared. They only found out about one, so the judge only gave me twenty years. When I get out, I'll still be in my fifties. I've been seeing the psychologists for ten years now, but how do I know I'm not still sick? Can I be cured at all? How do I know I won't do it again?

Maybe I'd be better off dead. Maybe I should tell some of the guys the real reason I'm locked up, so they can kill me... but I'm afraid of the pain. They won't do it quickly or easily, you know that. They hate people like me. They'll make me suffer.

How many? *(A long, long silence.)* F-f-fourteen. I see all their faces in my mind, Chaplain. I can't forget them. I can still hear them cry, every night as I lie in my bunk. They haunt my nightmares. I wake up every night in the small hours, and weep, and writhe, and hate my own guts, and curse myself for the filth that I am... but even after all these years, the memories still turn me on.

Is there any hope for me? Can I be forgiven? Or will God turn his back on me, and ignore my screams as I go into the fire?

You tell me, Chaplain. *Is there any hope for me?*

FRIDAY — 6:50 P.M.

The Duty Officer is a senior manager in the prison administration (usually a department head), who's in charge of coordinating any issues that may arise. He or she will call in other department heads and/or notify senior executives as appropriate. The duty rotates among our managers each week. The Duty Officer will normally get urgent information from informants like Kevin, and decide who should be called in if swift action is needed.

I telephone the Operations Lieutenant. "Dan, Peter here. Where's the Duty Officer, please? I have something urgent and confidential for him."

Dan understands immediately. "I'm not sure, Peter. Give me your extension. I'll find him, and have him call you."

"Don't mention my name or extension over the radio, please, Dan."

I give him my number and hang up. Within a few seconds, Dan comes on the radio. The Duty Officer replies, and Dan asks for his phone twenty. The radio goes quiet, and I know Dan's calling him. Within a minute or two my telephone rings.

"Peter, it's Simon. I'm Duty Officer tonight. What's up?"

"Hi, Simon. Inmate Kevin has asked to speak to you."

"OK. Put him on."

To anyone looking in through the windows, it'll appear that

I've just arranged an outside phone call for Kevin. He speaks with the Duty Officer for several minutes in a low voice. From what I can hear, it seems that some inmates have arranged to have a visitor bring in a shipment of drugs tomorrow morning. Kevin heard them discussing their arrangements. If his information proves genuine, he'll be rewarded with a few extra privileges for his good work tonight.

Some CO's and other staff look down on informants, treating them with a certain degree of contempt. I don't. I know the risks they're taking. If word got out to the inmates who are planning this drug deal that Kevin had betrayed them, they'd put out a contract on his life on the spot. He's risking everything to warn us about a potential danger, and I respect him for that. It makes our lives a lot safer to have people like him helping us — and in a prison like this, with the kind of inmates we have, it takes real courage on his part.

Kevin finishes his conversation, and looks at me. "The Duty Officer wants to speak to you again," he says, holding out the phone. I take it from him.

"Peter here, Simon."

"Thanks, Peter. I'll relay that information to SIS. Please make Kevin's presence seem as natural and normal as possible when he leaves — commiserate with him about his sick sister, you know, that sort of thing."

"I get it. Don't worry. We'll look after him."

We ring off with mutual good wishes. I look at Kevin as I replace the handset.

"Kevin, I'll speak with you as we go out. Your sister's sick and you've been talking with her, OK?"

"Sure, Chaplain. Her name's Sue, by the way."

"Thanks, I'll remember that. I know that SIS will look after you for tonight's work, but you've got an extra phone call from me whenever you need one, OK? Just my personal way of saying thanks."

He smiles. "Thanks, Chaplain, I appreciate it."

I enter Kevin's 'call to his sister' in the log, just in case an inmate sneaks a look at it. We leave together, making appropriate comments to mislead the inmates waiting in the lobby.

I check my watch. It's almost seven o'clock, and my next volunteer should be arriving shortly. I look at the two waiting to talk to me. "I'll have to go out soon to collect a volunteer, but if one of you has a simple problem, we might be able to resolve it before then. What about it?"

One of them stands. "I'll only need a couple of minutes, Chaplain."

"OK, Trevor, come inside."

Trevor comes into the office and sits down. He's got a problem with a CO, whom he claims is 'pushing him around' and trying to make trouble for him. He describes a few incidents that, from his perspective at any rate, seem to bear out what he's saying. I promise to look into the matter and see what can be done. He leaves, satisfied, and I consider for a moment. Trevor might have a legitimate complaint... or he might be trying to stir up trouble among the staff. It's impossible for me to say.

I decide to approach Dan and ask for his advice. He's a friend, and I know I can broach the subject in confidence. I call him, and brief him on the problem without identifying the inmate concerned.

"His complaint sounds potentially reasonable, Dan, but you know as well as I do that this could be an attempt to tie us up in knots. The inmate concerned doesn't have a track record of causing trouble, though. What do you think?"

"Hmm. I know the officer you mentioned. I've not had any other complaints about him. I'll call him in for a private, off-the-record chat, and see what he has to say. Will you be reporting this officially?"

"No, of course not. If anything official is to happen, the inmate will have to file a written complaint. I'm just passing it on to you off the record, to see whether we can resolve things via the 'buddy network'."

"I appreciate it, Peter. I'll see what I can do from my end."

"OK, Dan. This conversation never happened, and I don't know anything about it."

"Neither do I." We both chuckle.

As I replace the telephone handset, my radio crackles. "Control to Chaplain Grant."

"Chaplain Grant, go."

"One volunteer ready for you in the lobby, Chaplain."

"Thanks, Control. I'll be there shortly."

I stand and stretch. It's been a busy evening so far, with no let-up in sight. I lock my office door behind me, as I look at the last inmate waiting to see me. "Lewis, I have to collect another volunteer from the front. Please wait here. I'll be back as soon as I can."

"OK, Chaplain."

I step into the passage. As I do so, the doors to the Education Department swing open, and Harry walks through. He's heard the call from the Control Center, and headed over to keep an eye on the place for me. I leave him in charge as I walk down the corridor.

I'm back in ten minutes with the next volunteer, a Protestant minister from a local church. He'll be conducting a Bible study class for an hour, following the praise and worship service currently taking place. I relieve the Corridor Officer, who returns to the Education Department, and lead the minister to the lobby, where he takes a seat.

I invite Lewis into my office to hear his problem. It's fairly straightforward. He wants to undertake a correspondence course in Bible study from his denomination. I ask him to provide me with details of the course, the contact details for the supplier, and so on. I'll check it out with my boss, the Supervisory Chaplain. If he approves, we'll issue written permission for Lewis to keep the course materials with his personal property in his cell. If we don't do that, they might be regarded as contraband and confiscated when officers do a routine search.

"Who's going to pay for the course, Lewis?"

"I've got enough money in my commissary account to cover the cost, Chaplain. I'd like to put through a Special Purchase Order, if you'll help me to do that."

"OK. Let's see what my boss has to say on Sunday. If he approves, we'll get together next week and organize the paperwork."

"Thanks, Chaplain. I appreciate your help."

Special Purchase Orders are the means whereby inmates can buy approved items from outside suppliers. We issue the paperwork here, and it's forwarded to our accounting section. They confirm that the inmate has the funds available, deduct the amount concerned from his commissary account, and issue a check to the supplier. Everything is carefully scrutinized at several stages in the process, to ensure that there's no funny business involved. I think my boss will approve Lewis's request. Jay's a good man, and he encourages inmates to learn more about their respective faiths. He's been a friend and mentor to me as I settled into a chaplain's job, and I have a lot of respect for him.

Lewis leaves my office, and I check my watch. Almost time for the 7:30 move. I walk out and lock the office behind me, moving to the lobby with the Protestant minister. As we stand there, the praise and worship service comes to an end, and inmates begin to exit the main chapel. I ask them to wait by the locked doors to the corridor, and lead the minister into the main chapel, where he greets the two volunteers who've preceded him. They'll spend a few minutes working together, praying and talking with inmates.

I return to the lobby as the loudspeakers announce, "Ten-minute move. The move is open." I unlock the doors to the corridor, and watch as the inmates stream out.

The Chapel doesn't receive much incoming traffic during this, the penultimate move of the evening. About forty inmates from the Christian praise and worship service leave the Chapel, as well as those who've seen me about phone calls or other issues. A dozen others come in to join those who've stayed for an hour's Bible study. A couple more Native Americans arrive to join their comrades in the small chapel. They'll be planning their Sweat Lodge ceremony for the morning, preparing and practicing chants and songs. They'd like to use their drums to do so, but they've been told that they can't beat them inside the chapel. It would be too disruptive to other services going on at the same time.

The move comes to an end, and I glance down the passage at the Corridor Officer as he locks the door leading to the compound. He waves at me in acknowledgment, and a few minutes later, after checking the corridor, he enters the Chapel area. He'll watch it for me while I escort the two Protestant volunteers out of the prison. While I'm waiting for him, I take the opportunity to change my radio's battery. It's been getting quieter and quieter as the old one ran down.

I lead the volunteers down the corridor to the portal, and out through the slider at the wall. Here I usher them into a waiting area outlined in yellow paint next to the wall, then walk away from them, down the path towards the Control Center. One of the gun towers is sited to overlook this path and the waiting area. Everything is clearly visible to the officer on duty there. I pluck my radio from my belt, and call him on the tower frequency.

"Chaplain Grant to Tower 9. Two Religious Services volunteers waiting for clearance in the circle."

I continue walking until I come to a halt at the first slider leading to the Control Center. I know that the Tower officer will be carefully scrutinizing the volunteers on his monitor, with his camera set to high magnification , checking that their identification badges are clearly visible. The reason I've left them behind is that, if they were escaping prisoners who'd taken me hostage, they wouldn't allow me to get away. By walking away from them, I've indicated that I'm not under duress.

The radio crackles. "Tower 9 to Chaplain Grant. Your volunteers are clear."

I beckon the volunteers, who walk down the path towards me. As they reach me, the Control Center opens the first slider, and we step inside. The slider closes, and an officer comes to the window to check that the volunteers have the correct mark on their wrists as they hold their hands under the ultra-violet light. He takes their photographs from the rack and checks each volunteer against his picture, comparing their faces and the photographs on the identity cards they wear to those in his records. Satisfied, he nods to his colleague, who opens the outer slider for us. I collect their volunteer badges, and wish them a pleasant evening as we shake hands. I return the badges to the Lobby Officer.

The Control Center has me give them a key count while I'm there, then I head back into the institution, to take over the Chapel for the final hour of the evening.

WHY PRISONS?

*In a prison, the awe of the publick eye is lost, and the
power of the law is spent; there are few fears, there are no
blushes. The lewd inflame the lewd, the audacious harden
the audacious. Every one fortifies himself as he can against
his own sensibility, endeavours to practice on others the arts
which are practised on himself; and gains the kindness of
his associates by similitude of manners.*

— Samuel Johnson (1709-1784)

Long-term incarceration as a form of punishment for crime is
a relatively recent phenomenon in human history. It's been with us
for only a few hundred years. Ancient prisons were basically
holding areas for those not yet judged guilty of a crime. Once they
were convicted, punishment might involve enslavement (rowing
galleys, working in a mine, etc.) or bodily harm (e.g. branding, or
the loss of a limb). In certain societies, particularly those adhering
to Islamic Shari'a law, some of these punishments are still
common. Death was a not infrequent sentence, either by direct
execution, or by forcing the criminal to take part in exhibitions
such as gladiatorial games. Some penalties could be remitted if the
criminal paid a fine to the authorities, or compensation to the

victim(s). Criminals of sufficient rank or social standing (not to mention wealth) might be exiled; those of lesser status might simply be outlawed, and declared 'fair game' for anyone who might capture or kill them.

Through medieval and early Renaissance times, these practices continued. The situation was complicated by the fact that actions might be legally sanctioned, even encouraged, in one time and place (for example, the looting of captured buildings by soldiers), but illegal in another (as when those same soldiers returned home). A peasant might be executed for taking a deer from a lord's forest, but that same lord could take any animal from the peasant with little fear of any negative consequences — his word alone would be sufficient to dismiss charges. It was a time when 'might made right'. However, the concept of judicial settlement of disputes, and a national body of laws applicable to all, became more and more prevalent.

As early as 1166, King Henry II of England ordered the erection of jails in every county of his realm. They were initially viewed as holding-places for prisoners before their trial, but by the late thirteenth century, those refusing trial by jury (by claiming 'benefit of clergy', for example) would be held in prison, sometimes indefinitely. (Of course, they had to provide their own food, clothing and support — or starve. The authorities weren't very generous in those days.) By the fifteenth century, many towns and cities had prisons, and county jails were run by sheriffs. During this period, vagrants and those accused of 'idleness' might be incarcerated in jails or 'Houses of Correction' as punishment.

Gradually, imprisonment for a period of time became accepted as a legitimate punishment for minor crimes such as vagrancy and poaching. Debtors might also be thrown into prison, if they were unable to pay their creditors. By the seventeenth and eighteenth centuries, the rapid increase in population meant a corresponding increase in the number of convicts. Many crimes were still punishable by death (some of them incredible by modern standards — at one time, in England, the theft of a single sheep was deemed worthy of execution, and stealing a loaf of bread might lead to transportation to a 'penal colony' in the West Indies, as a slave in all but name). Prisons mostly remained dirty, stinking holes, with no facilities whatsoever except those provided by the prisoners themselves, out of their own resources.

The rise of the humanitarian movement during the Enlightenment of the eighteenth century brought new perspectives to crime and punishment. For the first time, people were proclaimed to be rational and responsible beings, with an innate dignity. Not all authorities agreed, but over time, punishment for crime grew less severe, and shorter in duration. Prison conditions were improved, and criminals were distinguished from one another by the nature of their crimes and their perceived potential for 'improvement'. Religious organizations such as the Quakers began to formulate new theories of crime and punishment, leading to radically different concepts of prisons and their purpose. Since the nineteenth century there has been a steady progression in such developments, and a constant evolution of new approaches to dealing with crime and criminals.

During the third quarter of the twentieth century, an overwhelming momentum built up around the theory that criminals are the product of social and environmental evolution. They were regarded as being not fully responsible for their propensity to commit crimes, which was viewed as a disease requiring treatment. Given this new approach, punishment for crime was also seen as something requiring reassessment. Retribution was no longer the primary motive: rather, punishment should be rehabilitative in nature, a means to an end. It should produce a moral or utilitarian improvement in the criminal, depending on one's perspective on the matter.

By the 1980's, this approach had been largely discredited. Widespread experiments to 'cure' criminals had produced no measurable success whatsoever. In reaction to this failure, a harder line against crime and criminals took hold in the United States. The number of those incarcerated grew dramatically, both in absolute numbers and as a proportion of the population. To illustrate this point, in 1980 there were a total of just over 1.8 million persons under correctional supervision in the US (i.e. on probation, in prison, or on parole). In 2005 this figure had risen to over seven million. The US imprisons its residents at a rate five to eight times greater than other major industrialized countries, and today has a higher proportion of its population in prison or under correctional supervision than any other nation on earth[12].

Vast numbers of new prisons have had to be built to accommodate this increase, and many new corrections employees hired. It's been pointed out that this has given rise to a 'prison-industrial complex', where the livelihoods of many institutions, corporations and individuals have become inextricably intertwined with the continued growth of the 'corrections industry'. In particular, a private prison industry has developed, which houses convicts for profit. I regard this 'prison-industrial complex' as being at least as unhealthy for society as earlier efforts to blame crime and criminal behavior solely on external factors. After all, if an 'industry' depends for its growth and financial well-being on the conviction and incarceration of an ever-increasing number of people, at least some elements of that 'industry' are likely to try to influence legislators and policy-makers to adopt approaches and laws that *ensure* such an ongoing increase. Can that possibly be good for our society and culture? I doubt it very strongly.

In order to find a solution to the problem, let's begin by analyzing where we stand at present. What is the current perspective on prisons and imprisonment? I submit that an excellent starting-point is the mission statement of the BOP[13]:

It is the mission of the Federal Bureau of Prisons to protect
society by confining offenders in the controlled environments

of prisons and community-based facilities that are safe, humane, cost-efficient, and appropriately secure, and that provide work and other self-improvement opportunities to assist offenders in becoming law-abiding citizens.

The mission statements of the various state corrections departments may differ from that of the BOP to some extent, but I think the general principles will be universal. Let's analyze this statement in detail, to see what prisons are supposed to be from the perspective of the authorities.

The task of the BOP is *to protect society*. It's not diagnosis, or treatment, or rehabilitation, or anything else. This 'what to do' governs any and every consideration of implementation, or 'how to do it'. The task will be accomplished by *confining offenders in controlled environments*. A prison has no other reason for existence. Having said that, we can see that the prison should meet a number of requirements: but *those requirements are secondary to its primary purpose or task,* and are implemented only insofar as they can be achieved without hampering or restricting that primary purpose. The protection of society is the objective, the focus, of everything the BOP does.

The secondary requirements are that prisons should:

1. Be safe;
2. Be humane;
3. Be cost-efficient;
4. Be appropriately secure;
5. Provide work and other self-improvement opportunities to assist offenders in becoming law-abiding citizens.

Every one of these requirements is important.

The concept of safety is relative. The primary objective is that *society* should be kept safe from those who threaten it, so the prison must accomplish that. Second only to society, the *staff* who work there — all of them law-abiding citizens, who represent the society seeking protection — should be safe. The third priority goes to the *prisoners* confined in the institution. They should be kept safe from harm, whether external or internal: but their safety is secondary to that of the staff, and tertiary to that of society.

This has many implications for the day-to-day running of a prison. Staff are required to keep dangerous prisoners confined at all costs. (That's why the BOP has a firm policy that no concessions whatsoever which might threaten public safety are to be made to inmates who take staff members hostage. If they threaten to kill the staff members unless they're allowed to leave, the hostages will have to take their chances until a rescue team can be organized.) Staff are expected to do all they can to protect inmates, *commensurate with their own safety*. If, for example, there's a riot on the compound, and inmates are stabbing one another with shanks, it's *not* required that staff risk their lives to save that of an inmate. If they have to withdraw until the violence dies down and they can re-establish control, that's unfortunate, but acceptable.

In its comments on what will be required to fulfill its vision statement[13], one of the goals the BOP sets for itself is that it 'ensures the physical safety of all inmates through a controlled environment which meets each inmate's need for security through the elimination of violence, predatory behavior, gang activity, drug use, and inmate weapons.' I regret to say that this idealistic pronouncement usually makes corrections staff laugh out loud. *It will never happen.* It's a fine-sounding piece of rhetoric, but it's meaningless in the context of the behavior of the inmates themselves. Even in minimum-security camps, you'll find drug use, a certain amount of predatory behavior, and a minimal level of violence. At high-security institutions, this is magnified a hundredfold. Even in Supermax, where inmates are locked down twenty-three hours a day, and never leave their cells without being chained hand and foot and escorted by multiple guards, these problems have not been eliminated. Certainly, inmates will be kept as safe as possible, and the problems identified in this target will be minimized: but they will never, *ever* be completely eliminated under the present system, and with our present inmates. The word 'humane' seems incongruous in this context. Dictionaries tell us that behavior and attitudes are humane when characterized by tenderness, compassion and sympathy, particularly towards the suffering or distressed. When one thinks of a prison environment, just about the last descriptions that come to mind are 'tender', 'compassionate' or 'sympathetic'! Certainly, the average inmate would probably break down in fits of hysterical laughter if asked to think of Correctional Officers in such terms. Why, then, does the BOP include this term in its mission statement? I think the answer can be deduced by looking at families. Parents may love their children, but they also set the limits of acceptable behavior, insist that their standards are met, and bring up their children in a 'humane' way within these boundaries. In a sense, the BOP acts *in loco parentis* to its inmates. It has to establish the rules and the boundaries within which prison society will function. These should be as 'humane' as possible, commensurate with the requirements of safety, but the latter remains the overriding priority. The term also implies elements of a humanist philosophy that has doubtless influenced correctional perspectives.

Next, the BOP's institutions should be 'cost-efficient'. This is a term that can be used in many ways. From the BOP's perspective, it will naturally refer to producing optimum results for the money spent on prisons: they should be economical in terms of the result or outcome they produce, their 'return' on that investment. What is this 'return'? *The safety of society*, of course. That's the only reason prisons exist. Any other objective — rehabilitation, education, treatment, whatever — could certainly be pursued in a different type of institution or setting. It's precisely because inmates threaten society that they're removed from it by incarcerating them. Thus, the BOP's institutions will justify their cost if they protect society… *but do they?*

Given the recidivism rate noted at the end of Chapter 4 and the crime rates described in this chapter, can we really argue that society is being 'protected' by the present system? I'm not sure. Should the 'protection' offered by prison not include some means to make it at least likely, if not reasonably certain, that recidivism will not be the most frequent result after inmates are released? From that perspective, prisons today are certainly *not* cost-effective. We spend a great deal of money to incarcerate criminals (it costs only a little less than the overall median annual personal income in the USA for the BOP to incarcerate one convict for one year[14]), but this expenditure doesn't appear to render that inmate any less likely to re-offend as soon as he's able to do so. In the majority of cases it buys society only a temporary reprieve. Could those funds be better applied? We'll return to that question later in this chapter.

In the absence of a better way of doing things, cost-efficiency can be achieved by incarcerating inmates at a level of security appropriate to the risk they represent; providing essential services but few luxuries; requiring inmates to contribute to the cost and effort of looking after them, by performing many of the tasks required to keep a prison functioning; and minimizing expenditure on areas not directly related to the BOP's primary mission. The Bureau does all these things, and it does them fairly well, in my experience. However, it then becomes the target for those who want the BOP to be 'all things to all inmates'. They complain that it's not spending enough on educational programs (whether academic or vocational), decry the limited opportunities for inmates to develop new interests, talents and aptitudes, moan that there isn't enough psychological and sociological support for inmates, and so on. All these areas *could* be better addressed by the BOP, *if* our politicians were willing to vote the funds for them. Generally, they're not: after all, voters want smaller government, lower taxes, and less expenditure. Therefore, the BOP has to attend to its first priority, the safety of society, and put less emphasis on (or do without) the other elements that are 'nice-to-haves'. It does the best it can with the resources allocated to it.

The fourth requirement is that prisons should 'be appropriately secure'. What does 'appropriate' mean in this context? Clearly, it's partly to do with the risk posed by each inmate. One who isn't dangerous to society can be housed in a minimum- or low-security facility. One who's violent and predatory needs the stricter and more secure (not to mention more expensive) confinement offered by a high- or maximum-security unit. The level of security of an institution will be appropriate to the type of inmate it houses. However, there's another aspect to 'appropriate'. Prisons have to provide appropriate environments for staff and inmate security, and that's very hard to accomplish at times. Our facilities are certainly good at keeping inmates inside, but no matter how hard their staff try, they can't always protect the inmates from one another, nor can they guarantee their own safety. Is it 'appropriate' to spend more on these areas? It may be... but politicians will have to appropriate the funds to do so. So far, they haven't.

The final requirement is that prisons should 'provide work and other self-improvement opportunities to assist offenders in becoming law-abiding citizens'. Note that it's not the *prison's* responsibility to produce change in inmates. It provides work and opportunities to assist them, but *the inmates have to accomplish the improvement themselves*, and become law-abiding citizens out of their own desire to change. As noted in Chapter 4, action follows thought; behavior follows personality. The prison can't force change on the inmates: *they* have to be prepared to think, and examine their own consciences, and want to change, not just their behavior, but the personality that gives rise to that behavior. We can't impose remorse from outside. No sentence or punishment can do that. It has to come from within. There are those who seem to think that prisons should somehow wave a magic wand, and transform offenders into model members of society. Unfortunately, we don't have any Hogwarts graduates in the BOP, so this expectation seems doomed to remain unfulfilled.

As for 'work and other self-improvement opportunities', there are a few of them, but there could certainly be many more. Regrettably, to provide them costs money: and unless our political leaders are prepared to make more funds available, the BOP will have to do the best it can with its present resources. Even at that, its programs are typically very much better than those of the average state corrections department, but there's definitely room for improvement.

Very well. We've examined what prisons should be in terms of the 'official' mission of our nation's premier corrections authority. We now have to ask: *is this 'official' mission adequate?* Given the abysmal failure of massive incarceration rates to greatly impact recidivism, should we not ask, very pointedly, whether building more prisons, and stuffing more and more people into them, is going to help? Could our tax dollars not be better applied to more appropriate solutions to crime?

It seems to me that the words of Dr. Johnson, quoted at the head of Chapter 4 ('Criminal Minds And Convict Culture'), are as true today as when he penned them, some three centuries ago. Many corrections authorities and leaders agree. To cite just one out of many who've commented on the subject, Robert Brown Jr. was director of the Michigan Department of Corrections from 1984-1991. He recently pointed out that crime prevention is a far better protection for public safety than imprisonment, and denounced the false assumption that increased incarceration will reduce crime. He cited figures showing that, despite an increase of over 250% in the incarceration rate in Michigan between 1984 and 1992, the crime rate actually *increased* slightly in that state during the same period. He also noted that imprisonment would not help those with mental health or substance abuse problems, or those lacking the skills necessary to find employment, to become, or function as, law-abiding citizens[15].

(Brown's emphasis on crime prevention is important. Too

often we regard it as the job of law enforcement officers and agencies to prevent crime. *This is impossible.* Law enforcement agencies can't *prevent* crime; they can only deal with its consequences, by arresting those who've committed it. That may be too late for the victims. The front line of crime prevention is the ordinary citizen, who secures his home and property and protects himself and his loved ones. This is an important lesson that many fail to heed. I'll have more to say about it in the Epilogue.)

Perhaps the best that can be said for our present policy of 'massive incarceration' is that it's a short-term panacea for a long-term problem. As long as we're neither willing nor able to deal with the factors underlying crime, we'll have to 'warehouse' criminals to keep them out of our hair. Furthermore, we all have to accept our share of responsibility for the immense increase in the number of those behind bars. Many of those in prison might well be more appropriately assigned to non-custodial punishment and treatment programs. As long as we're willing to increase the number of offenses qualifying for prison terms, and elect those who pass laws to that effect, we'll be stuck with the present untenable situation in corrections. It's no good blaming the BOP or other corrections agencies. They don't make the laws that the courts use to send people to prison. The courts and the prisons do what the authorities ask of them — and we, the people, elect those who oversee the authorities. The final responsibility rests in our hands alone.

Furthermore, if we permit the current growth in our prison population to continue, we're going to have to pay through the nose for it — and suffer serious consequences in our society and communities. To use the BOP as an example, in 1975 it had a budget of $208.3 million. Its 2008 budget request totaled $5,363.89 million, a twenty-five-fold increase over the intervening thirty-two years[16]. In 1975 it had an average daily inmate population of 24,860: in June 2007 it had almost 199,000 persons in its custody, an eightfold increase. Dividing its budget by the number of prisoners, in 1975 it spent approximately $8,400 per inmate. Its 2008 budget request allocated about $27,000 per inmate.

To obtain a fair comparison, we should adjust the earlier figures for inflation. I'm informed that the BOP's 1975 budget would amount to approximately $815 million in 2007 dollars. If this is correct, its 2008 budget request represents a six-and-a-half-fold increase in purchasing power over 1975, less than the eightfold increase in inmate numbers. Its spending per inmate in 2007 dollars was almost $33,000 in 1975, about 22% higher than it is today. Clearly the agency has achieved significant economies, for which it should be given due credit.

The BOP had just over 8,000 employees in 1975: in 2007 it had more than 35,000, well over a fourfold increase. At the time of writing, it houses inmates in 114 Federal facilities (180 if attached sub-facilities are broken out and listed separately) and 13 privately-managed facilities. Even with this number of prisons, as of January 2007 its facilities were '37 percent above rated capacity system-wide'[17]. State corrections departments and facilities have exhibited a similar expansion over the past few decades. If these trends continue, we're going to be in a very parlous position in the not too distant future.

I'll examine possible alternatives to incarceration, and other options to improve the safety and security of society, in Chapter 18: but what about prisons? It goes without saying that we *have* to have some way to separate incorrigible or dangerous criminals from society, so prisons in one form or another are always going to be required. Their basic mission, the protection of society, will also remain unchanged. However, is there any way to improve the *process* of incarceration, to develop a new concept that might reinvigorate and revitalize prisons as a place not only of confinement, but also of personal change?

I believe that there is an approach that might work. It relies upon the recognition and implementation of policies to address two distinct issues. First, **there will always be criminals in our**

society. Those who remain criminally inclined, and who cannot or will not reform, need to be permanently removed from our midst. Second, **rehabilitation and reform require both remorse and personality change on the part of the criminal.** These cannot be achieved, and will not be imparted, through teaching job skills.

I submit that recidivism can only be reduced if *both* of these issues are addressed. To do so will require an integrated approach, and a different perspective on crime and punishment; but I believe it's feasible. Of course, these are only one person's suggestions — others may come up with something better.

I suggest that the first step must be to drastically reduce the number of crimes qualifying for imprisonment. There are many that have been elevated to this level by legislative *fiat*. The 'War On Drugs' is a good example. Didn't we learn *anything* from Prohibition in the 1920's? Outlawing a substance doesn't stop its consumption. I'm fully in agreement that illicit drug use is at best undesirable, and at worst a real threat to society (just like, for example, excessive alcohol consumption). I'll support any worthwhile effort to deal with it, but imposing long prison sentences on low-level dealers and heavy users *simply isn't working*.

The proof is in the figures. The 'War On Drugs' has been in full swing for more than two decades. This nation reportedly spends up to sixty billion dollars on it every year[18] — about as much as the annual combined total of Federal, state and local expenditure on prisons and corrections[19] — yet the drug problem in the US is worse today than it's ever been. Literally as I write these words, I've clicked over to a major news Web site and seen a headline: 'Study: Parents in denial, despair as teens' drug use grows'[20]. Our efforts aren't working, even though we've locked up hundreds of thousands of people for drug-related offenses. If that's the case, why persist with a failed approach? Einstein pointed out that 'insanity is doing the same thing over and over again, expecting different results'. By that standard, the War On Drugs as presently waged is not just a failure, it's an *insane* failure.

207

Reducing the number of lower-level offenses requiring custodial punishment would be a good start. I'll have more to say about this later. However, I submit that the single biggest problem in dealing with our present situation is the *rate of recidivism*. It's been hovering at the two-thirds level in the USA for the past couple of decades at least. We can confidently predict that two out of every three convicts released from prison will be rearrested for another crime within three to four years of their release. Our present prison system is not dealing with this problem — and I submit that if it's to be considered a success, it *must* deal with it. Failure is not an option. If we allow this 'revolving door' to keep operating, we're going to spend ourselves into bankruptcy and social paralysis.

I submit that the solution to recidivism requires a two-pronged approach. The first acknowledges that there are, and always will be, those with a criminal mindset, who are utterly disrespectful of society's expectations. They don't want to change, and see no reason why they should. For individuals with a sustained record of criminal activity, I suggest the only solution that will effectively protect society is to permanently incarcerate them. If they won't change, they can't leave prison. They must never be allowed to reach the 'revolving door'.

The second 'prong' must address the programs and classes currently offered in our prisons. With few exceptions, such programs deal with the *what* rather than the *why*. There are many programs teaching inmates a particular skill, or how to get a job when released, or how to deal with drug addiction. There appear to be very few that directly and openly challenge them to examine their own personality, identify the elements of the criminal mindset thus exposed, and deal with those elements by *wanting* to change, and actively working on behavior modification. Most programs teach them to *do something* rather than to *be someone*. I submit that's precisely why we aren't reducing our recidivism rate.

In case this distinction isn't clear, let me use military training as an example. In the armed services of most nations, a recruit is put through basic training to teach him the fundamentals of discipline, military skills, techniques and requirements, etc. He'll get more unit-oriented instruction when he's assigned to his parent outfit, but he won't necessarily develop an *esprit de corps* unless he's fortunate enough to go to a unit or branch of service that emphasizes it. On the other hand, the best armed forces regard *esprit de corps* as more important than skills. The US Marine Corps is a good example. Its boot camp concentrates on making recruits into Marines. The skills they learn, and their Military Occupational Specialty, whilst very important, are secondary to what they become as individuals: proud members of the Corps, living representatives of its tradition, a true 'band of brothers' in the classic warrior sense. Skills without *esprit de corps* are worthless to the Marines, and recruits who don't 'get it' will very likely not be allowed to graduate. I submit that the difference between generic military basic training, and Marine boot camp, is analogous to the difference between, respectively, *doing something* and *being someone*.

I'd therefore suggest a change in the programs offered in our prisons. First and foremost, every inmate would be required to participate in classes and in-depth counseling sessions addressing issues of criminal personality, behavior modification and personal renewal. The elements of the criminal mindset (see Chapter 4) would be freely discussed with all inmates, and programs implemented to encourage each and every one of them to examine themselves, identify problem areas, and work seriously for change. It would be a fundamental principle that only those demonstrating real, sustained behavior modification and improvement would be permitted to move on to programs designed to equip them to start afresh after their sentence has been completed. Those who can't or won't demonstrate such improvement should not be permitted to enter the latter programs.

There are two potential approaches to character and behavior change. I regard them as complementary rather than alternatives. The first is a psychological approach, identifying the elements of the criminal personality, and challenging them to confront and deal with them. (See Note 2 for an excellent resource on such an approach.) The second is one designed to give them a new foundation for their lives. As a Chaplain, I naturally endorse and support faith-based initiatives in this regard, focusing on the need for repentance, conversion, and living according to the moral standards of one's faith. (My work with Felix is one example — see Chapter 4.) However, I'm aware that many object to this, and demand something more secular, free of religious 'bias'. That's fine with me. I see no reason why both avenues can't be offered. Let inmates make their own decision, and choose the path that best suits their personality, needs and outlook on life. There's no need to fight about it amongst ourselves. If an approach works, we should all support it. If it doesn't work, why bother with it? Let the proof of the pudding be in the eating. Let's not waste time in partisan argument amongst supporters of incompatible outlooks on life.

I can already hear snorts of disdain from experienced professionals in corrections. They're doubtless thinking that I'm being unrealistic and utopian — that a leopard can't change his spots, and a hardened criminal can't change his ways. To them I can only say, you may be right: but our present system is a failure. To have two out of every three released convicts re-offend and return to custody can't be described as anything else. We simply *have* to find a better way, and this is my suggestion. If you have a better one, let's hear it. Of course, change can't be imposed from outside: it has to be desired and actively pursued by the convict himself. However, if we provide a real incentive for them to change (by making it clear that unless they do, they're never going home, as I'll discuss in a moment), won't we have a better chance of producing this change?

I note that in Australia, where considerable emphasis has been placed on reform and re-training of inmates, the recidivism rate is down to about 40%[21]. Admittedly, that country's demographics differ from ours, but even so, if they can produce such results, why can't we? Think how much we'd save if we could bring the US recidivism rate down to the Australian level. Given our present two-thirds rate, of the two-million-odd convicts presently in Federal, state and local prisons, we can predict that more than 1,300,000 will be back in prison within a few years of their release. At the Australian rate of recidivism, that figure would be reduced to 800,000. That's a difference of over 500,000 inmates, who would no longer be a burden on the corrections system or the taxpayer. At an estimated annual cost to house one prisoner of between $20,000 and $30,000, that represents an annual saving of between ten and fifteen billion dollars — two to three times the entire annual budget of the BOP. Even a tenth of that saving would pay for a very substantial number of prison programs.

Cost saving in the prison system is only one aspect. Think of all the operators involved in the criminal justice system: the law enforcement agencies making the arrest, the institutions holding pre-trial inmates, the prosecuting authorities, the courts with their judges, bailiffs, public defenders and other staff, the expense of appeals, the probation and parole agencies, and so on. At present they're all having to deal with two out of three released inmates coming back into the criminal justice system, some of them over and over and over again. If we could reduce this workload, each of these agencies would be relieved of a great deal of pressure, and save a great deal of money. Even if we had to spend more on keeping unreformed recidivists in prison for the rest of their lives, the savings in these other areas should be more than sufficient to compensate for it.

I'm not ignoring the need to give inmates new life skills, over and above a change in their personality and behavior. It's been known for some time that released prisoners who can't find a job frequently return to crime as the only way of generating an income. If we can minimize that problem, we minimize the risk to them. As the International Center for Prison Studies has pointed out, there are more inmates from poorer neighborhoods and social strata than from wealthier classes. The former exhibit a range of social, health and community problems[22]. If we can equip such inmates to be able to better fend for themselves and their families, and help them to find work and earn a living, we make it easier for them to avoid re-offending.

If we can *first* help inmates to change their ways, and *then* provide them with education and training to escape the 'poverty trap', recidivism should drop rapidly. However, the first step is willingness on the part of the inmate to change, and to work at it. Only if he does that will it be worthwhile to invest time and effort in giving him the tools to build a new life. At present, that first step is being largely neglected in our incarceration system. It needs to be given primary emphasis, and a great deal of attention.

We've examined a change of focus in the programs offered in prisons. What of the prisons themselves? How can they be adapted to deal with the results of these programs?

I suggest that the present system of high-, medium- and low-security institutions be maintained, but with a somewhat different emphasis. At the 'top of the heap' there will be penitentiaries for high- and maximum-security inmates. Their primary purpose would be incarceration and strict control of dangerous and repeat offenders. Programs in such institutions would focus almost exclusively on the criminal mindset, and emphasize personal responsibility for change. Inmates would have to demonstrate such change over an extended period, earning the opportunity to move to lower-security facilities through good behavior, and compliance with the regulations governing their incarceration. I'd demand a high standard, perhaps as much as a year or two without a single disciplinary offense, even of the most minor sort, before such a move should be possible. I also propose that recidivists convicted of further crimes should be automatically assigned to such facilities at first, irrespective of the nature of their crime or the length of their sentence. If they won't 'get with the program', give them a tougher program.

I'll go further. I propose that *no-one should ever be released into society from a penitentiary.* To earn release, inmates in these facilities would be required to demonstrate sincerity and real progress in tackling issues of criminal personality, improved behavior, and compliance with prison regulations. If they do, they should in due course be sent to a medium-security facility, to continue their progress and receive training and education to help them reintegrate into society. Release should only be possible from such a lower-security institution. If inmates don't earn a transfer to one, when their release date approaches, the penitentiary administration should lay their records before a judge. If their behavior and attitudes have been so bad that they haven't been able to qualify for a move to a lower-security institution, the judge should be not only authorized, but required, to extend their sentence and keep them behind bars. This should be reviewed periodically, perhaps every three to five years: but if they persist in their wrong attitudes, they should stay locked up — indefinitely, if necessary. That would take care of a lot of recidivism right away. It would take legislation to accomplish this, but that can be done: for example, offenders could be given an open-ended minimum rather than a finite maximum sentence.

Some will object that this will inevitably mean a greater number of inmates confined in penitentiaries, increasing costs. However, I submit that this is not necessarily the case. Such inmates will no longer be moving in and out of prison, thereby increasing turnover. I daresay that at least a quarter of all those entering prison in any given year are recidivists. If they're no longer coming in (because they're already inside and will stay there), this will reduce throughput significantly, and simplify the system. In addition, they won't incur repeat costs in the pre-incarceration criminal justice system, as already noted.

Think of this in terms of a 'cell-day'. Let's define this as one prison cell, occupied by one convict, for one day. A convict coming into the system with a twenty-year sentence will use the same number of 'cell-days' as ten inmates, each sentenced to two years. If two to three of the ten can be removed from the criminal justice system by reducing recidivism, the short-term 'cell-days' they require will have been eliminated. Only seven or eight would now be admitted with short sentences: and the recidivists would stay in prison, and not rotate in and out. The overall number of 'cell-days' in the system would remain constant, but the number of inmates entering and leaving it would be reduced. I submit the expense incurred need not rise: indeed, given a reduction in turnover (with its associated processing costs), it might even be reduced over time. As we'll see later, if some inmates can be given non-custodial sentences instead of incarceration, costs will drop even further.

I'd have medium-security facilities to accommodate those whose offenses are serious, but who have demonstrated that they are committed to changing their basic mindset, and are working hard towards meaningful reintegration into society. At the 'bottom tier' of prisons I see low- and minimum-security institutions, but with an 'open prison' approach. I'll call them 'reform facilities' for want of a better term. I would actively seek to put low-level offenders (non-violent criminals, those who've been convicted only once and for relatively minor offenses, etc.) in such facilities, and move more serious offenders to them in due course, once they had demonstrated their sincerity and an improvement in their attitude and mindset.

Medium- and low-security institutions would offer the same programs dealing with criminal personality and behavioral issues as provided in penitentiaries. Inmates would be encouraged to actively work with instructors and mentors to overcome personal problems. In addition, after they successfully complete initial programs in these areas, and demonstrate real, sustained improvement, vocational training should be provided for those who need it. Inmates would be taught trades and professions,

214

including hands-on exposure to disciplines and crafts in high demand outside prison. Training should be provided for plumbers, electricians, mechanics, and other trades that are short-staffed at this time. Those with a more academic bent should be offered facilities to complete higher education, and qualify in areas of importance to society. I would specifically exclude 'soft' degree options, that are merely a piece of paper and not really required by the job market. In this area I'd look at teaching, nursing, EMT/paramedic work, and similar occupations as suitable offerings. (Obviously, security screening would be necessary to ensure that those whose offenses and/or proclivities render them unsuitable for certain positions are prevented from training for them.)

Programs such as those described above would be considerably more extensive — and expensive — than those presently offered. On the other hand, there would be fewer inmates requiring them, because hardened recidivists would be retained in penitentiaries where they won't be offered. Additional funding and co-operation could be obtained from major industries and commercial groups. For example, if there's a nationwide need for auto mechanics, it would make a lot of sense for vehicle dealers and manufacturers to support a training program in prisons. It would also make sense to have companies already providing such training to industry do the same in correctional institutions. This would save money by avoiding needless duplication, and also prevent undesirable competition between prison and commercial training establishments. I daresay quite a lot could be achieved over time. Initially, additional funding would have to be provided: but as I said earlier, unless we break the current spiral of incarceration, recidivism and 'corrections bloat', we're in deep trouble. Spending money now to save a great deal more money in future sounds to me like a worthwhile investment.

There's another way to assist with the reintegration into society of inmates who demonstrate real, meaningful personality improvement and behavior change. Given at least a year of good conduct, inmates in low-security facilities could be allowed to spend some weekends with their families (which would hopefully help to preserve family life and reduce divorces), and encouraged to find employment during the week. They should be eligible to keep up to a third of their wages or salaries. Another third should go to their families (if they have them), and the balance should be put into a savings account and held for when the inmate is released. This will give him a little financial security to begin a new life.

In addition, I'd like to see inmates in low-security facilities actively involved in work that supports the community. Examples might include working as firefighters or EMS personnel, providing basic assistance in schools and health facilities, training work dogs (as already happens in a number of correctional institutions), assisting at animal shelters, making furniture for those who can't afford it, working with organizations such as Habitat For Humanity, and so on. They could also be employed by municipal governments at a nominal wage, to tackle work that would otherwise be unaffordable. This would give the inmates a chance to use their newly acquired skills, and at the same time make a meaningful contribution to society.

I'd have a 'three strikes' policy in all levels of prison. Any infringement of regulations, no matter how minor, would count as one strike. Any inmate in a low-security facility who was found guilty of three 'strikes' within any twelve consecutive months would be sent to the stricter environment of a medium-security institution. Anyone in the latter who committed three offenses over a similar period would be sent to a penitentiary. This should be an automatic administrative procedure. 'Downward' movement from high- to medium-, and then to low-security facilities, should require a substantial period without any 'strikes' being recorded. Those who want to get out of prison should be required to demonstrate their fitness for release by good conduct. If they won't or can't do so, let them stay behind bars.

I submit that our present practice of throwing more and more banknotes, bodies and buildings at the correctional system is failing. The recidivism rate demonstrates this beyond any possible doubt. If we *have* to spend this kind of money, let's spend it on institutions and programs that will reduce recidivism. That, in turn, will reduce how much we have to spend on prisons, and the entire criminal justice system, in the longer term.

CONVICT TO CHAPLAIN VIII

THE HOPELESS

I leave here next month. I've been inside seventeen years, this time. My woman divorced me long ago. Took the kids and split — never told me where she was going. I got a son and daughter somewhere. They may think I'm dead. I'm afraid to try to trace them, in case they hate me. After all, when they needed their Daddy, I wasn't there for them. I screwed up their lives just as surely as I screwed up my own. I don't know if they ever forgave me for that.

I'm scared, Chaplain. I used to work as a printer before, but I can't go back to that — everything's done by computers now. In the parole system, they say you gotta have a job or go back to prison. What the hell kind of job can an old **** like me find? I'm fifty-four years old. Who's gonna want someone like me? I learned to cook in the kitchens here, but can you see any place hiring me to flip burgers? Hell, they can get pimply-faced kids off the street to do that at minimum wage — and the kids don't have a rap sheet! What chance do I stand?

I got no home to go to, no job waiting, no money. All I'll have is the release clothes they'll give me, and twenty bucks. I gotta begin again, in a town that's probably changed so much I won't

218

even recognize a lot of it. Yeah, yeah, I've heard all the **** about how the halfway house and my parole officer will help me to adjust. You don't believe that **** any more than I do. We're adults, Chaplain. No kids here needing a sugar-coated pill. You and I both know I've gotta make it on my own, or not at all. Sink or swim… and I'm scared I've forgotten how to swim. All these years I been doing my time, living hour to hour. The rule in here is, never plan ahead, never think about the future. Do that inside, you go buggy. Outside, you *gotta* do it, or you'll starve. I'm not real good at it any more.

You heard Tony's back behind bars? We're the same age, and did the same stuff on the street, and drew the same kinda sentence. He got out last year. He used to say to me, "Gene, we'll make it together" — but he didn't make it. His brother wrote me. Tony tried for six months, but he couldn't get his **** together. He started dealing again, and they caught him. With his priors, he's lookin' at a twenty to thirty stretch. 'Habitual offender', that's what they'll call him. He'll die in a place like this now.

You know what's scariest of all, Chaplain? That starts to look like the best choice for someone like me. At least, in here, we get three hots and a cot. We need a pill, or want to wash our clothes, or whatever, it's all here. Hell, most people my age are within a few years of retiring. I'll be starting from scratch, just like a kid out of school. How the **** will I ever be able to afford to retire?

So tell me, Chaplain… why shouldn't I take the easy way out, and deal some ****, and let them catch me and put me back in here? What hope have I got for anything else?

FRIDAY — 7:45 P.M.

As I walk down the long corridor my radio comes to life. "Duty Officer to Chaplain Grant."

"Chaplain Grant, go."

"Phone twenty?"

"Negative. I'm on my way back to the Chapel after escorting volunteers out of the institution. May I call you in five?"

"OK. My phone twenty is 1234."

I reach the Chapel and relieve the Corridor Officer. Going into my office, I call Simon. "Peter here, Simon. What's up?"

"Peter, Inmate Andrew's in a bad way. They've got him in Intensive Care down at the hospital. He's being guarded by Lieutenant **** and two CO's. He's registered as a member of your faith group, so I wondered whether you'd like to drop in at the hospital after you finish up here tonight. From what they tell me, he probably won't last till morning."

"Thanks for the heads-up. I'll go there when I leave the prison. Do you want me to call you from the hospital?"

"Not necessarily, only if there's something I need to know. I'll be leaving here at nine, but you can reach me through the Operations Lieutenant if you need to. Remember, we change shifts at ten, so if you call after that time, Lieutenant **** will be on duty."

"OK. What about notifying Andrew's family?

"I've checked his file, and spoken to his Unit Counselor. Andrew's been behind bars for over twenty years this time around. His parents are dead, he has no siblings, and his wife divorced him and remarried after his incarceration. She's listed as the person to be notified if he dies, but I doubt she'll be interested. She took out a court order forbidding him from having any contact with his kids while they were minors. They'll be grown now, of course, but they've never tried to reach him, as far as we know, and there's no record of his trying to get in touch with them. We have no contact information for them."

I sigh. "I guess one of us will have to call his former wife in the morning. Hell of a lonely way to die, isn't it?"

I can almost feel him shiver over the telephone. "You said it!"

I hang up, sigh, and rub my eyes. I'm tired, and I've got another long day ahead of me tomorrow: but if one of our charges is on his last legs then, as Chaplains, we owe it to him to be there. If we were in his shoes, we'd hope there'd be someone who cared enough to be with us for a while at the end… and this is where the Golden Rule most assuredly applies: 'Do unto others as you would have them do unto you'.

I step out of the office and lock it. The Wiccan group leaders at their desk notice my expression, and their priest asks, "Is everything OK, Chaplain?"

I look at him wearily. I wouldn't normally discuss this with inmates, but these three have demonstrated their sincerity in matters of faith.

"There's an inmate in hospital, and — "

He nods. "That's Andrew, yeah. I saw them take him out earlier on a stretcher. Is he going to be OK?"

"They took him straight to the hospital. It looks pretty bad. I know you guys aren't of his faith, but if you want to say a prayer for him, tonight would be a really good time to do so."

They all nod simultaneously. "We'll get on it right away,

Chaplain, if you don't mind us praying round the desk here."

I smile in gratitude. "Of course not, guys, go ahead. I'm going to do rounds of the chapel. Say one for me while you're at it. I'll visit Andrew when I leave here tonight."

They nod, and turn towards one another, 'closing the circle' as they call it. I really appreciate their prayers. They're not praying to God as I know or understand him, but I trust he'll accept their sincerity, and hear their prayers for their fellow inmate. At a time like this, I'm sure Andrew, like most of us, would want all the help he can get, if he were able to ask for it.

I do rounds. The Protestants in the main chapel, the Native Americans in the small chapel, the Asatru and Jehovah's Witness groups in two classrooms, and the Jewish group in the conference room, are all engaged with their respective activities. There's no-one waiting to ask for a phone call, no-one needing me — most unusual for an evening shift. I go back to the office and pour myself another cup of coffee, sipping slowly. I switch off the coffee machine, and take the pot out to empty it. Our three Wiccan leaders look at it eagerly. I smile and nod, and they grab styrofoam cups. I fill their cups, then pour the dregs down the sink in the inmate bathroom. Better to use it than waste it, I reckon.

I spend a few moments filling in my activity log for the day. It's been more hectic than usual. I take the folder containing details of the notification I provided to Phil in the Hole, and use my notes to complete a formal Notification Of Death form, which I forward via e-mail to all those concerned with his case. One of us will follow up with SHU in the morning, to ensure that he's OK. I pick up the phone, and call Sally in her office.

"Sally, it's Peter. How's Phil doing? Any further news?"

She sighs. "He was given his booster shot, and that's tranked him out for the evening. I'm not sure how he'll be in the morning. He may not even remember our visit. I've left a note for my relief to check on him."

"Thanks, Sally. One of us will check as well. If he wants to call his sister again, please ask the Duty Psychologist to contact myself or Ken — we'll both be here tomorrow. Thanks for helping me with him. You went the extra mile by coming down to the Hole with me. I really appreciate it."

"You're welcome. Do the same for me sometime."

I type a brief e-mail to the Chief Psychologist, drawing his attention to Sally's help, and officially thanking his department. He'll take that into account at her next performance review. She's earned our gratitude, not just on this occasion, but on others when she's helped us out.

I put the desk in order, pack my black bag with my notes and belongings, and tidy up the place. It's almost time to go. As I finish, the speakers announce, "Yard Recall. Yard Recall."

I go out to supervise the last move of the night. Inmates pour out of the rooms where they've been sitting, and head for the corridor. I open the storage cupboards for those who need to replace items, and lock them when they're done. I switch off the lights and lock the various rooms, ensure that all the equipment's been put away, and check for any stray inmates. Meanwhile, the four volunteers gather in the lobby, waiting for me.

At last I reach for my radio. "Chaplain Grant to Corridor Officer. Chapel area clear of all inmates."

"Ten-four, Chaplain. Have a good night."

I pick up my bag, lock my office, and collect the volunteers. We go out into the corridor and I lock the department's doors for the last time, then we head for the portal. Wearily I add up the distance I've walked today. With all the running around involved in this job, I often cover a couple of miles during a shift, but today's been more than usual — probably at least three miles. No wonder my feet are sore! With hard, unyielding concrete floors underfoot, our legs and feet take punishment here.

I usher the volunteers into the holding area, then walk towards the Control Center, calling the Tower Officer to clear them. Eventually he does so, and I motion them forward as the slider opens. Their stamps all check out, and they're soon processed out of the building. I hand in their volunteer ID cards at the Control Center — the Lobby Officer has gone inside already. I take my radio from my belt, remove the belt clip and pocket it, take my keyring off its chain and count the keys one last time, and hand them in along with the radio and spare battery. I wait for the officer to return them to their places and bring me my chits, which I clip onto my keyholder in readiness for the morning.

"You working tomorrow, Chaplain?" he asks, passing my chits through the two-way drawer beneath the window.

"Yes, Ray. 'No peace for the wicked', as they say in the classics! Hope it stays peaceful for you tonight."

"From your lips to God's ears, Chaplain! Sleep well."

We grin at one another. I turn away, flip over my token on the staff board to show that I'm no longer in the prison, and walk out through the steel door into the warm, muggy night air. I'd normally head home to bed now, to get up early tomorrow and be back here by 7:30 a.m. However, tonight there's still one more job to be done. It's a long drive to the hospital where Andrew's lying in the Intensive Care unit. I glance at my watch. With luck, and if traffic in the city isn't too heavy, I can be there in less than an hour.

I reach my truck, and slide wearily behind the wheel. I start the engine and flick on the air-conditioning. The interior of the truck is still blood-warm from the heat of the day. I wind down the window to let out some of the hot air, and reverse out of my parking slot. The barrier pole lifts as I approach the exit, and I accelerate gently down the road towards the highway.

ALTERNATIVES?

We can't solve problems by using the same kind of thinking we used when we created them.

— Albert Einstein (1879-1955)

We've looked at prisons, and I've given a few ideas as to how they could be adapted to deal with the present situation. However, prisons are only one element in the criminal justice system — and prisons don't decide for themselves who to admit, and who to discharge. They take their orders from the legislative branch of government, which makes the laws; and from the executive branch, which applies them; and from the judicial branch, which enforces them. Reform must take place in these three arms of government before it can have an effect in and on our prisons.

Are there any alternatives to prison? What other measures can be implemented to reduce our emphasis on incarceration? What else can be done to handle 'corrections bloat'?

I submit that the very first thing necessary is to streamline the way the criminal justice system handles cases. It desperately needs to be rationalized and made more objective. Right now, there are far too many subjective elements that affect cases, everything from the mood of an individual anywhere in the chain, through to plea-bargaining and influence from external individuals and/or agencies. As a result, it's almost impossible to find a single jurisdiction that's completely fair and objective in how cases are handled. Even the Federal system, which is very good compared to many state and local criminal justice systems, is not without its flaws. (If you doubt this, consider that all US Attorney positions — the individuals who initiate and pursue Federal prosecutions — are political appointments. They are usually replaced during each change of Presidential administration, as the new incumbents of power, to quote H. L. Mencken's famous dictum, 'turn the sitting rascals out and let a new gang in.' Since they're political appointees, it can be taken for granted that many of them will allow political considerations to influence the main focus of their attention, and the priorities of their staff.)

I'm sure many readers are shaking their heads, and saying that I'm completely unrealistic and utopian in my expectations. The present system is so entrenched, they'll say, that changing or fixing it is nothing more than a pipe-dream. It may be that they're right... but the present system of criminal justice administration is what's got us into this mess. If we don't fix it, we won't be able to get rid of the mess. Somehow, we as a nation *must* find the social and political will to do this, or else live with a broken system that costs us more and more every year. I selected the quotation from Einstein at the head of this chapter for a reason... because it's true.

There are so many variations, across so many different systems, that I can't possibly go into them without writing a book on that subject alone (which would also be very boring). However, there are certain common elements that can be identified, and certain common solutions that could be implemented.

First, we need to simplify the classification or stratification of crime. The two basic divisions are felonies (serious crimes) and misdemeanors (minor crimes). Over the years we've had 'classes' introduced to sub-divide them, so that one can have a 'Class 1' or 'Class 2' or 'Class 3' offense in either category (even, in some jurisdictions, a '2A' or '3B'). Punishments will vary according to division and class of offense. Plea-bargaining is another factor: an offense might carry a significant penalty, but if the prosecution doesn't want to go to the trouble and expense of a full trial, it might agree to allow the defendant to plead guilty to a lesser charge, carrying a minor penalty (perhaps not even a jail sentence). This might be completely unjust from the point of view of the victim, but in all too many cases, the reality is that *the prosecution doesn't care about the victim.* All they want is to get a conviction as quickly and as cheaply as possible. If they're overloaded with other cases, or low on budget and can't afford the expense of a major trial, or don't have enough investigators to nail down all the evidence they'll need, they'll frequently settle for a plea-bargained minor conviction.

I submit that we need to minimize the sub-division of categories of crime, and ensure that they are handled consistently. This will require a clear and unambiguous definition of the seriousness of an offense, and the appropriate punishment for it. It will also involve the end of most plea-bargaining. If prosecutors aren't serious about dealing with crime, they won't be able to keep us safe. If a murder can be plea-bargained down to manslaughter, or even a charge of simple assault, the lesser penalties for the latter crimes mean that those responsible can be out on the streets, and perhaps killing again, before too long. I accept that a certain amount of plea-bargaining will still take place, but in general, the prosecuting authorities should be *required* to prosecute criminals to the fullest extent of the law, and be held accountable if they fail to do so. Leniency has got us nowhere.

We also need to simplify the laws themselves. In both Federal and state legal systems, they've built up into a tangled mess over many decades and centuries. Many politicians rush to deal with a social problem by passing new laws to criminalize it, or impose stiffer penalties, or restrict the judiciary's discretion in sentencing by imposing mandatory requirements. A good example is so-called 'hate crime' legislation. *This is nonsensical.* A murder is a murder, irrespective of whether it's committed out of hatred of someone's race, or religion, or sexual orientation, or whether it's plain old-fashioned criminal violence. Is the victim somehow more dead, if killed out of hatred? Less dead, if hatred wasn't a factor? Of course not. A criminal can only be convicted of an *act,* not a thought. To pretend otherwise is to imply that one victim of crime is 'more important' than another victim of an identical crime. That insults both victims, and also demonstrates contempt for the concept of equality under the law.

Another example is laws that blame an object rather than a person, such as those mandating sentence enhancements if a firearm is used in a crime. Once again, the crime (say, armed robbery or assault) is the same. It's irrelevant whether the criminal used a firearm, a knife, an axe, a baseball bat, a chainsaw or a nuclear bomb — the crime is still armed robbery or assault. To say that it may be more or less severe, depending on the instrument used, is simply ridiculous. A gun has no will of its own. If I put a loaded, cocked gun on my desk right now, as I type these words, pointed directly at me, it will do nothing at all. It'll just sit there unless a human operator picks it up, aims it, and pulls the trigger. It takes an operator to wield a baseball bat or a chainsaw, too.

To make an inanimate object the criterion for sentence enhancement, as if it had some kind of moral volition of its own, or were somehow to blame for making the crime worse, is no more rational than adjusting the criminal's sentence based on his astrological 'star sign', and arguing whether or not his horoscope was to blame for his actions. Besides, it matters not whether your skull is perforated by a bullet, or pulverized by a baseball bat: you're still the victim of the same criminal act (and remember, it's the *action* that leads to conviction, not the instrument, the intention or anything else), and you're just as badly hurt either way. *The instrument is irrelevant to the crime.* To base sentencing laws on the former merely makes our criminal justice process less rational, less streamlined, and more complex. It's pointless.

This carries over into the sheer number of laws on our statute books. There are far too many of them. For example, instead of having a single omnibus or 'umbrella' law dealing with addictive, narcotic and intoxicating substances, we have hundred — *thousands!* — of laws addressing each substance in detail, and prescribing penalties and sanctions for its use. The problem is the same as that identified in the previous paragraph: *such laws target and penalize the 'thing', the object, rather than the crime itself.* This has led to the ridiculous situation of some non-violent, minor-league drug dealers being sentenced to terms of imprisonment two to three times longer than those given to murderers, or a dealer in one form of a drug (crack cocaine 'rocks') being subject to far harsher penalties than a dealer in a different form of *exactly the same drug* (cocaine powder). The sense of proportion about the criminal act itself (dealing in illegal narcotics) has been completely lost.

Given that, it's no wonder that so many people exhibit widespread disrespect for the law — not to mention outright disobedience. As Winston Churchill pointed out, 'If you have ten thousand regulations you destroy all respect for the law'. (Or, as H. L. Mencken observed with tongue in cheek, 'Say what you will about the Ten Commandments, you must always come back to the pleasant fact that there are only ten of them'.) Instead of passing more and more laws, why not consolidate them into fewer laws governing the classes of problems or crimes involved, and add a 'schedule' to each? If, for example, a new illicit drug is encountered, it can be added to the 'schedule' by a simple vote in the Legislature. As things stand at present, the new drug will end up being the inspiration for ten new laws, twenty new regulations and several dozen political-patronage jobs (at taxpayer expense, of course) before the year is out — and none of them will do a thing to solve the problem.

Assuming we elect politicians who will revise and rationalize the laws of the land, what about their judicial enforcement? Here

I'd suggest that we cut through the tangle of bureaucracy and conflicting approaches, and simplify things radically. I propose that a misdemeanor crime should *never* be punished by a sentence of incarceration. Some States already do this: others have prison sentences for more serious misdemeanors. Let's remove this class of criminal from our prisons once and for all. They don't need to be there, and there are plenty of alternative punishments for them. If a crime's serious enough to warrant imprisonment, it's serious enough to be classified as a felony. (That includes imprisoning someone who persistently refuses to comply with the non-custodial sentence imposed for a misdemeanor crime. We can define such defiance as a felony offense in itself, and for that offense he can and should go to prison. If he won't do it the easy way, he can do it the hard way.)

I further propose that the 'revolving door' of the present justice system be slammed shut. There are far too many offenders who've accumulated multiple arrests, misdemeanor convictions, plea-bargains, alternative sentences, and so on. They may have forty or fifty such convictions on their records, but carry right on doing the same thing every day. This is a major reason why our crime and prison statistics are so skewed. Such behavior needs to be nipped in the bud. I propose that any individual accumulating more than, say, three to five convictions for misdemeanor crimes (excluding administrative punishments such as speeding tickets, etc.) should receive a final warning from the court at that point. He should be told bluntly that if he commits another crime — *any* crime, even at misdemeanor level — he *will* be charged as a felon, and face a prison sentence. The felony charge might be called 'persistent criminal behavior' or something like that, and should carry a minimum sentence sufficient to deter 'casual criminals'. It would be a charge over and above that brought for the actual criminal behavior in question, and its sentence would be imposed in addition to the punishment for the latter offense.

I'd take this further, and suggest that something like

California's 'three strikes' law should be applied throughout the country. Anyone with more than a few convictions, even minor ones, should be subject to a felony 'habitual offender' charge the next time they commit a crime. Penalties can be graduated, so that a first conviction might earn two to three years imprisonment, a second eight to ten years, and a 'third strike' result in twenty years to life. We simply can't afford to let the current situation continue whereby individuals can accumulate hundreds of arrests and scores of convictions. According to one District Attorney with whom I've spoken, over 50% of her office's caseload is taken up with such recidivists and repeat offenders. If we take them out of society, we'll ease the burden on our judicial system to an enormous extent — and we'll give it the space and time it needs to concentrate its attention on new offenders, who can be helped and turned around before they progress to the repeat offender stage. They're the ones who really need our help. As for those whose actions mock and scorn the system, by all means let them continue to do so — from behind bars.

I can already hear some readers arguing, "But that will increase corrections expenditure! Didn't you say you wanted to reduce it?" Yes, indeed: and despite possible short-term cost spikes, I believe that this approach *will* reduce it, in the long run. At the moment we have many offenders who spend a few months every year, or a few years every decade, in prison. They keep coming back, over and over and over again. Our intake figures are skewed out of all proportion, because we keep cycling the same people through our systems. I believe that if we give them a stark choice — reform and give up your criminal lifestyle, or spend the rest of your life in jail — this recycling will gradually come to a halt. Yes, I daresay there will be a short-term increase in the number of long-term inmates who can't or won't 'get with the program': but, over time, admissions to prison will drop dramatically as the 'revolving door' shuts down. We'll also save an enormous amount by no longer repeatedly processing such individuals through the criminal justice system, sometimes several times each year.

Furthermore, if we can put in place programs and interventions that truly and meaningfully address the problem of criminal personality traits and mindset, and release inmates who are much better prepared and equipped to live a different life outside the prison, we have a real chance to reduce recidivism and the 'culture of crime' that's taken hold in so many of our cities. No single step in isolation will solve the problem: but together, I think they can do so.

We should also work to get rid of the misguided notion that some things, currently classified as crimes, are in fact *not* crimes, but matters of individual choice. I refer, of course, to the recreational use of drugs. We have to realize that drug use has permanent consequences, not only for the user, but for the whole of society — accidents caused by drug users who can't control their vehicles; crimes committed by those trying to get money to buy drugs; the enormous strain on our health facilities and services, as drug users seek treatment for related health issues; and so on. (The same problems apply to those addicted to alcohol, of course. The problem of Fetal Alcohol Syndrome is yet another example of how their irresponsibility affects us all.)

To give just one example (they are legion) of what such addictions cost, a nurse has said to me that up to 50% of the patients coming to the Emergency Room where she works are crystal meth users seeking treatment for abscesses, agitated delirium, brain bleeds, endocarditis, pain of various kinds, septicemia, and other ailments. She also sees those sickened by the poisonous residues of the chemicals used to make methamphetamines, which linger in carpeting or walls, or are carried into the ecosystem by illegal dumping. For those who say that drug use should be a matter of personal choice, not a crime, what are you going to do to get rid of those side-effects? Your taxes and mine have to pay for them, not to mention our sky-high medical insurance premiums, and the grossly inflated prices we pay to hospitals for surgery and treatment — prices which have to cover those who can't pay for themselves. Effectively, responsible citizens are being robbed to pay for the irresponsible. Clearly recreational drug use has ramifications and consequences far beyond any question of individual choice.

This illustrates another very serious problem that we'll have to confront if we want to be serious about crime. We live in a self-indulgent, self-centered, even self-obsessed society. Far too many people have been raised by parents who gave them anything they wanted. (To give just one illustration, North American parents spent *ten times more than the world average* on toys for their children in 1999/2000[23]. If US figures were isolated from those in Canada and Mexico, I'm sure the former would be higher still.) They've never learned self-control, never learned to judge the importance (or otherwise) of anything: instead, they've become accustomed to instant gratification.

Many of our criminals are afflicted with this myopic, irrational approach, and they frequently come from strata of society where it's the norm rather than the exception. Any meaningful criminal reform program, in focusing on criminal personality and traits, will also have to address this issue, and point out that if we want something, we have to be able to afford it. 'Afford' isn't only a monetary concept: it also refers to the time we'll devote to whatever we want. Can we legitimately take that time if it should be devoted to other things, such as family, work, etc.? Our sense of priorities has to be sound, and our life has to be in balance, if we're to escape the trap of 'I want it all, and I want it now'. Just for a start, our television programming is crammed full of that perspective — after all, advertisers want us to perpetuate that myth in our lives. How about turning off the TV for a month, and focusing on real life?

It's perhaps appropriate to mention our youth judicial and correctional systems at this point. I won't go into them in depth, as this would require a book of its own: but they often fail to deal effectively with younger criminals. Frequently, the latter are given a judicial 'slap on the wrist' and released to commit further crimes. This can lead to truly disastrous consequences for them. I've met a number of inmates in adult prisons who are bitter and angry at their long sentences. They point out (with considerable justification, from my perspective) that they committed the same crimes, several times, when they were classified as juveniles. They received only minor punishment. The next time they committed that same crime, they were classified as adults, and pulled a multi-year sentence in an adult prison. The contrast in punishments is stark. Clearly, something needs to be done in the juvenile justice system to deter such criminals before they decide to continue the same pattern in later life.

We've looked at the underlying situation confronting us in society. We've also looked at how prisons might be restructured, to more effectively deal with the problems that presently exist. Now, how to manage the misdemeanor offenders among us? There are far more of them than there are felony offenders, and most of the latter started off with misdemeanor offenses. If we can help misdemeanor offenders to change their ways early, they may never 'develop' into hardened criminals at all.

There are many possible 'decision points' at which intervention is possible. I'm going to list a number of them, to illustrate the vast number of points at which choices can be made and alternatives selected.

As soon as an offense is observed or reported, a law enforcement officer can issue a citation, or make an arrest, or decide that the offender is in need of informal assistance through diversion to facilities for the mentally ill, juveniles, etc. If a warrant for arrest is requested, the judge or magistrate may issue it, or issue a summons requiring a court appearance, or refer the complainant to extra-judicial resources.

Once an offender's been arrested and brought to the jail, the staff there might divert him to extra-judicial services (particularly where mental illness is suspected), or make a citation release requiring the offender to appear in court at a later date, or set bail according to a schedule prepared by the court. In the latter case, the bail magistrate may ask for additional information in order to make a better informed decision.

The prosecutor can carefully screen cases, to decide whether the original charge should be pursued, or reduced charges made, or even to abandon the prosecution altogether. The quicker this is done, the less time the offender will be a financial burden on the system. Diversion is important at this stage too. The offender might be offered a deal whereby, if he accepts assignment to a treatment or behavior modification program, charges will be dropped. (Of course, this will include a clause to the effect that if he doesn't satisfactorily complete the program, and/or re-offends within a certain time, the original charges will be reinstated.)

The initial court appearance offers another opportunity to divert the case to extrajudicial channels. Various types of bail or release on recognizance can be implemented; the judge can facilitate a diversion deal, as described in the previous paragraph; and prosecution and defense attorneys can consult, to determine possible outcomes to everyone's advantage. Of course, the defendant's prior criminal record should be taken into account in making any decision. It would be at this point that a repeat offender might have a felony charge of 'habitual criminal behavior' added to the charges he's already facing. That would immediately elevate him to a felony offender category, and make any extrajudicial treatment options much less likely.

Between the initial court appearance and the trial, there may be a number of additional hearings concerning bail, background investigations, pretrial motions and so on. These offer additional opportunities for extrajudicial intervention or diversion of the case. At the trial itself, the same considerations apply. If the defendant is found guilty, a multitude of non-custodial options become available. Traditionally, these might include one or a combination of the following (listed in alphabetical order):

'Boot Camp': This is a popular option for younger offenders. They are confined in a residential facility that offers a strict regimen of classes, discipline and exercise.

Community Service: The offender may be required to perform a given number of hours service to the community in a government or private organization. The duration of community service is often calculated by dividing the 'value' of the crime by the minimum wage per hour to obtain the number of hours of service to be performed.

Electronic Monitoring: This involves the use of an ankle bracelet with a transmitter allowing the offender's movements to be tracked. He may be forbidden to frequent certain places and confined to his home during certain hours of the day or night.

Fine: A cash penalty, depending on the actual damages incurred and the defendant's ability to repay them. The fine might be paid to the government, or to a charity or private organization working in the field affected by the crime (e.g. animal abuse might be punished by a fine paid to the Humane Society).

Non-custodial confinement: This could make use of a so-called 'halfway house' where offenders are required to spend some or all of their nights, but are free to go to work during the day. Programs offered in such a facility can address the specific issues of the offender's crime.

Probation Supervision: Imposing conditions of limited association, restitution, etc. and requiring the offender to report regularly to a probation agency until they are fulfilled.

Restitution: A requirement that the offender pay to the victim, or to society, an amount sufficient to compensate for the loss caused by his crime. Services may be substituted for a cash payment.

Suspended Sentence: The penalty is held in abeyance pending restitution, completion of one or more programs of treatment or behavior modification, supervision by a probation agency, etc. It will typically also include a provision that the offender not commit another offense within a specified period.

Treatment: The offender can be required to undergo a course of treatment on an in- or outpatient basis to address one or more of his particular problems (this option is discussed in greater detail below).

In the light of what's been said earlier in this book, I'd like to focus on two of these options. First, I suggest that treatment should be a mandatory part of any sentence, and should emphasize identifying the elements of the criminal personality and mindset, as discussed earlier. Offenders should be taught to recognize any of these elements that exist within themselves, and shown how they affect their behavior and lifestyle. Effective intervention at this point may help them to reform before they commit more crimes and wind up behind bars. This is more easily (and much more cheaply) accomplished at this stage of proceedings.

The other very important option is the so-called 'boot camp'. I'm sure many readers will have found, as I did, that military service tends to knock a good deal of nonsense out of one. I know that when I went into the military, I was a cocky, know-it-all, somewhat silly teenager. When I came out some years later, I was a man. It was a hard transformation, parts of which I certainly didn't enjoy, but it did me a world of good. I'm sure many of my readers who are former service personnel are nodding their heads in understanding as I say that. If we could obtain the services of veterans to serve as instructors, and have them run a concentrated 'boot camp' environment for younger offenders, I think it might have salutary results.

This could be taken further. There are many young offenders who've been in and out of the courts and juvenile programs without any change in their behavior being evident. What if a 'Service Corps' could be established specifically for such youngsters? If they were to spend a year or more under strict discipline, enduring hard (but not inhumane) training, would this not jerk many of them out of their old ways? In times past, young offenders were frequently given the option by judges to either go to jail, or join the military. I think there was a lot of wisdom in that option. Today, the Armed Forces usually won't recruit anyone with a criminal record: but if a formally-established Service Corps could be organized, and provision made that successful service in that Corps, for a given period of time, would lead to the expunging of juvenile criminal records (and perhaps even misdemeanor-only adult records), a path for service in the Armed Forces would open up for such individuals. Given their problems in recruiting suitable and sufficient personnel, I'm sure the Armed Forces would be delighted to have such graduates available, particularly if they came with discipline, fitness and a 'right mindset' already inculcated. Who knows? They might even be willing to assign some of their instructors to help the Service Corps. There may be real possibilities here.

Where could such a Service Corps be employed? I'd ask, rather, where it could *not* be employed! Every year there are natural disasters requiring assistance; there are fires to be fought across tracts of timberland in numerous States; there are National Parks and wildlife reserves needing cleanup and maintenance; there are inner-city neighborhoods requiring renovation and restoration; there are organizations such as Habitat For Humanity that could make very good use of the Service Corps... the possibilities are almost endless. All these activities would also offer members of the Corps a very wide-ranging introduction to potential career opportunities, and the real needs of society.

I believe that if the proposals made in this chapter could be implemented, and the prison system reformed as discussed in Chapter 16, we could turn around the present unacceptable situation within five to ten years. We'd be left with a significantly larger proportion of hard-core long-term inmates, who won't accept the need to change; a reduced number of inmates in medium- and low-security facilities, going through intensive programs to identify the elements of the criminal personality they exhibit, and help them to modify them into something more appropriate; and no misdemeanor prisoners at all, these having been diverted to non-custodial punishment, with an allied emphasis on helping them to change right away, before they can 'graduate' to felon status. I believe that at the end of a decade, our prison population might have been reduced by between a quarter and a third, and our recidivism rate would hopefully have dropped to at least Australia's level of 40%, if not further.

We have to be realistic, and accept that there will always be those who won't reform. Criminals have been with us since the beginning of recorded history (see the Epic of Gilgamesh[24] and the book of Genesis[25] for early examples). They will be with us until the end of time. For those who won't reform, we'll have penitentiaries, and we'll have to make sure that after they've been given a reasonable number of chances to reform, they spend the rest of their lives in them. I see no reason why we should allow them to continue to prey on us. If they refuse to change, let's put them where their only option is to prey on one another. On their own heads be it.

I predict fierce opposition to many of the ideas I propose. This opposition will come from three groups. There will be conservatives, who'll decry any easing of sentences or penalties (as recommended for misdemeanor offenders) as being 'soft on crime' or 'a danger to the community'. To them I can only say that lifetime incarceration of all hard-line recidivists is hardly 'soft on crime'. Also, our present system is not producing any improvement in recidivism. Since the present system is failing, why not try something new? I repeat: 'Insanity is doing the same thing over and over again, expecting different results.' It would be insane to continue with the present state of affairs.

The second group of opponents will be those of a more liberal bent, who will object to my contention that there are going to be many criminals who can't or won't reform, and who will therefore be condemned to indefinite incarceration in high-security facilities. They'll doubtless regard this as 'inhuman' and 'cruel and unusual punishment'. I beg to differ. The same opportunities for reform and real, meaningful personal change will be offered to everyone in the correctional system. Only those who refuse to avail themselves of those opportunities will be affected. Their continued incarceration will be as a result of their own choices and their own actions (or the lack thereof). I believe that our primary objective must be the safety of society. If these individuals persist in threatening that safety, then let them be permanently separated from the society they threaten. I see no reason why innocent people should suffer because of their intransigence, whether voluntary or involuntary.

The third group of opponents will be from the 'prison-industrial complex' I referred to earlier. There are today many individuals, organizations, pressure groups and alliances that depend for their livelihood on an ever-expanding corrections sector. Any reduction in expenditure in this area, any downsizing of facilities, will be economic setback for them. I therefore predict that they'll fight tooth and nail to prevent any meaningful reform. The *status quo* is very much to their advantage.

I can only say to them that it may be to *their* advantage, but it's an unmitigated disaster for the rest of us. If a criminal hurts or kills anyone, the repercussions spread far beyond the immediate victim to affect families, employers, and the general economy.

It's time we got our priorities straight, and put our house in order. I've offered my suggestions as to how this might be achieved. Now, dear reader, it's up to you to come up with your own ideas, and join in the national debate to find the best way forward.

CONVICT TO CHAPLAIN IX

THE HOPEFUL

Dear Chaplain Grant,

Sorry it's taken me so long to write to you. I guess I was too shy before now. Maybe I was ashamed, because you knew me the way I used to be. Anyway, I figured it was about time.

Three years ago, when I told you how scared I was to leave, you promised me you'd contact a local church and get me some help. You came through for me. I'll never forget that. Pastor John came to see me in the halfway house, and fixed me up with a trailer near the church.

I've been working in prison ministry with his team for two years now. I teach them what it's really like behind bars, and they all reckon I've helped them become a lot more effective. It's good to be needed like that. Maybe those years inside won't be a total waste after all. It still feels funny to visit a prison, and be allowed to leave again! Your letter to the local jail really helped. Without it, they'd never have approved an ex-con like me as a religious volunteer.

My time in the prison kitchens sure came in handy. Pastor John organized a job for me as a short-order cook at a local place. The owner's a member of his church. I knew how to make some of them fancy Italian sauces and casseroles, thanks to what the wise guys taught me. I cooked some for the owner, and she liked them so much we now have 'Italian Day' once a week. Tell Vinny I'm in charge of the kitchen for that. He'll crack up.

The owner's a widow. She and I been going out for a year now. I've taken it real slow and careful, like you advised, and Pastor John's been a big help. We're talking about swapping rings next year.

Life ain't so bad on the outside. I make enough to get by, and if Beth and I get hitched, we'll have enough between the two of us to be OK. She has her own home already, which helps. I don't want you to think that's why I'm seeing her, though. I really like her, and she likes me. It's strange, having a woman in my life again after so many years surrounded by men, but I'm enjoying it. I could get used to this. She wants me to try to trace my kids, too. I'm scared, but Pastor John agrees with her. It would be good to be a family again, and she says if we get hitched, she wants them there along with her three. Wouldn't that be great?

I never forgot your last words to me, Chaplain. As you shook my hand, you looked me straight in the eye. You said, "Gene, I know you've had trouble believing in God sometimes, but God doesn't have any trouble believing in you. If you come to a place where things are dark, and you've got no hope left, remember that. *God believes in you, Gene.* So do I. Believe that, believe in God, and don't let him or me down by refusing to believe in yourself."

You were right, Chaplain. I'm believing in God, and in myself, and I'm learning. It helps to have Beth believing in me, too, and Pastor John — and you. You were the first.

Thank you.

FRIDAY — 9:45 P.M.

I pull into the parking area in front of the charity hospital. The building's old and dilapidated. It badly needs a complete overhaul, if not demolition and replacement with a modern structure, but there are no funds available for the purpose. Like so much of this country's infrastructure, it's been neglected due to the ever-increasing cost of entitlement programs. Ironically, those who use this hospital are mainly the beneficiaries of those same entitlement programs — so while they're getting more money, giving them that money is simultaneously producing sub-optimal health care for them. I don't suppose the politicians have ever thought about it in those terms, though. A new hospital building doesn't buy votes. Bigger monthly pay-outs do.

I guess it's a bit like the prison system. Voters like the sound of 'get-tough' laws, increased sentences, and locking offenders away, out of sight and out of mind. However, they hate spending money on prisons. A retired Warden once put it to me like this: "The old proverb talks about cutting one's coat according to one's cloth. Well, in our line of business, the politicians describe the coat in minute detail, from material, to length of sleeves, to the number of pockets. They then order us to make it, but give us only half the cloth we need to do so. When we don't succeed, they blame us, and look for another tailor — then they do the same to him."

I approach the entrance, walking slowly, wearily. The security guard at the entrance sees the name badge on my shirt, and nods a greeting as I hold out my ID wallet to him. He checks it briefly. "Thanks, Chaplain. I guess you're here to see the prisoner who was brought in earlier this evening?"

"That's right."

"He's in ICU. You know the way?"

"I know it, thanks. I've been here before."

I walk through the dingy, worn lobby to the elevator, and press the button. With much creaking and groaning the old car grinds down from the upper levels, and the doors open. I take the elevator to the appropriate floor, and walk down the passage to the ICU doors. A Lieutenant and a Correctional Officer are seated on a bench outside, pistols holstered at their waists. It's an unusual sight: inside the walls, no-one's ever armed (except those in the gun towers), for fear that an inmate might get his hands on the weapon. Staff are armed only for escort duties like this. They rise as I come towards them.

"Hi, Chaplain. How's it going?"

"Hi, guys. I came down to see how Inmate Andrew's doing. What's the latest?"

The Lieutenant grimaces. "I don't think he'll last another hour. He only made it to the hospital on CPR. The doc says his brain's suffered irreversible damage from oxygen starvation. They've called the prison to inform them of their intention to take him off life support."

If a prisoner has designated next of kin, who've accepted legal responsibility for such decisions, they'd have to make the call (and pay all medical costs from that point onward if they decided to keep life support going): but Andrew has no-one designated as such on his file. That means the decision will be in the hands of our executives. In a case like this, where the prognosis is so unequivocally terminal, they're sure to approve the hospital's intention to shut down life support.

"I'll go in and see him. Is anyone in there right now?"

"Only George."

I nod. It's standard policy that any high-security inmate must have three armed guards, commanded by a Lieutenant, if he leaves the prison to go to a hospital for treatment. Even though Andrew's dying, regulations require that at least one of them must be in the room with him at all times.

I push through the swinging double doors. The ICU is darkened, quiet, the soft hiss of air-conditioning and the muffled clicking and beeping of medical equipment the only sounds. Two beds are occupied in curtained-off alcoves on either side of the room. I walk to the nurses' station, identify myself, and ask for Andrew. The nurse at the desk nods towards one of the alcoves.

"He's in there, Chaplain. We're just waiting on confirmation from the prison before we switch off life support. He's unconscious, but you can go in if you like."

I thank her, and slide back the curtain. George comes to his feet, looking at me. He's a young Correctional Officer, still in his first year on the job, and I can see he's a little upset at being so close to imminent death. It's probably the first time he's encountered such circumstances. In this line of work, it certainly won't be the last — and not always under such aseptic and clinical conditions, either. I shiver slightly as I remember some of the stabbing victims I've seen immediately after a prison assault. Blood everywhere. You wouldn't think the human body could hold that much of it — and the throat-grabbing metallic stench of it seems to linger in your nostrils for days afterward.

"Hi, George. Relax. I'm just here to check on Inmate Andrew."

He nods, and sinks back into his chair. I look at Andrew. A breathing mask covers his mouth and nose, tubes leading to a pulsing, hissing machine. There's a drip in his arm, and wires run from electrodes on various parts of his body and head to more softly beeping electronic units next to the bed. His heartbeat is shown as a steady, monotonous blip, sustained by the machines plugged into and onto his body. Andrew's skin is pale and waxen, his wispy gray hair tousled and unkempt. His bristly cheeks seem shrunken, hollow, as if his face had fallen in on itself, and his eyes are closed. A handcuff encircles his left wrist, attaching it to the metal bed frame. Even though he's helpless and near to death, regulations insist that he be treated as an escape risk.

Andrew's been behind bars in local, state and Federal prisons for well over half his life. His crimes were many and increasingly vicious, until the explosion of evil that led to his last, lifelong prison sentence. He's been a real hard case behind bars, too, like many other members of his biker gang, and he's caused a lot of trouble for the authorities. That's over now — he won't be causing any more. He's on the threshold of the Judgment that we all must face one day. I've no idea whether the faith into which he was baptized as a baby means anything to him, but I hope that somewhere, in the innermost recesses of his soul, he's found at least some ability to repent of his sins. If he hasn't done so before, it's probably too late now.

Quietly, in my mind, I recite the prayers for the dying. I ask for mercy for Andrew, and for those he injured through his crimes, be that injury physical, mental or spiritual. I've already given him the Last Rites, so there's no need to do that again. As I pray, I hear the telephone ring at the nurses' desk behind me. I hear the light clicking of her heels on the floor as she goes to the door and summons the Lieutenant. I hear him come in, the heavy clumping of his boots very different from the sound of her shoes. He murmurs into the telephone, then hands it back to her. She makes another call, and in a few moments a doctor comes into the ICU. A brief conversation, then they pull back the curtains and enter Andrew's cubicle. The Lieutenant and the other CO follow them.

"Good evening, Chaplain," the doctor greets me quietly. "I guess this man is your department now. We've been authorized to shut down life support."

247

I nod, and look at the Lieutenant. "Please remove his handcuffs."

He hesitates. "We're not supposed to do that until — "

"I know, Lieutenant, but you can see for yourself that he's not going anywhere. I'll take the responsibility if anyone argues. Please remove his handcuffs."

The Lieutenant nods at George, who takes a key from his pocket and opens the cuff around Andrew's wrist. He removes the other ring from the bed frame, and places the cuffs in a pouch on his belt. I daren't tell them my thoughts, because they'd think I was crazy: but I don't think any man, no matter how guilty, should have to die in chains. Whimsy? Stupidity? Call it what you will.

We stand back as the doctor and nurse go to Andrew's bedside. The doctor flicks switches, presses buttons, turns dials, and enters commands into the medical equipment and monitor unit by his bedside. The nurse shuts off the drip into his arm, removes the breathing mask, and detaches several electrodes from his body. They step back, and the doctor turns to me.

"It's done. His heart will stop of its own accord within a few minutes."

"Thank you, Doctor. I'll wait."

The Lieutenant and the CO's go out with the doctor, and I hear them talking in low voices at the nurses' station as they prepare the paperwork to take back to the prison.

Andrew will be buried in a pauper's grave in the local cemetery, unless his former wife is prepared to pay for his body to be disposed of in some other way. I doubt very much whether she'll be willing to do that. He'll have no-one at his funeral except the grave-diggers. If I'm on duty and can't be there, his committal will be conducted by a minister who's never known him, or even heard of him, and almost certainly won't be from his denomination. I make a mental note to ask a couple of local pastors to pass the word to their congregations, as soon as I learn the date and time of his funeral. I hope at least some people will attend, to pray for his soul.

Most of the machines are quiet now, their lights no longer flickering, their screens blank. The breathing unit no longer hisses and pulses.

I take Andrew's clammy, unresponsive hand lightly in mine, and watch, praying, trying to utter on his behalf the appeal for Divine mercy he can no longer make for himself.

The traces outlining his heartbeats become shorter, wavering, and draw further and further apart on the last active screen as the numbers drop steadily. His breathing becomes labored and jagged. The death rattle is in his throat. It's unmistakable — I've heard it before. He gasps and splutters, his chest heaving.

A sudden tremor runs through his body, from head to toe and back again… then all movement ceases.

The monitor emits a low, unbroken tone as the heart display flat-lines.

I reach out and trace the Sign of the Cross on his forehead.

After all those years behind bars, Andrew is at long, long last a free man.

EPILOGUE

Thank you for joining me in the pages of this book. I hope you understand prison life better now, and I trust you'll become one of the many people trying very hard to find solutions to the pressing problems confronting us. It's going to be a long and difficult road... but together we can — we *must* — find a way forward.

As you go about your daily life, spare a thought for those who are keeping you safe by ensuring that the bad guys stay locked up. Think of the former criminals who have genuinely reformed, and are struggling to make new lives for themselves in a world that's very seldom sympathetic and supportive towards them. Think, too, about the former convicts who are out on the streets again, and who *aren't* trying. They'll offend again soon, and will probably end up back behind bars. Pray that they don't decide to pick you for their next target.

Learn to protect and defend yourself in case they do — including equipping yourself with suitable and effective tools. Don't trust the minimalist panacea 'solutions' touted by many. Violent assault isn't easily stopped, certainly not by whistles, or screams, or martial arts, or running fast, or calling 911. Even measures such as pepper spray aren't foolproof — I've seen hardened convicts eat the stuff, and keep coming. Your safety is in your own hands, no-one else's. Be watchful, and be careful. I know all too well how many violent criminals are released from prison each year. I don't want you to be their next victim. There are those who claim that we should rely on police and law enforcement agencies to protect us. I'm afraid that's nonsense. I have the highest respect for our law enforcement officers, but they have *no legal obligation whatsoever* to protect individuals, except under certain very restricted and limited circumstances. A lot of people don't realize this, but it's true. Our courts have explicitly ruled that it's a 'fundamental principle of American law that a government and its agents are under no general duty to provide public services, such as police protection, to any individual citizen'[26]. Anyone who tells you otherwise is either misinformed, or lying. If a 'politically correct' spokesman urges citizens not to resist criminals, but rather to leave things to law enforcement, consider the matter in the light of this cold, hard truth, and act accordingly.

Furthermore, all too often police can only get to the scene of a crime in time to fill out the forms and clean up the mess. To give just a few examples: in 1999 in New York City, NY, according to statistics released by the Mayor's office, the average amount of time it took a police officer to respond to a 911 call was 10.3 minutes[27]. Kansas City, MO police reported their average response time as 'five to ten minutes' in 2005[28]. In the same year, Priority One responses to 911 calls in Atlanta, GA and nearby counties took an average of nine to fifteen minutes[29]. If the *average* response times are that long, this means there are many calls that take even longer. Dear reader, remember that you've got to get to a phone in the first place, and call 911, before the police can respond at all! What if you can't? What if the criminals have cut the telephone line, or the cellphone battery is flat, or the cell tower is out of range? Also, if you think that even the average response times aren't enough for a determined, violent attacker to beat, rape or murder you (and perhaps your family as well), you're deluded. I have personally witnessed a club-wielding attacker kill a fit, strong man in less than ten seconds. Yes, it's that fast if the assailant, like many violent criminals, knows what he's doing. Plan accordingly when thinking about defending yourself and your loved ones.

For those who think I'm being unduly alarmist, I invite you to inspect your local crime statistics at the DA's office, or through your law enforcement agencies. Remember that, even in the safest areas, criminals can arrive without warning (as Wesley did — see his story in Chapter 2 — and as some cities and towns found out to their cost when they accepted evacuees from Hurricane Katrina in 2005[30]). Ask about average response times to 911 calls in your area. If local authorities can't or won't provide the figures, you might want to ask yourself, "Why not?" Is it because they're abysmally slow? Follow the local news (particularly the police blotter), and look for reports of violent crimes. In the past month alone, I've counted over a hundred within half an hour's drive from my home. Remember, the odds of being a victim of violent crime during adulthood in the USA are better than two to one (see Chapter 2). With all this information, you'll be able to objectively assess the risks you face in your particular environment, and decide what precautions are appropriate and suitable to guard against them. If you truly think you don't need any, there's a bridge in New York City I'd like to sell you. Cash only, please — small bills preferred.

I'm no longer working for the BOP. I had the misfortune to suffer a serious job-related injury, and after two surgeries, I've been left permanently partially disabled. The Bureau decided that I had to accept medical retirement. I'm really sorry about that. I'd much rather have continued my work with them, but I would no longer be capable of responding to or assisting in an emergency. I understand that's a deal-breaker for the Bureau. I'd be a liability rather than an asset in such circumstances, and that's not fair to those who might have to put themselves at risk to help me.

I'll find new ways to contribute to corrections work and ministry, and I hope to continue to make a difference in the lives of inmates. I'd also like to help people like you, dear reader, to understand the reality of life behind bars. That's why I wrote this book. We're all directly affected by this 'shadow world' in many ways, from paying taxes to support it, to hearing and seeing dramatic highlights from it on the news, to being potential (or — God forbid! — actual) victims of those destined for it or hardened by it. The better we understand it, the better we can work together to fix it. Let's also try to elect politicians who will work to find and implement solutions to the problems in the system today, and keep up the pressure until they do so.

I hope you'll consider volunteering to help at a prison near you. Talk to the chaplains there. Find out whether your church, or another local community organization, has any sort of outreach program. I highly recommend that if possible, you arrange to go through the volunteer training offered by the BOP or local facilities. I also suggest that you get one or two of the books mentioned in the first and second end-notes. They'll give you a very good picture of what you'll be dealing with as a volunteer. Use the resources of the Internet to find out more. (However, please note that Web sites run by convicts or their supporters are likely to be highly biased against the 'system'. On the Internet, much 'information' is worth only what you pay for it.)

Thanks once again for joining me. I appreciate it.

STATISTICS

This section lists some statistics about the USA's correctional population, provided by the Bureau of Justice Statistics of the US Department of Justice. This Bureau's reports may be found at URL http://www.bjs.gov/.

Please note that other sources of data (see, for example, Note 12 in the next section) may offer different statistics, determined by alternate methods of data collection and/or calculation. Those interested in statistics about the correctional population in individual states should consult their prison administrative authorities, who will usually provide this information on their official Web sites.

1. Number of Adult Persons under Correctional Supervision.

YEAR	PROBATION	JAIL	PRISON	PAROLE	TOTAL
1980	1,118,097	183,988	319,598	220,438	1,842,100
1990	2,670,234	405,320	743,382	531,407	4,350,300
2000	3,826,209	621,149	1,316,333	723,898	6,445,100
2010	4,055,514	748,728	1,518,104	840,676	7,076,200

2. Number Of Sentenced Inmates Incarcerated Under Federal And State Jurisdiction.

(NOTE: These figures are supplied by the US Bureau of Justice Statistics. Others — see, for example, Note 12 in the next section — are significantly higher. These figures exclude those incarcerated while awaiting trial and those under local jurisdiction, such as in town or county jails for offenses against purely local statutes. They also do not take into consideration those arrested for probation or parole violations whose cases have not yet been adjudicated, and who may be returned to prison when that is done. The figures in this table represent only those who were serving a term of imprisonment in the year indicated for violating Federal and/or state laws.)

NUMBER OF SENTENCED INMATES UNDER STATE AND FEDERAL JURISDICTION (RATE PER 100,000 POPULATION)	
YEAR	**RATE**
1980	139
1990	297
2000	478
2010	500

3.   Recidivism.

Two major studies released in 1983 and 1994 provide the most comprehensive figures for this topic and are as close as one can get, in terms of official statistics, to determining a national recidivism rate. The figures obtained by the Department of Justice for re-arrest of released inmates were:

RECIDIVISM					
YEAR	ALL RELEASED PRISONERS	VIOLENT CRIMES	PROPERTY CRIMES	DRUG CRIMES	PUBLIC ORDER CRIMES
1983	62.5%	59.6%	68.1%	50.4%	54.6%
1994	67.5%	61.7%	73.8%	66.7%	62.20%

The press release accompanying the 1994 figures is reproduced in full below, as it provides a detailed analysis and breakdown of the percentages involved.

ADVANCE FOR RELEASE AT 4:30 P.M. EDT
BJS 202/307-0784
SUNDAY, June 2, 2002
TWO-THIRDS OF FORMER STATE PRISONERS REARRESTED FOR SERIOUS NEW CRIMES
WASHINGTON, D.C. — Sixty-seven percent of former inmates released from state prisons in 1994 committed at least one serious new crime within the following three years, the Justice Department's Bureau of Justice Statistics (BJS) announced today. This was a rearrest rate 5 percent higher than that among prisoners released during 1983.
State prisoners with the highest rearrest rates were those who had been incarcerated for stealing motor vehicles (79 percent), possessing or selling stolen property (77 percent), larceny (75 percent), burglary

(74 percent), robbery (70 percent) or those using, possessing or trafficking in illegal weapons (70 percent).

Those with the lowest rearrest rates were former inmates who had been in prison for homicide (41 percent), sexual assault (41 percent), rape (46 percent) or driving under the influence of drugs or alcohol (51 percent).

About 1 percent of the released prisoners who had served time for murder were arrested for another homicide within three years, and about 2 percent of the rapists were arrested for another rape within that period.

Within three years, 52 percent of the 272,111 released prisoners were back in prison either because of a new crime or because they had violated their parole conditions (e.g., failed a drug test, missed a parole office appointment).

Men were more likely to be rearrested than were women (68 percent, compared to 58 percent), blacks more likely than whites (73 percent vs. 63 percent) and non-Hispanics more than Hispanics (71 percent vs. 65 percent). Younger prisoners and those with longer records were also more likely to be rearrested.

Post-prison recidivism was strongly related to arrest history. Among prisoners with one arrest prior to their release, 41 percent were rearrested. Of those with two prior arrests, 47 percent were rearrested. Of those with three earlier arrests, 55 percent were rearrested. Among those with more than 15 prior arrests, that is about 18 percent of all released prisoners, 82 percent were rearrested within the three-year period.

The 272,111 inmates had accumulated more than 4.1 million arrest charges prior to their current imprisonment and acquired an additional 744,000 arrest charges in the 3 years following their discharge in 1994 — an average of about 18 criminal arrest charges per offender during their criminal careers.

These charges included almost 21,000 homicides, 200,000 robberies, 50,000 rapes and sexual assaults and almost 300,000 assaults.

Almost 8 percent of all released prisoners were rearrested for a new crime in a state other than the one that released them. These alleged offenders were charged with committing 55,760 new crimes in states other than the imprisoning state within the three-year period. New York, Arizona and California had the most arrests of out-of-state offenders in this study.

The data were from the largest recidivism study ever conducted in the United States, which tracked prisoners discharged in 15 states representing two-thirds of all state prisoners released in 1994. They were 91 percent male, 50 percent white, 48 percent black, 24 percent Hispanic (of any race) and 44 percent were younger than 30 years old.

Most of them had been in prison for felonies: 22 percent for a violent offense (such as murder, rape, sexual assault or robbery), 33 percent for a serious property offense (mostly burglary, motor vehicle theft or fraud), 33 percent for a drug offense (primarily drug trafficking or possession) and 10 percent for public order offenses (mainly drunk driving or weapons crimes).

Most former convicts were rearrested shortly after getting out of prison: 30 percent within six months, 44 percent within a year, 59 percent within two years and 67 percent by the end of three years.

The study findings are based upon the prison and criminal records of an estimated 272,111 discharged prisoners in 15 states who were tracked through fingerprints records made at various points of contact with the justice system, both within the state in which they had served time and other states to which they traveled.

The BJS special report, "Recidivism of Prisoners Released in 1994" (NCJ-193427) was written by BJS statisticians Patrick A. Langan and David J. Levin. Single copies may be obtained by calling the BJS Clearinghouse at 1-800/732-3277. After the release date, this document can be accessed at: http://www.ojp.usdoj.gov/bjs/abstract/rpr94.htm Additional criminal justice materials can be obtained from the Office of Justice Programs homepage at: http://www.ojp.usdoj.gov

NOTES

(**IMPORTANT NOTE:** URL's for information resources were correct at the time they were accessed, but are subject to change. If those supplied no longer lead to it/them, an Internet search for the resource(s) by title and/or author should locate it/them. The author has retained copies of these resources, as downloaded or printed at the time of using them, for future reference.)

1.   <u>Inmate manipulation of staff:</u> see, for example:

Allen, B. & Bosta, D.
GAMES CRIMINALS PLAY: How You Can Profit By Knowing Them
Rae John Publishers, 1981.

Cornelius, G. F.
THE ART OF THE CON: Avoiding Offender Manipulation
American Correctional Association, 2001.

Elliott, B. & Verdeyen, V.
GAME OVER: Strategies For Redirecting Inmate Deception
American Counseling Association, 2003.

Another excellent book that gives examples of inmate manipulation (along with a detailed look at some convicts in depth) is Early, Pete, 'THE HOT HOUSE: Life Inside Leavenworth Prison', Bantam, 1993.

2. The criminal mind: For a particularly thorough and in-depth examination, see Samenow, Dr. Stanton E., 'INSIDE THE CRIMINAL MIND', Crown Books, New York, 1984.

3. Department of Justice statistics for 15 states: US Department of Justice, Office of Justice Programs, Bureau of Justice Statistics, 'CRIMINAL OFFENDERS STATISTICS', last revised August 8th, 2007. Retrieved on August 22nd, 2007 from URL:

ojp.usdoj.gov/bjs/crimoff.htm

4. SIS: the Special Investigative Supervisor, also the name of his department in the prison. SIS serves Federal prisons in the same way that the FBI serves the law enforcement community. It's an intelligence-gathering and investigation unit that supports the Corrections function in dealing with problems and issues.

5. HIPAA: the Health Insurance Portability and Accountability Act of 1996, which imposes strict privacy provisions on the exchange of health-related information.

6. Lawsuits filed by inmates: For an excellent review of this problem and its impact on the legal system, see Schlanger, Prof. M., 'INMATE LITIGATION', Harvard Law Review, Vol 116 no. 6 (April 2003), pp. 1555-1706.

7. Court cases connected with the Church of the New Song: See *Theriault v. Carlson*, 339 F. Supp. 375, 377 (N.D. Ga. 1972), vacated, 495 F.2d 390 (5th Cir. 1974); also *Theriault v. Silber*, 453 F. Supp. 254, 260, 261 (W.D. Tex.), appeal dismissed, 579 F.2d 302 (5th Cir. 1978), cert. denied, 440 U.S. 917 (1979); also *Remmers v. Brewer*, 494 F.2d 1277 (8th Cir.) (per curiam), aff'g 361 F. Supp. 537 (S.D. Iowa 1973), cert. denied, 419 U.S. 1012 (1974).

8. Moynihan Report: Moynihan, Daniel P., 'THE NEGRO FAMILY: THE CASE FOR NATIONAL ACTION', Office of Policy Planning and Research, US Department of Labor, 1965. Retrieved from URL:

http://www.dol.gov/oasam/programs/history/webid-meynihan.htm

Available from numerous other sources on the Internet as well.

An excellent article examining the Moynihan Report four decades after its release, and comparing the present situation in black communities to that found by its author, is: Kay S. Hymowitz, Kay S., 'THE BLACK FAMILY: 40 YEARS OF LIES', City Journal, Summer 2005. Retrieved from URL:

http://www.city-journal.org/html/15_3_black_family.html

9. Child Protective Services: News reports about failures (some local, some widespread) in local, state and Federal welfare and protective services are not uncommon. An excellent and objective overview of the problems in one field may be found in a report by the General Accounting Office of the US Government to Hon. Nydia Velasquez of the House of Representatives dated July 1997,

entitled 'CHILD PROTECTIVE SERVICES: COMPLEX CHALLENGES REQUIRE NEW STRATEGIES'. Retrieved from URL:

http://www.gao.gov/archive/1997/he97115.pdf

The cited quotation from that report is from the section 'Results In Brief' on Page 2.

10. Lord Of The Flies: A dark allegorical novel by William Golding published in 1954. It describes a group of boys stranded on a desert island. They try to form a civilized democratic society but eventually revert to totalitarianism and primitive savagery where only the strongest and most violent survive and prosper.

11. The 'Charlemagne technique' of evangelization: It's reported by some sources that Charlemagne (742-814 A.D.), the first of the Holy Roman Emperors, was declared a Saint by a local Bishop soon after his death. (Whether this was due to Charlemagne's innate sanctity, or the sword of his son at the Bishop's throat, is a question open to historical debate.) At any rate, one of the arguments that was supposedly advanced in support of this proclamation was Charlemagne's success in converting to Christianity the survivors of conquered Hun, Goth and Vandal tribes. He would allegedly line them up next to the nearest body of water and give them a choice: be baptized in it — or be drowned in it. Apparently the spontaneous (?) cries of *"Hallelujah! Now I see it!"* (or however Huns, Goths and Vandals expressed such sentiments) were deafening. Of course, the questions of whether and/or for how long the 'converts' stayed 'converted' after Charlemagne led his army home again are also matters for historical (not to mention ecclesiastical) debate…

12. US incarceration rates: There are two primary sources for this data. The first is a report by The Sentencing Project of the Soros Foundation, 514 10th Street NW Suite 1000, Washington DC, 2004: www.soros.org. It's titled 'COMPARATIVE INTERNATIONAL RATES OF INCARCERATION: AN EXAMINATION OF CAUSES AND TRENDS'. Retrieved from URL:

http://www.opensocietyfoundations.org/reports/comparative-international-rates-incarceration-examination-causes-and-trends

The second source is the 'WORLD PRISON POPULATION LIST' (9th edition) of the International Center for Prison Studies of King's College London, 26-29 Drury Lane, London WC2B 5RL, UK. The Center's Web site is www.prisonstudies.org. Report retrieved from URL:

http://nicic.gov/Library/025827

The top 10 comparative rates of incarceration (number imprisoned per 100,000 population) as of May 2011 are given by the World Prison Population List as:

USA — 743
Rwanda — 595
Russia — 568
Georgia — 547
US Virgin Islands — 539
Seychelles — 507
St. Kitts & Nevis: — 495
British Virgin Islands — 468
Belize — 439
Dominica — 431

Contrast the USA figure to the (much lower) number provided by the Bureau of Justice Statistics, as cited in Section 2 of the 'Statistics' chapter immediately preceding these Notes. I'm unable to determine which figure is more accurate.

13. BOP Mission Statement: This is taken from the Web site of the BOP. Retrieved from URL:

http://www.bop.gov/about/mission.jsp

The full text at the time of writing is as follows:

Mission Statement

It is the mission of the Federal Bureau of Prisons to protect society by confining offenders in the controlled environments of prisons and community-based facilities that are safe, humane, cost-efficient, and appropriately secure, and that provide work and other self-improvement opportunities to assist offenders in becoming law-abiding citizens.

Vision Statement

The Federal Bureau of Prisons, judged by any standard, is widely and consistently regarded as a model of outstanding public administration, and as the best value provider of efficient, safe and humane correctional services and programs in America.

This vision will be realized when:

– The Bureau provides for public safety by assuring that no escapes or disturbances occur in its facilities.

- The Bureau ensures the physical safety of all inmates through a controlled environment which meets each inmate's need for security through the elimination of violence, predatory behavior, gang activity, drug use, and inmate weapons.
- Through the provision of health care, mental, spiritual, educational, vocational and work programs, inmates are well-prepared for a productive and crime-free return to society.
- The Bureau is a model of cost-efficient correctional operations and programs.
- Our talented, professional, well-trained, and diverse staff reflect the Bureau's culture and treat each other fairly.
- Staff work in an environment free from discrimination.
- A positive working relationship exists where employees maintain respect for one another.
- The workplace is safe, and staff perform their duties without fear of injury or assault.
- Staff maintain high ethical standards in their day-to-day activities.
- Staff are satisfied with their jobs, career opportunities, recognition, and quality of leadership.

14. The overall median annual personal income in the USA (without demographic distinction) in 2005 was $28,567. This figure is taken from the Current Population Survey (CPS) 2006 Annual Social And Economic Supplement, a joint project between the Bureau of Labor Statistics and the Bureau of the Census. It may be found in the document 'PINC-05. Work Experience in 2005-- People 15 Years Old and Over by Total Money Earnings in 2005, Age, Race, Hispanic Origin, and Sex'. Retrieved from URL:

http://pubdb3.census.gov/macro/032006/perinc/new05_001.htm

The BOP's estimated cost per inmate per year is approximately $27,000. See also Note 16.

15. Robert Brown Jr.: '**Brown: Prevention, Not Prisons, Best Serves Public Safety**', in the August 12, 2007 edition of the Lansing State Journal, Lansing, MI. Retrieved from URL:

http://www.lsj.com/apps/pbcs.dll/article?
AID=/20070812/OPINION02/708120497/1085/opinion

16. BOP budget figures for 1975 were obtained from the US Department of Justice Budget Trend Data. Retrieved from URL:

http://www.usdoj.gov/jmd/budgetsummary/btd/1975_2002/btd02tocpg.htm

Budget proposals for 2008 were obtained from the US Department of Justice FY 2008 Congressional Budget Submission. Retrieved from URL:

http://www.usdoj.gov/jmd/2008justification/

17. Quotation from BOP 2008 budget proposal, '**FY 2008 PERFORMANCE BUDGET, Congressional Submission, Salaries and Expenses**', Part 1: Overview, page 4. Source URL provided in note 14 above.

18. War On Drugs: statistics taken from a Cato Institute report, '**The Drug War Toll Mounts**' by Rodney Balko, December 2, 2004. Retrieved from URL:

http://www.cato.org/publications/commentary/drug-war-toll-mounts

19. Annual US expenditure of $60 billion on corrections: statistic from Lynn Bauer, '**Justice Expenditure And Employment In The United States**'. Bureau of Justice Statistics, US Department of Justice, Washington DC, 2002. Retrieved from URL (subscription required):

http://www.icpsr.umich.edu/cocoon/NACJD/STUDY/04365.xml

20. Headline from the CNN Web site, August 16, 2007. Retrieved from URL:

http://www.cnn.com/2007/HEALTH/08/16/teens.substance.abuse.ap/index.html

21. Australian recidivism rate: the figure of 40% was taken from the report '**Tough On Crime Versus Drug Treatment: A VAADA Briefing Paper**', p. 4. This report was prepared by the Victorian Alcohol And Drug Association for submission to the Parliament of Australia's House of Representatives Standing Committee on Legal and Constitutional Affairs on 9 September 2002. Retrieved from URL:

http://www.aph.gov.au/house/committee/laca/crimeinthecommunity/subs/sub107and107_1.pdf

In the Parliament of New South Wales on 15 November, 2006, Ms. Catherine Cusack MP cited the Australian national recidivism rate as 38.4%. Retrieved from URL:

http://www.parliament.nsw.gov.au/prod/parlment/hansart.nsf/5f
584b237987507aca256d09008051f3/31388b75fb59d92eca2572360
0075353!OpenDocument

22. Source: International Center for Prison Studies, '**Justice Reinvestment — A New Approach To Crime And Justice**', p. 5. Retrieved from URL:

http://www.kcl.ac.uk/depsta/rel/icps/justice-reinvestment-2007.pdf

23. Source: International Council of Toy Industries, Industry Statistics, '**Total Toys And Video Games**'. Retrieved from URL:

http://www.toy-icti.org/resources/wtf_2001/06.htm

24. The Epic of Gilgamesh, Tablet I: a trapper speaks to his father.

"Father, a certain fellow has come from the mountains.
He is the mightiest in the land,
his strength is as mighty as the meteorite of Anu!
He continually goes over the mountains,
he continually jostles at the watering place with the animals,
he continually plants his feet opposite the watering place.
I was afraid, so I did not go up to him.
He filled in the pits that I had dug,
wrenched out my traps that I had spread,
released from my grasp the wild animals.

He does not let me make my rounds in the wilderness!"

(The culprit, of course, was Enkidu.)

25. The book of Genesis, chapter 4, verse 8 (King James translation):

"And Cain talked with Abel his brother: and it came to pass, when they were in the field, that Cain rose up against Abel his brother, and slew him."

26. Citation from *Warren v. District of Columbia,* 444 A.2d 1 (D.C. Ct. of Ap., 1981). There are many similar rulings. See, for example, *Hartzler v. City of San Jose,* 46 Cal. App. 3d 6 (1st Dist. 1975); *DeShaney v. Winnebago County Department of Social Services,* 109 S.Ct. 998 (1989); *Balistreri v. Pacifica Police Department* (901 F.2d 696 9th Cir. 1990).

27. Source: Cooper, Michael; '**Police Are Criticized for Responding More Slowly to 911 Calls**'. New York Times, September 24, 1999. Retrieved from URL:

http://query.nytimes.com/gst/fullpage.html?
res=9B0CEED9123FF937A1575AC0A96F958260

28. Source: Report in the Kansas City Star, cited on various law-enforcement-related Web sites. Retrieved from URL:

http://www.kansascity.com/mld/kansascitystar/news/local/states
/missouri/counties/cass_county/11699774.htm

29. Source: Report on the Web site of the Fox 5 Atlanta television station, cited on various law-enforcement-related Web sites. Retrieved from URL:

http://www.fox5atlanta.com/iteam/911.html

30. The FBI noted an increase in 'crime migration' to other cities after Hurricane Katrina: "For example, we saw a significant spike in gang activity in Houston after Katrina, so we teamed up with the Houston Police Department and went after those gangs." Retrieved from URL:

http://www.fbi.gov/news/stories/2006/september/burrus_09010 6

Also, many news reports cited an increase in crime caused by refugees from Hurricane Katrina in various cities. Among many examples found on the Web are the following:

http://abcnews.go.com/WNT/story?id=1320056

http://news.yahoo.com/s/nm/20060107/us_nm/hurricanes_hou ston_dc

http://www.npr.org/templates/story/story.php? storyId=5178286&ft=1&f=1003

GLOSSARY

(NOTE: Words in *italics* refer to another entry in this section.)

Benefit of clergy: In the Middle Ages clergy were exempt from trial or punishment in a civil court. One could claim this benefit and demonstrate clergy status by reading a psalm, usually the 'Miserere' (Psalm 51, or 50 in the Douay version), as usually only the clergy could read in those days. (However, since many could recite that particular psalm from memory, this didn't always accurately indicate clergy status.)

BOP: Acronym for the Federal Bureau of Prisons, an agency within the US Department of Justice.

Bug/buggy/bugging: Slang term for 'insane' or 'crazy'. One who is insane is a 'bug'; if he's acting in an insane manner he's 'buggy' or 'bugging'.

CO: Acronym for *'Correctional Officer'*.

Commissary: The shop run by the prison for the inmates. Can also refer to supplies bought at the shop, as in "I got my commissary today".

Correctional Officer: The title or rank of a prison guard in the *BOP*.

CPR: Acronym for 'Cardio-Pulmonary Resuscitation'.

Crawfish: Slang term meaning 'to back down' or 'to submit'. Can also mean 'to withdraw from a previously agreed arrangement'.

DA: Acronym for 'District Attorney', the prosecuting authority in most US local or county jurisdictions.

De facto: A Latin term meaning 'in fact' or 'in reality'.

EMS: Acronym for 'Emergency Medical Services', usually referring to medical technicians or paramedics on ambulances.

Fiat: A Latin word meaning an authorization, sanction or order, as in 'a legislative fiat' or 'a royal fiat'.

Fish, fresh fish: A newly-incarcerated convict, one with no previous experience of prison life.

Flagrante delicto: A Latin term of medieval origin meaning literally 'while the crime is blazing'. To be caught 'in *flagrante delicto*' indicates that one has been discovered or apprehended in the very act of committing the offense.

FLETC: Acronym for 'Federal Law Enforcement Training Academy', the institution that trains new BOP personnel (among others from many different agencies). Its main campus is at Glynco, on the northwestern edge of Brunswick, Georgia. There are several satellite campuses.

Hogwarts: 'Hogwarts School of Witchcraft and Wizardry' is the principal setting for J. K. Rowling's 'Harry Potter' novels.

Holding tank: A temporary detention cell used to hold inmates who are to see the Operations Lieutenant or another officer, usually concerning disciplinary infractions or investigations.

Hole, the: Slang name for the *Special Housing Unit*.

Homey(s): Also known as 'homeboy(s)' — originally a term meaning someone from the same town or locality, but it's come to be used as a slang term to refer to a fellow member of the same gang or a criminal associate.

Incident Report: The formal document used to report any incident in the prison. Also used to initiate disciplinary action against any inmates involved in the incident, if necessary.

In loco parentis: Latin phrase meaning 'in the place or role of a parent'.

Jumah: The name for Friday of the Muslim week, and also of the noon prayer service on Friday that all adult, male, free Muslims are obliged to attend.

Lock(ed) down: When prison inmates are confined to their cells. It can either be for the duration of an emergency and the subsequent investigation, affecting a given housing unit or even the entire prison, or on a permanent basis in *Supermax* or the *Special Housing Unit*, where it's interrupted only by a period of exercise (usually one hour per day) in a secure, tightly controlled area.

Malum in se: a Latin phrase meaning 'something that is wrong or evil in itself'.

Malum prohibitum: a Latin phrase used in law to refer to conduct that constitutes an unlawful act only because a a statute or regulation forbids it (e.g. parking in a loading zone), as opposed to conduct that is evil in and of itself (see *malum in se*).

Meds: Slang abbreviation for 'medicine(s)' or 'medication(s)'.

Mirabile dictu: A Latin term meaning 'strange to say' or 'marvelous to relate'.

Mob, the: Slang term for the Italian-American or Sicilian-American Mafia (but not the Mexican Mafia).

Modus vivendi: A Latin term meaning 'a manner of living', 'a way of life', 'a lifestyle'.

Muezzin: The person who chants or intones the call summoning Muslims to prayer. This is usually done from the tower or minaret of a mosque, but in prison it's performed in the chapel by one of the participating inmates.

Mule: Slang term for a person who's smuggling drugs.

Nelsonian blind eye: Vice-Admiral Horatio Nelson of the Royal Navy (1758-1805) lost the use of his right eye as a result of wounds received in 1794. At the Battle of Copenhagen (1801) he was signaled to break off the action, but disagreed with the order. He is reported to have held his telescope to his blind eye and remarked to his Flag Captain, "I really do not see the signal!" His force continued the action and won a famous victory, which excused his disobedience.

Nibelungen cycle: The cycle of four operas by Wagner concerning Germanic paganism. The operas are 'Das Rheingold', 'Die Walküre', 'Siegfried' and 'Götterdammerung'.

Operations Lieutenant: The officer in charge of a shift of Correctional Officers at a Federal correctional institution.

Posted Picture File: A record containing pictures and details of all inmates considered dangerous or a security risk or a threat to the safety of staff. Nowadays it's usually online, but if on paper, it's usually kept in the office of the *Operations Lieutenant*.

Prima facie: A Latin term meaning 'on the face of it' or 'ostensibly' or 'at first sight': literally, 'self-evident'. Of course, when the matter is more carefully investigated 'self-evident' truths may turn out to be not so true after all.

Rabbit: Prison slang term. In some prison systems it refers to an inmate who is 'owned' or dominated or controlled by another inmate or a gang. In other prison systems it can refer to an inmate who is likely to, or who has, escaped; or to one with homosexual proclivities.

Rep: Slang abbreviation for 'reputation' (or notoriety).

Shank: A home-made knife, usually manufactured by prison inmates who take a stiff object made of metal or thick heavy plastic and sharpen its point and/or edge by rubbing it against concrete or brick.

Shari'a: An Arabic word referring to Islamic religious law. The word means literally 'the way' or 'the path to the source of water'.

Shot: Slang term for an *Incident Report.*

SHU: (Pronounced 'shoe') See *Special Housing Unit.*

Sotto voce: A Latin term meaning 'in soft tones, not intended to be overheard' or 'in an undertone'.

Snitch, snitching: Being an informant. Snitches are hated by other convicts, who'll usually retaliate against them in any way possible, up to and including physical violence, even murder.

Special Housing Unit: A segregation and isolation unit where the most troublesome inmates are kept *locked down* (sometimes in solitary confinement) for security reasons or for punishment. Similar facilities are known by different names in other prison systems.

Status quo: A Latin term meaning 'the existing state of affairs' or 'the present condition'.

Street cred: Slang for 'street credibility' or a reputation among one's peers. See also *rep.*

Supermax: Slang term referring to the Administrative Maximum prison at Florence, Colorado, the most secure prison in the *BOP* at the time of writing (and probably in the entire USA).

Ten-four: A shorthand radio code meaning 'OK' or 'Roger'.

Twenty: A shorthand radio code meaning 'location', as in 'What's your twenty?', which asks 'Where are you?'.

URL: Acronym for 'Uniform Resource Locator': a protocol for specifying addresses on the Internet.

Wise guy: Slang term for a member of the Mafia (specifically the Italian-American or Sicilian-American criminal enterprise of that name, not the Mexican Mafia).

Yard Recall: The term used in the Federal prison system when all inmates are recalled to their residential units. It happens three times per day at scheduled intervals, and can be called at any time in an emergency.

ABOUT THE AUTHOR

Peter Grant was born in South Africa in 1958. The state censor board did not allow television until 1973, and his parents didn't get one until 1974; so he grew up with books. Lots of books. He started out after school as a military man, moved into commercial information technology, and assisted with humanitarian work during South Africa's prolonged civil unrest that led to the end of apartheid in 1994. After having traveled all over Africa, he emigrated to the USA in 1997, married a pilot from Alaska, and settled in Tennessee.

Visit him at his Amazon.com author page, or his blog at:

http://bayourenaissanceman.blogspot.com

Made in the USA
Columbia, SC
17 April 2018